fun with the family
Metro New York

hundreds of ideas for day trips with the kids

First Edition

Mary Lynn Blanks

gpp®

travel

Guilford, Connecticut

To buy books in quantity for corporate use or incentives, call **(800) 962-0973** or e-mail **premiums@GlobePequot.com**.

Editor: Amy Lyons
Project Editor: Lynn Zelem
Layout: Joanna Beyer
Text design: Nancy Freeborn and Linda R. Loiewski
Maps: Rusty Nelson © Morris Book Publishing, LLC
Spot photography throughout © Photodisc and © RubberBall Productions

Library of Congress Cataloging-in-Publication Data is available on file.

ISBN 978-0-7627-5339-0

Printed in the United States of America
10 9 8 7 6 5 4 3 2 1

Contents

About the Author

An avid explorer and experienced world traveler, Mary Lynn Blanks toured and trekked across almost every continent during her childhood. After attending Florida State University on a theater scholarship, she moved to New York City and joined the casts of ABC's *All My Children* as Tara and later CBS's *As the World Turns* as Annie. Fulfilling a lifelong dream, she then ran away with the circus . . . writing and coproducing original television and radio programs and commercials for Ringling Bros. and Barnum & Bailey Circus. Unofficially known as the "Vanna White of Concacaf," she is also an FAA-licensed pilot, a PADI-certified scuba diver, and the proud mom of sons Christopher and Nicholas. She is also the author of *Fun with Family Upstate New York*.

Acknowledgments

Researching the riches of New York would not have been possible without the assistance of the wonderful people at the tourist offices, parks, and attractions listed. You'd be hard-pressed to find a more helpful and enthusiastic group, and I urge you to contact them for more information.

A special thanks to my editor Amy Lyons, who guided me through this edition with wit, wisdom, and infinite patience.

To all my friends and family who supported and sustained me through this journey, I am deeply indebted. Their faith in my talent allowed me to believe in myself and find my voice. A very special thanks to Chuck Blazer, Elaine Kaufman, Dr. Ruth Westheimer, Donna de Varona, Robin Eisenmann, Callan White, Cece Verardi, Shelley Tahlor-Levine, Nina Chertoff, Nicole Orth-Pallavicini, Kathy Schultz, Beverly Monsky, Leo Bookman, Bobby Supino, my soccer, Concacaf, and FIFA family of fabulous females, Marci, Stuart, Jason, Samantha, Dylan, Drew, Logan, Cameron, and my wonderful sons, Chris and Nick.

And finally, to my mom and dad, Lola and John Blanks, and my sister, Lisa, all presently touring another dimension, I owe perhaps the most. From London to Leningrad, Istanbul to Indonesia, my parents journeyed with us to just about every Pan American port of call, encouraging our exploration of new experiences and different cultures. It was their gift of the world when I was young that sparked the fire of adventure and discovery within me and nurtured my sense of wonder. My hope is to pass this gift on to my children and perhaps to yours. Enjoy the trip!

Introduction

In 1524, Giovanni da Verrazzano sailed into what is now New York Harbor and was met by a lot of Lenape Indians in canoes. A hundred years later the Dutch founded their first and only colony in America, New Netherland, which reached from New Amsterdam on the southern tip of Manhattan all the way up the Hudson River to Fort Orange, today called Albany. One hot August day in 1664, four English frigates sailed into New York's harbor and demanded the Dutch give it up. They did so, without a fight, as they didn't really have an army to defend themselves, and the area was renamed New York. After the American Revolution, the former colony became the eleventh state in the nation, and today the metropolitan area is home to almost 20 million people.

For this edition, the metro area is divided into three regions. At its heart is New York City, a bouquet of five boroughs blessed with a diversity, soul, and temperament that make it the "Capital of the World." It is a mecca for doers and dreamers—a place where nearly 170 languages are spoken and where all is possible. To the east lies Long Island, the longest and largest island in the continental United States, and bigger than Rhode Island. Stretches of sandy beaches and primeval pine barrens await exploration, along with majestic mansions and sites rich in history. To the north are the fjords of the Hudson Valley, where the scenery and unique light gave inspiration to the artists of the nineteenth-century Hudson River School. Although space doesn't allow the inclusion of every attraction, this guide will give you the keys to the original magic kingdom, and open the marvelous metro area to you and your family.

Unlike solo travels, where there's a footloose freedom, family travel requires a bit more planning and flexibility. Everyone should be included in the process. As New York is perennially renewing and re-creating itself, things change. Contact the places listed, either by phone or Web site, to get up-to-the-minute information about special events and vacation packages; to confirm hours of operations, admissions, and reservations; and to ask about accommodations for special needs your family may have.

At the beginning of each chapter is a quick reference map, and each region is explored in a circular loop, but to open your options and customize your route, you'll

More Family Fun in Upstate New York

If you will be spending time in the Upstate New York—including the Catskills, Mohawk Valley, Finger Lakes, North Country, and Western New York—be sure to pick up a copy of the companion book in this series, *Fun with the Family Upstate New York* (GPP Travel).

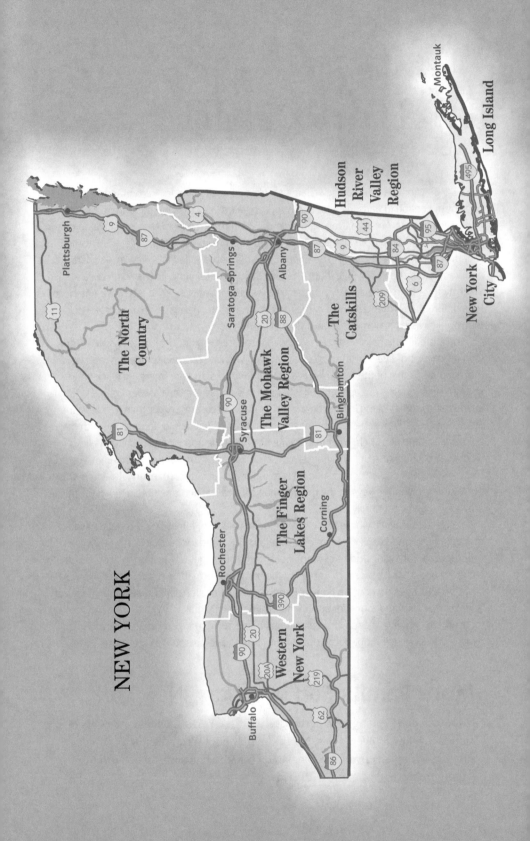

want to get a detailed road map. The age recommendations are pretty subjective, but you know your children best. It's a plus if you can tour historical sites relevant to their school studies, especially when festivals or special events are scheduled. Revolutionary War encampments, pioneer days, and powwows can transform a dry history lesson into a virtual reality time travel trip worthy of Jules Verne and H. G. Wells.

Each chapter has a short list of suggested children's books relevant to that region. While many are fictionalized accounts of the area's history or folklore, they add a depth and richness to the tapestry of traveling that a mere guidebook cannot. It's tough to top sharing the storybook about Eloise while having high tea at the Plaza in Manhattan, or reading *Treasure Island* around a beach bonfire.

As you travel around New York, think of yourselves not as tourists but rather as explorers. As Henry David Thoreau wrote, "The question is not what you look at, but what you see." By sharing the adventure of discovery with your family, you will discover much about each other as well. These are fleeting years, so get out there, have fun with your family, and collect a treasury of memories.

Rates for Attractions

$	up to $6
$$	$6 to $11
$$$	$12 to $20
$$$$	more than $20

Rates for Restaurants

$	most entrees under $10
$$	most $10 to $15
$$$	most $16 to $20
$$$$	most over $20

Rates for Accommodations

$	up to $100
$$	$100 to $150
$$$	$151 to $200
$$$$	more than $200

Attractions Key

The following is a key to the icons found throughout the text.

SWIMMING		**FOOD**	
BOATING/BOAT TOUR		**LODGING**	
HISTORIC SITE		**CAMPING**	
HIKING/WALKING		**MUSEUM**	
FISHING		**PERFORMING ARTS**	
BIKING		**SPORTS/ATHLETICS**	
AMUSEMENT PARK		**PICNICKING**	
HORSEBACK RIDING		**PLAYGROUND**	
SKIING/WINTER SPORTS		**SHOPPING**	
PARK		**PLANTS/GARDENS/NATURE TRAILS**	
ANIMAL VIEWING		**FARM**	

New York City

Friends of mine from out of town always seem amazed I choose to raise my children in New York City. True, it's crowded, expensive, sometimes pretty gritty, and my sons don't have their own tree house or a big dog, but there are other perks. Their backyard playhouse is a castle in Central Park; they're on a first-name basis with the zoo's polar bears; they can see the best of Broadway, off Broadway, or street performers; there's always a parade, festival, or movie filming around town; they can sample the cuisine of dozens of cultures or get a pizza delivered anytime; and they're ten minutes from the best dinosaurs and mummies in the country. For us, New York City is the original magic kingdom. Anything you want to buy, see, do, or dream is possible here.

Divided into the five boroughs of Manhattan, Brooklyn, Queens, the Bronx, and Staten Island, each section is again divided into a mosaic of unique neighborhoods. This is a city that is constantly reinventing itself and always offering opportunities to see, experience, or understand something new and different. Pick up a MetroCard, your transportation key to the kingdom, a good map of the town, and prepare your family for a wonderful whirlwind adventure in glorious Gotham.

DRIVING TIPS

Don't. Don't drive in Manhattan, at least. New York City is blessed with an arguably efficient subway and bus mass-transit system, accessible by the customized MetroCard, and unless you know the streets, you will spend a lot of boring, exasperating time in traffic jams and a fortune on parking and parking tickets. Leave the driving to the yellow medallion taxis, most operated by knowledgeable drivers; fasten your seat belt; and get a receipt. The subway is the fastest way around the boroughs, but the slower buses offer more scenic views. Unless you want to experience the premier thrill ride of this international theme park. For that, board the first subway car on the train, stand in front of the front window, hold on tight, and ride the subterranean city rails through spooky darkened tunnels. Very cool. New front train cars will no longer have this configuration, and older cars will be phased out, so catch this ride while you can. As for the best way to get around

NEW YORK CITY

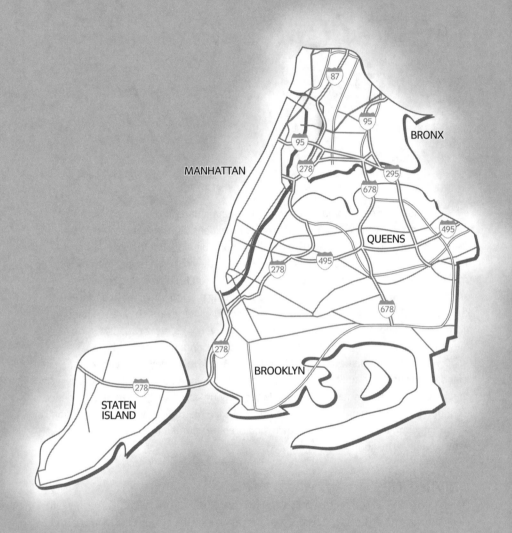

BRONX

MANHATTAN

QUEENS

BROOKLYN

STATEN
ISLAND

town, walking wins. Don't despair on crowded sidewalks, for the pedestrian polka can be mastered with practice.

The Bronx

Once the tribal lands of the Weckquasgeek Indians, the area was settled in the mid-seventeenth century by a Scandinavian sea captain named Jonas Bronck. Remaining rural until the late nineteenth century, the construction of the subway brought waves of new immigrants from Europe, building the borough into a multicultural stew of more than a million people.

Bronx Zoo (International Wildlife Conservation Park) (all ages)

2300 Southern Blvd.; (718) 220-5100 and (718) 367-1010; www.bronxzoo.com. Open daily Apr through Oct, 10 a.m. to 5 p.m. weekdays, 10 a.m. to 5:30 p.m. weekends; Nov through Mar, 10 a.m. to 4:30 p.m. daily. Closed Thanksgiving, Christmas, New Years Day, and Martin Luther King Day. General admission $$$, Total Experience ticket $$$$ (includes seven admissions to rides and attractions); 2 and under free, and donate what you wish on Wed.

Possibly the country's premier urban zoo, with more than 6,000 animals living in large landscaped natural habitats and environmentally controlled ecosystems, this wildlife park celebrated its 110th birthday in 2009. Little feet can get tuckered out traversing the 265 acres of abodes, so plan your visit in advance with online itineraries available from the Web page or pick up a map at the gate and plot your course for family favorites, particularly the feeding demonstrations.

At the wonderful Children's Zoo, you can crawl through a prairie dog den, climb a giant spider web, or pet a plethora of farm animals. Traipse through a tropical rain forest at JungleWorld, ride on a camel, then hop aboard the Wild Asia monorail and glide by gaurs, elephants, and rhinos. Take a trek across the African Plains, past lions and a pack of African wild dogs, toward the dens of big grizzly bears Betty and Veronica and their arctic cousins, the polar bears. The former Antelope House now houses giraffes, a colony of curious pygmy mongooses, and Arthur and Doris, two new nocturnal aardvarks. Visit the World of Birds for an afternoon Bee-Eater Buffet of live crickets, and see penguins perform, along with other aquatic bird antics at the Aitken Sea Bird Colony. Head over to the "African Alps" and the Baboon Reserve, one of the largest primate exhibits in the country. Snakes of all sizes slither at the World of Reptiles, along with a massive prehistoric alligator snapping turtle. The Mouse House is home to a collection of rare and local rodents, and the seasonal Butterfly House, along with a spin on the year-round Bug Carousel, is breathtaking. Hike to the Himalayan Highlands, home to endangered red pandas and snow leopards, then head into the Congo Gorilla Forest, a six-and-a-half-acre fern and waterfall–bedecked primate paradise that's home to more than twenty western lowland gorillas. At the Monkey House, daily primate training demonstrations are held, and at Tiger Mountain, a re-created natural habitat of the Amur (Siberian) tiger, three tiger enrichment sessions are offered every day. Sea lion feedings are fun to watch in the morning and afternoon at their Beaux Arts Astor Court habitat, and nearby in the former lion house are the newest neighbors, the inhabitants of Madagascar, with up-close looks at lemurs, lizards, furry fossas, and cave-dwelling Nile crocodiles. To get a bird's-eye view of the park's vast reserve, skim the treetops inside Skyfari "skybuckets," or take the terrestrial tram for a trip around the perimeter.

Special programs for families are scheduled year-round, including opportunities to investigate careers as a zoologists, animal-tracking adventures, Boo at the Zoo, and Sleepovers with the Creatures. In winter, evening hours are extended during Holiday Lights, a magical display of thousands of twinkling lights sculpted into giant animal shapes scattered throughout the park, with ice-sculpture demonstrations and hot chocolate. The main restaurant, the Dancing Crane Café, serves a variety of hot and cold dishes year-round, and five other seasonal cafes are located throughout the park.

New York Botanical Garden (all ages)

200th Street and Kazimiroff Boulevard; (718) 817-8700; www.nybg.org. Open year-round Tues through Sun, Apr through Oct, 10 a.m. to 6 p.m.; Nov through Mar and Monday holidays, 10 a.m. to 4 p.m.; please call to confirm hours on day of your visit, as special events may preempt the regular schedule. $, under 2 free.

Located next door to the Bronx Zoo, this 250-acre verdant oasis offers fifty plant collections within its indoor and outdoor gardens, ranging from rose to rock to rhododendron. The jewel of this horticultural haven is the Enid A. Haupt Conservatory, the country's largest Victorian crystal palace, filled with the fragrance of exotic and unusual tropical and desert plants from around the world. Outside, trails wind through stands of 300-year-old trees and past the only freshwater river in the city. Discovery carts dot the paths, offering interesting flora facts and hands-on activities. The wonderful Everett Children's Adventure Garden, a twelve-acre nature discovery zone for families, and the Ruth Rea Howell Family Garden offer everyone a chance to play in the dirt, dig up worms, and learn about the fun of gardening every day. Hands-on activities include seasonal programs such as Buzz about Bees, Global Family Gardening, and Goodnight, Garden. In winter the glorious glass house of Haupt hosts "A Victorian Holiday," with G-scale trains running past dozens of miniature replicas of New York's most famous century-old mansions, built entirely from leaves, twigs, and acorns. When the tootsies get tired, hop aboard the narrated tram traversing the trails of the garden or stop for a snack at the Garden Café, then step into the gift shop for gifts that keep on giving, from seed packets to garden supplies.

Yankee Stadium (all ages)

East 161st Street at River Avenue, Highbridge; (718) 293-6000; www.newyork.yankees.mlb .com. Tours year-round Mon through Fri 10 a.m. to 4 p.m., Sat 10 a.m. to noon. Tours limited when team is in town. Admission varies with seat location. $$$–$$$$.

Home of the 2009 World Series champions, the New York Yankees (for the twenty-seventh time!), this new stadium, the most expensive in the country, replaces the 1923 "House that Ruth Built" with the "House that Jeter Built." While the field dimensions are the same, the billion-plus-dollar coliseum has more legroom, upscale amenities, and a steak house. Ticket prices are a bit steeper, but it is a beautiful ball park, seating 51,000 diehard fans of the American League team that has won more World Series than any other team in history. In the footprint of the old stadium will be a new ball field with the same alignment, complete with bleachers, as part of the new Heritage Field and Ruppert Plaza Complex, which will connect to the nearby Macombs Dam Park. Tours of the new stadium are available for an extra fee in season, and the Web site has information about promotional days, with hat, bat, T-shirt, and glove giveaways scheduled throughout the year, and special ticket packages. The pinstriped Bombers play from Apr through Oct—so take your family out to the ball game, buy them some peanuts and Crackerjacks, and see the best ballplayers in the business, right here in the Bronx.

Edgar Allan Poe Cottage (ages 7 and up)

2640 Grand Concourse; (718) 881-8900; www.bronxhistoricalsociety.org. Open Mon through Fri 9 a.m. to 5 p.m., Sat 10 a.m. to 4 p.m., and Sun 1 to 5 p.m. $.

Once surrounded by farmland, this was the home of master writer Edgar Allan Poe and his wife, Virginia, from 1846 to 1849. Poe moved to the Bronx hoping the fresh air would restore Virginia's health, and it was here, "in a kingdom by the sea," that he wrote "Annabel Lee," the haunting poem inspired by his beloved wife. The cottage is currently undergoing a major renovation and restoration, and a new state-of-the-art visitor center is being constructed, due to open in 2010. Check the Bronx County Historical Society for current updates and alternative programming sites.

Bronx Museum of the Arts (all ages)

1040 Grand Concourse at 165th Street; (718) 681-6000; www.bronxmuseum.org. Open year-round Thurs, Sat, and Sun 11 a.m. to 6 p.m., and Fri 11 a.m. to 8 p.m. $, free on Fri.

More than 800 multicultural twentieth- and twenty-first-century works of art are exhibited at this museum, and special programs and workshops are offered for families throughout the year, including hands-on activities, guided tours, concerts, screenings, and surprises.

Museum of Bronx History (ages 7 and up)

Bainbridge Avenue and 208th Street; (718) 881-8900; www.bronxhistoricalsociety.org. Open Mon through Fri 9 a.m. to 5 p.m., Sat 10 a.m. to 4 p.m., Sun 1 to 5 p.m. $.

Once the home of blacksmith Isaac Valentine, this 1758 fieldstone farmhouse was the scene of several skirmishes between the Americans and the British troops during the Revolutionary War. Now the home of the Bronx Historical Society, the main floor of the Valentine-Varian House has several rotating local heritage exhibits, and a small gift shop.

Riverdale Park (all ages)

Hudson River, West 254th Street, Palisade Avenue (718) 548-0917; www.nycgovparks.org. Check Web site for safe directions to access points, depending on your transportation.

This Hudson River slice of shore stretches along the river for over a mile, adjacent to Wave Hill.

Twenty-seven species of birds live year-round in the wetlands and forests, and the billion-year-old bedrock, Fordham gneiss iced with marble, is the oldest formation in town. Within the park is the Raoul Wallenberg Forest, designated Forever Wild, and filled with ancient trees, dense thickets of blackberry bushes, grapes, and wild roses, and a good place to spot woodpeckers, white-throated sparrows, and red-tailed hawks.

Wave Hill (all ages)

675 West 252nd St., Riverdale; (718) 549-3200; www.wavehill.org. Open mid-Apr through mid-Oct, Tues through Sun 9 a.m. to 5:30 p.m., Wed until 9 p.m. during June and July; mid-Oct through mid-Apr, Tues through Sun 9 a.m. to 4:30 p.m. $, children under 6 free; Sat mornings, Tues, and all of Dec through Feb are free for everybody.

Perched on a bluff overlooking the Hudson River, this twenty-eight-acre estate is a wonderful place to play. With plush rolling lawns, spectacular views of the New Jersey Palisades, and formal gardens and woodland nature trails to explore, Wave Hill is a pastoral place of grace and beauty. The two mansions on the grounds, Wave Hill House and Glyndor House, once a peaceful retreat for Mark Twain, Theodore Roosevelt, and others, serve today as cultural centers, offering workshops, concerts, and art exhibits. Free gallery, garden, and tree tours begin at the Perkins Visitor Center. An artist-in-residence leads the year-round Family Art Project, a series of creative eco-art explorations, and master storytellers weave their magic into folktales from nature.

Concrete Plant Park (all ages)

Bronx River, between Westchester Avenue and Bruckner Boulevard; (212) NEW-YORK; www.nycgovparks.org. Free.

Another link in the chain of the Bronx River Greenway, this seven-acre park, once a concrete mixing plant and later an industrial wasteland, is New York City's newest waterfront play place, with a multiuse recreational path lining the western shore of the Bronx River.

Van Cortlandt Park (all ages)

246th Street and Broadway; (718) 548-0912; www.nyc.gov/parks. Park is open daily year-round. Nature Center open Wed through Sun 10 a.m. to 4 p.m. Van Cortlandt House Museum (718) 543-3344; www.vancortlandthouse.org.; open Tues through Fri 10 a.m. to 3 p.m., Sat and Sun 11 a.m. to 4 p.m.; closed Mon and major holidays, and free to the public on Wed. $. Park is free, golf fees separate.

This 1,146-acre nugget of nature abutting the northern border of the Bronx has a hodge-podge of habitats, ranging from woodland to swamp, and red foxes, bald eagles, and even coyotes have been seen here. This is New York City's fourth largest park, and numerous nature trails loop through the woods, past the borough's largest freshwater lake and wetlands, and along an abandoned railway bed. Visit the Van Cortlandt Nature Center for maps and information about activities. The easy John Kieran Nature Trail takes hikers past some of the more scenic sights, including Van Cortlandt Lake, with markers noting ecological and historical information. There are several areas for kids, but two newly renovated favorites are the Classic Playground, a creative climbing adventure through cargo nets and catwalks, and on board swings, slides, and seesaws, and the Sachkerah Woods Playground, a golf-themed play place next to the Moshulu Golf course, with sprinklers, sprays, and sand traps. The Van Cortlandt Golf Course is also here, opened in 1895, and is officially the oldest public course in the country. The Parade Ground, once the site of a Native American village, a Dutch village, a military training area, and a polo field, has undergone a $15 million state-of-the-art renovation of its twenty-six soccer fields, and its baseball/softball, and cricket fields. Recently volunteers planted and cared for 9,000 new tree saplings, painted benches, and weeded and wood-chipped the paths. Athletic events, including marathons and cross-country runs, and nature activities, from birding to photography, are offered year-round.

In the midst of this is the eighteenth-century Van Cortlandt House Museum, a restored estate house filled with authentic antiques, and exhibits exploring the lives lived here, from family slaves to prosperous plantation heirs. As he was a friend of the family, George Washington slept here before engaging the British at the Battle of White Plains. Special events at the museum include a February celebration of President Washington, an Easter Eggstravaganza in spring, history camps in summer, harvest festivals, Haunted Happenings, eighteenth-century celebrations in autumn, and concerts and candlelight tours at Christmas.

Pelham Bay Park (all ages)

895 Shore Road, Pelham Bay Park; (718) 430-1890. Orchard Beach Nature Center (Section 2 of the Beach); (718) 885-3467. Center open Memorial Day through Labor Day, Wed through Sun 10 a.m. to 4 p.m.; www.nyc.gov/parks. Pelham/Split Rock Course; (718) 885-1258. Turtle Cove Mini Golf, 1 City Island Rd.; (718) 885-2646. Bronx Equestrian Center, 9 Shore Rd.; (718) 885-0551; www.bronxequestriancenter.com. Park is free and open year-round; fees for trail rides and golf course.

Nestled in the northeast corner of the Bronx and encompassing 2,766 acres, this is New York City's largest park. Once the site of a 1638 settlement founded by liberal religious leader Anne Hutchinson, today the area attracts sun worshipers to the popular "Riviera of New York," Orchard Beach. The Kazimiroff Nature Trail loops through the rocky Hunter Island Marine Zoology and Geology Sanctuary, and the Split Rock Trail meanders through the Goose Creek Marsh and the Thomas Pell Wildlife Sanctuary, the home of numerous wading birds and the third highest osprey sightings spot in the country. Overlooking the lagoon and Long Island Sound is the nineteenth-century Greek Revival Bartow-Pell Mansion, filled with period antiques and surrounded by formal gardens. Two of the country's oldest public golf courses are here as well, the forgiving Pelham Bay and challenging Split Rock Courses, plus the family-friendly miniature golf course at the Turtle Cove Golf Center. The Aileen B. Ryan Recreational Complex, on the site of the former Rice Stadium, offers a running track, ball fields, and the Playground for All Children, designed for children of all abilities. Take a trail ride, English or western style, atop a horse from the Bronx Equestrian Center, or ride a pony if you're under 4½ feet tall. Special events throughout the year include historical hikes, art exhibitions, concerts, Dutch Days, and Seal-shore Safaris.

City Island Nautical Museum (all ages)

190 Fordham St., City Island; (718) 885-0008; www.cityislandmuseum.org. Open year-round Sat and Sun 1 to 5 p.m. Donation.

Similar in some ways to a small New England fishing village, City Island has a rich maritime heritage. The recently restored museum has interesting exhibits on the lives of the islanders, and the boats they built, including a number of America's Cup winners. Along the main road, City Island Avenue, there are several charter fishing boats and sailboats for hire, as well as good seafood restaurants. My personal favorite for three decades is the one at the end of the road, Johnny's Reef, with outdoor picnic tables, self-service baskets of fried fish, calamari, and clams, soaring seagulls, and panoramic views of the city across the Sound.

Fulton Fish Market at Hunts Point (all ages)

800 Food Center Drive; (718) 378-2356; www.newfultonfishmarket.com. Open Mon through Fri 1 a.m. to 9 a.m.; closed Sat, Sun, and major holidays. $.

Known as the "New York Stock Exchange of Seafood" and recently relocated from its original 180-year home at the South Street Seaport, this is the second largest fish market in the world, after Tokyo's Tsukiji wholesale market. At the new $86 million state-of-the-art facility, the largest consortium of seafood wholesalers in the country handles millions of pounds of seafood daily, with annual sales of more than a billion dollars. Families may visit during operating hours, and see hundreds of varieties of fish, but no photography is allowed.

There's a Farmers' Market, where you can purchase your personal catch of the day, or refuel at the friendly Fulton Cafe with diner delights.

Brooklyn

This was home to the Lenape and Canarsie Indians until the Dutch arrived and began building Breuckelen and other farming villages in the early seventeenth century. In 1898 Brooklyn became a part of New York City, and today some 2.5 million people of more than a hundred ethnic cultures reside in this 71-square-mile borough. For an awesome view, stroll across the famous Brooklyn Bridge, the unique link between Kings County and Manhattan.

Brooklyn Children's Museum (all ages)

145 Brooklyn Avenue; (718) 735-4400; www.brooklynkids.org. Open Wed through Sun 11 a.m. to 6 p.m., 11 a.m. to 5 p.m. during school days and some public school holidays, but closed for other major holidays. $$, free on Wed afternoons.

Founded in 1899, this was the world's first children's museum, and it inspired more than 300 other children's museums around the globe. Renovated and reopened in late 2008, it's doubled in size and is New York City's first "green museum," with photovoltaic panels and a geothermal heating and cooling system. Housed in an underground four-level maze of interconnecting tubes and tunnels, there are dozens of hands-on and interactive exhibits that will excite and enchant all ages, and the museum's collection of more than 30,000 natural-history specimens and cultural artifacts is fascinating.

A new addition is the wonderful World Brooklyn, a kid-size cityscape of stores and activities, from shopping for faux food at an international grocery, performing on the Global Beats stage, to carnival celebrations and dragon dancing. Another new exhibit, TOP SECRET: Mission Toy, offers opportunities to research, engineer, and try spy-style field training with toys from around the world, using puzzles, photographs, and pronunciations. Neighborhood Nature is a chance to check out the plants and animals, from fish to raccoons, living in freshwater ponds, saltwater beaches, urban woodlands, and community gardens. Be an eco-DJ by mixing the sounds around us, and touch a horseshoe crab and sea star.

Outside is the Greenhouse, filled with exotic flowers and unique plants, and nearby lies the famous Fantasia, the museum's 20-foot-long bright yellow albino Burmese python. If you're five or under, you and a lucky adult can enter Totally Tots, a play place of pretend, landscaped with sparkly Cookie Monster–blue sand, padded structures, and a wonderful water table, offering arts and crafts activities and creative play, plus dress-up dramatics. New for 2010 will be a terrific tree house exhibit, Out On A Limb. Highlighting the multicultural diversity of New York, family programs and workshops are offered year-round, and range from scavenger hunts and apple talks to science experiments and international festivals.

The Brooklyn Bridge (all ages)
Access from Brooklyn side at Tillary and Adams Streets, Sands and Pearl Streets, and exit 28B of the eastbound Bronx-Queens Expressway; (718) 222-7259; www.nyc.gov. Free.

This is one of the oldest suspension bridges in the country, and once the longest suspension bridge in the world when first built in 1883. Designed by John Roebling and his son Washington Roebling, it took thirteen years to complete construction. Unfortunately, John was injured before work had actually begun, and his son Washington developed decompression sickness soon after, so the bridge was essentially built under the supervision of Emily Warren Roebling, Washington's wife, who became an accomplished mathematician, engineer, and contract negotiator. When the bridge opened eleven years later, she was the first person to walk across it, and was honored in a speech noting "her capacity for that higher education from which she has been too long disbarred." I highly recommend you re-create that walk some morning, via the wide pedestrian bridge spanning the East River, head east to west, and watch the sun rise reflected on the buildings of the Big Apple. Breathtaking!

Look **Up!**

Sometime around 1968, a crate of Quaker parrots, also called monk parrots, escaped from JFK International Airport, or so one story goes. Colonies of them clustered around the boroughs, but they found Brooklyn to be their favorite area. Now, thousands of them live in nests atop gates, on fire escapes, stadium lights, and trees. For more information, and for parrot safaris, check the website www.brooklynparrots.com.

New York Aquarium (all ages)

Surf Avenue and West Eighth Street, Coney Island; (718) 265-3400 or (718) 265–FISH; www .nyaquarium.com. Open daily year-round at 10 a.m. Closing time varies by season. $$$.

One of the best aquariums in the Northeast, it is also the oldest continuously operating aquarium in the country. More than 8,000 animals of more than 350 species live here, including scary sharks, huge sea turtles, schools of candy-colored fish, electric eels, and graceful anemones. Alien Stingers explores the mysterious world of iridescent, phosphorescent *cnidarians,* the official name for sea jellies. Enter Explore the Shore to experience a 400-gallon tidal wave crashing into you (while you stay dry) and get an underwater view of a saltwater marsh, or touch a horseshoe crab and sea star. Head over to Glover's Reef and Conservation Hall to speak with underwater scuba divers in a massive tank full of coral and exotic fish. Sea Cliffs, a re-creation of 300 feet of the North Pacific's rocky coastline, is home to seals, otters, walruses, and penguins, and the daily feedings are not to be missed. Also a big family favorite is the Sea Lion Celebration at the Aquatheater, an interactive musical training demonstration. Reef, sand, and nurse sharks, along with stingrays and sea turtles, inhabit the floor-to-ceiling 90,000-gallon Shark Tank, and daily feedings here are also very popular. The newest attraction, Planet Earth: Shallow Seas, is a 4-D Experience using 3-D glasses, wind, mist, scents, and dramatic lighting to transport you digitally into the virtual deep. Family events and activities are offered throughout the year, often with a holiday or environmental theme, and there's a SeaSide Café serving hot and cold dishes and snacks year-round.

Coney Island Boardwalk (all ages)

1000 Surf Ave., Coney Island. Museum (718) 372-5159; www.coneyisland.com. Astroland (718) 265-2100; www.astroland.com. Deno's Wonder Wheel Park (718) 449-8836; www .wonderwheel.com. Keyspan Park (Brooklyn Cyclones), 1904 Surf Avenue; (718) 449-8497; www.brooklyncyclones.com. Beach and boardwalk open year-round, with lifeguards on duty from Memorial Day to Labor Day. Rides and attractions individually operated, and usually open weekends Easter to Labor Day, and all week from Memorial Day through Labor Day. $–$$$$.

Long before the debut of Disneyland, Coney Island was the apex of the amusement park world. Once, fantasy islands called Luna Park and Dreamland dotted the boardwalk, but today Deno's is the sole survivor of that magical era. After several years of real estate wrangling, the city has recently purchased portions of the boardwalk, in a plan to revive the area with year-round rides, attractions, and games. For a unique aerial perspective of Manhattan, climb into the 1920s Wonder Wheel or brave the wonderfully rickety Cyclone roller coaster. There are dozens of rides for all ages here, as well as an assortment of pinball and video games at the arcades. "Sideshows by the Seashore" is a ten-in-one tribute to the grittier circus-style shows that once graced the boardwalk, and upstairs is the Coney Island Museum chronicling this legendary seaside park. The classic-style circus of Ringling Bros. and Barnum & Bailey performs ocean-side every summer with its Coney Island Boom-A-Ring show, and the Brooklyn Cyclones, affiliates of the New York Mets, take the field at Keystone Park for their tenth year. A **free** fireworks show is presented every Fri night, but the high-light of the summer is the annual irreverent Mermaid Parade, presided over by a celebrity King Neptune and his Mermaid Queen. This being the birthplace of the hot dog, you must not leave before stopping at Nathan's Famous for some authentic Coney Island cuisine.

Brooklyn Botanic Garden (all ages)

1000 Washington Ave., between Empire Boulevard and Eastern Parkway; (718) 623-7200; www.bbg.org. Open Mar through Oct, Tues through Fri 8 a.m. to 6 p.m., Sat and Sun 10 a.m. to 6 p.m.; Nov to Mar, Tues through Fri 8 a.m. to 4:30 p.m., Sat and Sun 10 a.m. to 4:30 p.m. Closed Mon (except holidays), Thanksgiving, Christmas, and New Year's Day. Adults $$, students 12 and up $, under 12 free.

A lot of trees grow in Brooklyn, but perhaps the most beautiful ones grow in this 52-acre urban oasis. With the finest cherry blossom gardens outside of Japan, a spectacular 5,000-plant rose garden, and the second largest collection of bonsai trees in the country, this is a little slice of paradise. The $25 million glass Steinhardt Conservatory contains eight ecosystems that simulate the global habitats required by this extensive botani-cal collection. Several thousand rare orchids, a cacti-filled desert, a 6,000-square-foot rainforest complete with waterfalls and lush exotic tropical plants fill this crystal palace. Two acres divided into eight geographical zones comprise the Native Flora Garden, show-ing what's growing within a hundred-mile radius of the city. The Japanese Hill-and-Pond Garden is one of the oldest gardens of its kind outside Japan, and the first to be planted inside an American public garden. It was created by master Japanese landscape designer Takeo Shiota in 1915, who later died in a Japanese internment camp in 1943.

South of the Japanese Garden is the Celebrity Path, a trail tribute to over a hundred great Brooklynites, their names paved in leaf-accented stones. The Shakespeare Garden grows more that eighty plants mentioned by the Bard in his sonnets and plays, and in the Fragrance Garden, let your senses celebrate. There are other specialty gardens as well, including the Italian-style Osborne Garden, the Rock Garden built around boulders left behind by retreating glaciers, the pungent Herb Garden, and the 150-specimen Lilac Collection.

The Children's Garden, the first ever established in a botanical garden anywhere in the world, is nurtured by 800 young gardeners from the city schools every year. The Discov-ery Garden is a hands-on place for families to explore nature, either on woodland walks, or during drop-in seasonal activities that may include arts, crafts, and storytelling. The

Terrace Café offers light lunches, and the Garden Gift Shop has a variety of kid-friendly gardening supplies, toys, and books.

Brooklyn Museum of Art (all ages)

200 Eastern Parkway, at Washington Avenue; (718) 638-5000; www.brooklynmuseum.org. Open Wed through Fri 10 a.m. to 5 p.m., Sat and Sun 11 a.m. to 6 p.m. The first Sat of the month is sometimes free, open 11 a.m. to 11 p.m. Closed Thanksgiving, Christmas, and New Year's Day. $$, children under 12 free.

More than 1.5 million works of awesome art from all over the world, spanning some 5,000 years of creative expression and culture, are housed inside this 560,000-square-foot Beaux Arts building, the second biggest art museum in the country. The Egyptian Collection, spread over seven galleries, complete with a real mummy, is one of the best in the West, and kids will enjoy exploring the twenty-eight fascinating American-period rooms. This was the first museum to display African objects as art instead of artifacts, and the Native American collection is impressive as well. Curators have amassed one of the best collections of paintings, prints, and sculpture in the country, with the works of Degas, Rodin, Matisse, van Gogh, Picasso, and the Hudson River School represented. Because the museum's collections are so extensive, one solution was the creation of the Visible Storage Study Center, where thousands of objects are densely stored in transparent glass bays, rotating an ever changing array of objects for public view. Special programs for children ages four through eighteen are offered seasonally, and there are drop-in art activities such as Arty Facts, dance parties, concerts, gallery walks, and special Meet the Museum tours for tots throughout the year.

New York Transit Museum (all ages)

Boerum Place and Schermerhorn Street; (718) 694-1600, tours (718) 694-1867; www.mta .info. Open Tues through Fri 10 a.m. to 4 p.m., Sat and Sun noon to 5 p.m. $.

Housed in a historic 1936 subway station, this is the largest museum devoted to urban public transportation history in the country. The story of New York's subway system is presented here with photographs, artifacts, and videos, and there's a continuous screening of *River of Steel* in the theater. Surface transportation is highlighted at the On the Streets exhibition, with child-friendly street furniture, bus cabs, and a miniature trolley. The Clearing the Air exhibit explores the evolution and environmental impact of fuel technologies, and the Dr. George T. F. Rahilly Trolley and Bus Study Center has more than fifty detailed models of trolleys and work cars. On the platform level is a century's collection of over twenty restored vintage subway cars, and special nostalgic tours and train rides are offered throughout the year.

Urbanglass (all ages)

647 Fulton St.; (718) 625-3685; www.urbanglass.org. Gallery and store open Tues through Fri 10 a.m. to 6 p.m., and Sat and Sun 10 a.m. to 5 p.m.; check Web site for open house schedule and reservations for events. Free to watch, but fees for projects, some suitable for older children only.

MetroCard **Magic**

Catch the A train or any of the other subways in the largest underground fleet in the world with the magnetic MetroCard. The Card works on all the local buses, as well, and provides free transfers. Available for single rides, currently $2.50 per trip, or the money-saving Unlimited Ride Card with a 1-Day Fun Pass ($8.25), or a 7-day ($27.00), 14-day ($51.50), and 30-day ($89.00) option. Up to three children 44 inches tall and under ride free on subways and local buses when accompanied by a fare-paying adult. MetroCards are available at vending machines in subway stations and from many local merchants. For more information check the Web site at www.mta.info.

At this glassworks studio, the largest in the world, visitors can watch artisans magically mold hot globs of glass and electric neon into crystalline creations of color and light. Seasonal Saturday open houses offer families the opportunity to paint on glass, custom design a sandblasted jar, or step up to the "glory hole" and make a one-of-a-kind paperweight.

Brooklyn Academy of Music (BAM) (ages 4 and up)
30 Lafayette Ave., between St. Felix Street and Ashland Place; (718) 636-4100; www.bam .org. Box office open Mon through Fri 10 a.m. to 6 p.m., Sat noon to 6 p.m. Ticket prices vary with event.

As the oldest and possibly the most innovative performing arts center in America, BAM blends the traditional with the contemporary in over 200 dance, theater, music, opera, literature, and film events annually. For nearly three decades the Next Wave Festival has presented cutting-edge artists and their work, and once a year BAM hosts Takeover, an all-night house party with live music, dancing, Ping-Pong, and four movie marathons. Designed to inspire the next generation of young artists are the popular, year-round BAMfamily programs. The BAMfamily Concert Series features award-winning rock, blues, and jazz stars, including Guy Davis and Dan Zanes. At the BAMfamily Book Brunches, families can meet their favorite writers and illustrators, ask questions, and get the artist's current book autographed. The BAMkids Film Festival is an incredible showcase of dozens of international children's films from over twenty countries. The multigenerational and multicultural Sounds Like Brooklyn Music Festival takes place in Feb, with over a hundred shows over two weeks, at thirteen venues around the borough. The eclectic BAMcafe offers **free** live music on Fri and Sat nights, and it's also a good place to grab a bite to eat.

Prospect Park (all ages)
95 Prospect Park West and Grand Army Plaza; (718) 965-8900 or (718) 965-8951; www .prospectpark.org; zoo (718) 399-7339; www.prospectparkzoo.org. Park is open daily

year-round, 5 a.m. to 1 a.m.; **free.** House is open various hours due to school group visits; **free.** Kensington Stables (718) 972-4588; $$$$. Zoo opens daily at 10 a.m., closes at 5 p.m. weekdays Apr through Oct, 5:30 p.m. weekends and holidays, and at 4:30 p.m. daily Nov through Mar. Adults $$, children $, under 3 **free.**

Centered around the terminal moraine of a retreating glacier, the 585 acres of this rustic retreat from the Brooklyn streets is like a trip to the country. Designed by Frederick Law Olmstead and Calvert Vaux, the same landscape architects who created Central Park, this pastoral place features a mile-long meadow, a sixty-acre lake, and the only forest in the borough. Enter the park at Grand Army Plaza and pass underneath the striking stone Civil War Soldiers and Sailors Memorial Arch, inspired by Paris's Arc de Triomphe. Head south toward the child-friendly Prospect Park Zoo, home to over 400 animals of more than eighty species ensconced in natural habitats. Special events there include a Spring Fleece Festival and an Autumn Boo at the Zoo. Nearby is the 1912 vintage carousel, with fifty-one carved creatures and two dragon-pulled chariots. The Lefferts Historic House, once an eighteenth-century Dutch farmstead, is now a fun museum filled with pre-colonial crafts and agrarian artifacts, and offers seasonal activities of candle-making, butter churning, and storytelling.

Head over to the Audubon Center at the boathouse on Prospect Lake to the Learning Lab, home to some live local creatures, and for maps of the four interpretive nature trails, event information, and electric boat tours of the Lullwater aboard the *Independence*.

Also in **the Area**

Marine Park. East 33rd Street and Avenue U; Salt Marsh Nature Center (718) 421-2021; www.nycgovparks.org.

Sunset Park. Seventh Avenue at 43rd Street; (718) 965-6533; www.nycgov parks.org.

Fort Greene Park. Myrtle Avenue, Cumberland Street, DeKalb Avenue; (718) 722-3218;www.nyc.govparks.org.

Red Hook Park. 155 Bay St.; (718) 722-3211 or (718) 722-7105; www.nycgov parks.org.

Herbert Von King Park. 670 Lafayette Ave.; (718) 622- 2082 and (718) 965-6567; www.nycgovparks.org.

Puppetworks. 338 Sixth Ave., Park Slope; (718) 965-3391; www.puppet works.org.

The Old Stone House. 336 3rd St.; (718) 768-3195; www.theoldstonehouse .org.

Pedal boats can be rented at Wollman Rink, which freezes into a popular polar palace in winter. Seven state-of-the art playgrounds dot the perimeter, each uniquely decorated with dragons or frogs spouting water, with storytelling sessions, and arts and crafts activities in summer. The Bandshell is the main stage for live outdoor entertainment, with 2,000 seats and room for 5,000 more on the lawn, and it's also one of the largest outdoor cinemas in the world, with a 21-foot-by-50-foot movie screen. Tennis can be played year-round, on courts covered by big white bubbles in winter. Ball fields for baseball, soccer, and softball are located in Long Meadow, and horse and pony rides are available at Kensington Stables. In addition to special activities at the zoo and house, Prospect Park also sponsors a variety of **free** family events, workshops, gallery shows, and naturalist-led Discover Tours.

Plum Beach (all ages)

Belt Parkway, just after the Knapp Street/Sheepshead Bay exit; (718) 338-3799; www.nyc audubon.org and www.nps.gov/gate. Open daily year-round. Free.

Another slice of the **Gateway National Recreation Area,** this shoreline was created by sand fill from Rockaway Channel to ease erosion. Somehow a honeymoon haven for horseshoe crabs was created, and every spring during the new and full moons, they arrive in droves to lay millions of eggs.

Weeksville Heritage Center (all ages)

1698 Bergen St.; (718) 756-5250; www.weeksvillesociety.org. Open year-round Tues through Fri 1 to 3 p.m., Sat 11 a.m. to 3 p.m.; closed Sun and Mon. $.

In 1850 this was the second largest African American community in pre–Civil War America, with its own schools, churches, and newspaper, and home to more than 500 families. A hundred years later it was all but forgotten, until a historian and a pilot decided to do an aerial search for signs of the town in 1968. From above, they spotted a cluster of wood-framed houses hidden from the main road, and subsequent archeological digs confirmed them to be the historical houses of Hunterfly Road. Tours are offered of the houses, furnished to interpret the nineteenth- and twentieth-century lives of the African Americans who settled here. Special events throughout the year include African Heritage Month celebrations, a Summer Salon Series of outdoor concerts, the annual Weeksville Family Day celebration, and a Holiday Tree Lighting.

The Waterfront Museum and Showboat Barge (all ages)

290 Conover St., at Pier 44, Red Hook; (718) 624-4719; www.waterfrontmuseum.org. Open Thurs 4 to 8 p.m., Sat 1 to 5 p.m. Donation.

Housed on a historic floating barge that occasionally heads up the Hudson River towed by a tug, this charming museum has displays on harbor geography, tides, maritime shipping, commerce, and commuting. A recent exhibit highlighted the history of American showboats, the vehicle used to transport theater, music, and vaudeville throughout the country.

Empire-Fulton Ferry State Park (all ages)

26 New Dock St.; (718) 858-4708; www.nysparks.state.ny.us. Open year-round, dawn to dusk; **free.**

Running along the East River waterfront, sandwiched between the Brooklyn and Manhattan Bridges, this nine-acre park has picture perfect picnic places with panoramic views of the majestic Manhattan skyline.

Jamaica Bay Wildlife Refuge (all ages)

Ryan Visitor Center at Floyd Bennett Field; (718) 318-4340. Floyd Bennett Field (718) 318-3799. Aviator Sports & Events Center (718) 758-7500; www.aviatorsports.com. Jamaica Bay Riding Academy (718) 531-8949; www.horsebackride.com. Jacob Riis Park & Fort Tilden (718) 318-4300; www.nps.gov/gate. Open daily year-round dawn to dusk; visitor center open 8:30 a.m. to 5 p.m. **Free.**

This refuge is part of the Gateway National Recreation Area and the first national urban park in the country. More than 300 species of birds stop or stay here, despite the proximity of JFK International Airport. The William Fitz Ryan Visitor Center is currently closed for renovations, and will reopen in late 2010, but until then, maps, books, permits, and information can be obtained at the Ranger Station near the entrance to Floyd Bennett Field. Trails wind past ponds and through marshes where diamondback terrapins nest, and migrating monarch butterflies fly by in autumn. Summer is the season for swimming at Jacob Riis Park, with day-use passes for beach cabanas, swimming pools, and family recreational facilities at the Breezy Point Surf Club and Silver Gull Club. A new attraction is the twenty-five-acre Aviator Sports & Events Center, a 170,000 square foot indoor facility offering a variety of sports, plus public skate time on the ice rink, rock climbing, bicycle rentals, flight and roller-coaster simulators, Euro bungee, and video games. Horseback riding for equestrians of all abilities is available through Jamaica Bay Riding Academy and Seaside Therapeutic Riding. Nature walks and special events are scheduled year-round, from Irish, Italian, and Native American festivals to medieval Renaissance Faires.

Queens

Named for Catherine of Braganza, seventeenth-century queen of England, this is the biggest borough, encompassing 109 square miles and a rainbow of cultures. From Steinways to stained glass to the silver screen, Queens produced a plethora of products and extended a royal welcome to two World's Fairs.

Alley Pond Park (all ages)

Alley Pond Environmental Center. 228-06 Northern Blvd., Douglaston; (718) 229-4000; www.nycgovparks.org. Environmental Center open Mon through Sat 9 a.m. to 4:30 p.m., Sun 9:30 a.m. to 3:30 p.m.; closed Sun in July and Aug and some holidays. Alley Pond Adventure Center (718) 217-4685 or (718) 217-6034. Adventure Course open to the public **free** May through Nov, Sun at 10 a.m. and 1:30 p.m. Alley Pond Golf Center. (718) 225-9187; www.alleypondgolfcenter.com. $.

Although this 657-acre preserve has been chopped up by several major highways, the resulting mosaic of wetlands, woodlands, and ponds provides a diverse habitat for more than 300 species of birds and wildlife, from fiddler crabs to great blue herons. Begin at the Alley Pond Environmental Center, which offers a small petting zoo and eco-exhibits, then follow the Cattail Trail boardwalk that opens onto a viewing platform set over a green salt marsh. Numerous half-mile color-coded trails wind through hardwood forests, ponds, and freshwater wetlands from here. To the west is the 15,000-year-old, spring-fed, thirteen-acre glacial kettle pond known as Oakland Lake, and nearby are stands of oak and beech trees several centuries old, and a 155-foot tulip tree that's taller than the Statue of Liberty. Four playgrounds, several ball fields and courts, and two recently renovated miniature golf courses offer plenty of activities. A recent addition is the Alley Pond Adventure Course, a state-of-the-art challenge course, the first in the city and the largest in the metro area, complete with ropes, swings, nets, and zip lines. Also new is the Adventure Program, a one-day or overnight fun educational experience, where folks over eight and their families learn how to canoe, fish, use a compass, and experience natural New York for a small fee. **Free** family camping experiences and other events are also offered by the Urban Park Rangers, in a variety of the city's parks, on Fri and Sat nights in July and Aug.

Museum of the Moving Image (all ages)

35th Avenue at 37th Street, Astoria; (718) 784-0077; www.movingimage.us. Open Tues through Fri 10 a.m. to 3 p.m., with extended hours until 5 p.m. on some holidays, but closed Christmas Day and Thanksgiving Day; $$, under 8 free.

Before Hollywood there was Astoria, the birthplace of big-screen entertainment, where stars Rudolph Valentino, the Marx Brothers, and Gloria Swanson got ready for their close-ups. Saved from destruction in the 1970s by concerned film folk, today the Kaufman-Astoria Studios complex includes the largest sound stage outside of Hollywood, as well as seven smaller stages, and film and television production is booming again in the Big Apple. *Sesame Street* is taped here, although studio tours aren't available. You can, however, have lunch at the Studio Cafe, where the cast and crew of features filmed here sometimes stop by for a bite. The wonderful museum next door to the studio has amassed over 130,000 artifacts of the art, history, and technology of the moving image. The core of the collection is displayed in the Behind the Screens exhibit, with photographs and memorabilia from famous films and TV shows. Interactive stations allow kids to animate pictures, add sound effects, and be the stars of their own photo flipbooks. Fourteen classic arcade games, from Asteroids to Space Invaders can be played, and the cinema classic *The Red Balloon* is screened daily in Tut's Fever Movie Palace. The museum is currently undergoing a major expansion, with a three-story addition paneled in pale-blue aluminum, a new state-of-the-art 264-seat movie theater with orchestra pit, a smaller screening room for seminars and education programs, a video-screening amphitheater for changing art exhibitions, and a special screening room on weekends for families. Check the Web site for current schedules and weekend workshops.

Isamu Noguchi Garden Museum (ages 6 and up)

9-01 33rd Road (at Vernon Boulevard), Long Island City; (718) 545-8842; www.noguchi.org. Open year-round, Wed through Fri 10 a.m. to 5 p.m., Sat and Sun 11 a.m. to 6 p.m.; closed Mon and Tues, and Thanksgiving Day, Christmas Day, and New Year's Day. Adults $$, students $, under 12 free. First Fri of every month, pay what you wish.

Housed in a converted photo-engraving plant, this was the studio of the famed Japanese-American modern sculptor, Isamu Noguchi. Recently renovated, the museum is divided into thirteen galleries circling a tranquil courtyard garden dotted with his sculptures. Almost 300 of Noguchi's works of art are on display, created from stone, metal, wood, and clay, as well as some of his mulberry-paper Akari lamps. Free tours are offered every afternoon, in several languages.

Socrates Sculpture Park (all ages)

32-01 Vernon Blvd. at Broadway, Long Island City; (718) 956-1819; www.socratessculpture park.org. Open daily year-round 10 a.m. to sunset. Free.

This is a hands-on hodgepodge of fantastical contemporary creations of cement, stone, tile, wire, and whatever. Established by local artist Mark di Suvero and friends on five acres of an abandoned trash-strewn lot in the 1980s, today it's a wonderful place where children are encouraged to touch, climb, and explore. Special events occur year-round, from Kite Flights, creations crafted from recycled paper, to Summer Solstice celebrations, with drop-in family workshops in rag-doll and mask making, tin can treasures, and Martian-metropolis model building. In July and Aug, bring your picnic blanket, as free classic international films are screened outdoors at dusk, with the skyline of Manhattan in the distance.

Citi Field (all ages)

Citi Field, Roosevelt Avenue, Flushing; St.(718) 507-6387 or (718) 507–TIXX; www.newyork .mets.mlb.com. Ticket prices depend on seat location. $$–$$$$.

This brand-new 2009 baseball stadium, home to the National League's New York Mets, is the replacement rookie for the beloved Shea Stadium. With a capacity for 41,800 fans, it offers wider seats, better sightlines, more restrooms, larger hallways, two and a half acres of Kentucky Bluegrass turf, five restaurants, numerous food concessions serving classic coliseum cuisine of peanuts, pretzels, popcorn, and Cracker Jacks, plus Nathan's hot dogs, Brooklyn Burgers, sushi, seafood, barbecued ribs, pizza, pasta, veggie quesa-dillas, and twenty-eight kinds of beer. On the Field Level is the Mets 2K Sports Fan Fest, featuring team mascot Mr. Mets's Kiddie Field, a small scale version of Citi Field, plus batting cages, a base-running challenge, video-game kiosks, a dunk tank, and a DJ spinning sounds. The Fan Fest opens two and a half hours before all home games, weather permitting, and remains open until the seventh inning. It's fun and it's free, and fortuitous when little leaguers need a second-inning stretch. The season runs from Apr to Oct, and tickets can usually be purchased on game day.

P.S. 1 Contemporary Art Center (all ages)

22-25 Jackson Ave. at 46th Avenue, Long Island City; (718) 784-2084; www.ps1.org. Open Thurs through Mon noon to 6 p.m. $–$$.

This is one of the country's oldest and largest nonprofit contemporary art institutions. More of an exhibition space than a collecting museum, the center's merger with the Museum of Modern Art has created a cultural corridor between boroughs and a closer connection with emerging artists. More than fifty exhibitions are presented each year, from artists' retrospectives and site-specific installations to a variety

New York **in Song**

New York has inspired hundreds of songs, and although the current official state song is "I Love New York," here are a few more of my favorite tunes that tout the town:

"New York, New York"

"Native New Yorker"

"I Happen to Like New York"

"Give My Regards to Broadway"

"The Sidewalks of New York"

"The Only Living Boy in New York"

"Scenes From an Italian Restaurant"

"On Broadway"

"Manhattan"

"New York State of Mind"

"Lullaby of Broadway"

"Autumn in New York"

"Summer in the City"

"Arthur's Theme"

"At The Zoo"

"Broadway"

"The Brooklyn Bridge"

"Chelsea Morning"

"Diamonds and Rust"

"Downtown"

"Empire State of Mind"

"42nd Street"

"52nd Street"

"How About You?"

"Hello, Dolly!"

"NYC"

"Rent"

"Summer in the City"

"Taxi"

of music and performance programs. An annual family summer event is Warm Up, a multisensory mix of music and architecture, now in its tenth year. The Le Rosier Café is open during regular hours and has light snacks and desserts.

Queens County Farm Museum (all ages)

73-50 Little Neck Parkway, Floral Park; (718) 347-3276; www.queensfarm.org. Open year-round weekdays 10 a.m. to 5 p.m. outdoors only, Sat and Sun 10 a.m. to 5 p.m. Closed major holidays. Farm Museum free, except during special events. Green Meadow Farm: (718) 470-0224; www.visitgreenmeadowsfarm.com. $$.

This is the only working historical farm in the city, occupying forty-seven acres of the last remaining undisturbed farmland in town, and the longest continually farmed site in New York State. The 1697 complex includes historic farm buildings, greenhouses, planting fields, an orchard, a vineyard, and a herb garden. Sustainable organic agriculture is practiced, and the produce is sold at their seasonal farm stand, the Union Square Greenmarket, and local restaurants, and donated to City Harvest and local food banks. A variety of heritage breed livestock live here, including sheep, goats, chickens, ducks, pigs, rabbits, and Daisy the Ayreshire cow. The flock of grass-fed Rhode Island red hens lay about ten dozen brown eggs a day, and the Cotswold sheep provide fine wool for a new fiber farm project. The grounds are open weekdays, but free guided tours of the farmhouse are available on weekends, as are hayrides. Next door is the petting zoo portion of the farm, operated by Green Meadows, with cow milking, pony rides, and furry photo ops. In autumn, get a stalk talk before entering the three-acre interactive corn maze, and check the Web site for schedules of special events throughout the year, including wildlife weekends, spring carnivals, farm fests, the Queens County Fair, and the city's oldest and largest Native American gathering, the Thunderbird American Indian Pow Wow, an intertribal dance-off featuring forty tribes.

Flushing Meadows–Corona Park (all ages)

Grand Central Parkway, Van Wyck Expressway, Flushing; (718) 760-6565; www.nycgov parks.org; park open year-round. Tennis Center (718) 760-6200; www.usta.com. Golf (718) 271-8182; www.golfnyc.com. Aquatic Center, Avery Avenue and 131st Street; (718) 271-7572. World Ice Arena, 125-40 Roosevelt Ave.; (718) 760-9001; www.worldice.com. Park is free, but separate fees for some facilities.

Once the nineteenth-century dumping grounds for Brooklyn's garbage, this 1,255-acre parkland was created by the legendary Robert Moses in the 1930s. With the world on the brink of war, he envisioned an international exposition proclaiming peace and prosperity, and Flushing Meadows became the site of the 1939 World's Fair. In 1964 the World's Fair made a second appearance here, anchored by the 380-ton gilded globe called the Unisphere. Wonderful remnants of those fairs remain and house museums of art and science today. The park is the also the location of the US Open Grand Slam tennis tournament, played annually at the newly renamed Billie Jean King National Tennis Center. For most of the rest of the year, the thirty-three courts are available for public use. Eight playgrounds pepper the park, along with numerous ball fields and courts, a driving range, a miniature golf course, and the largest lake in the city, summer scene of the amazing Dragon Boat

Festival. A recent addition is the $66 million, 110,00-square-foot Flushing Meadows-Corona Park Aquatic Center and World Ice Arena, the largest of its kind ever built in a city park, with an indoor, adjustable-floor, Olympic-size public pool, diving tank, and a year-round indoor NHL ice hockey and skating rink.

Queens Zoo (all ages)

53-51 111th St., inside Flushing Meadows Corona Park; (718) 271-1500; www.queenszoo .com. Open Apr through Nov, Mon through Fri 10 a.m. to 5 p.m., Sat, Sun, and holidays 10 a.m. to 5:30 p.m.; Nov through Apr, daily 10 a.m. to 4:30 p.m. Adults $$, children, $, under 3 free.

Giant twenty-six-pound Flemish rabbits, 14-inch-tall deer, Andean spectacled bears that nest in trees, and flocks of endangered thick-billed parrots live here, surrounding an enormous sea lion pool, the site of three daily feeding demonstrations. Spiral up a walkway through the Aviary, where ducks and turkeys waddle on the ground, up to the treetop habitat of prickly porcupines and elegant egrets. Prowl the Great Plains to see a herd of American bison, pronghorn antelope, and a pack of coyotes, including Otis, found lost in Central Park. Meander through a wetlands marsh, past sandhill cranes and alligators, then take a walk past woodlands wildlife, from pumas and Canadian lynx to half-ton Roosevelt elks. Feed the llamas, sheep, and goats at the domestic animal area, and visit the Discovery Center, an indoor activity room with a library of animal-themed books and games, and nature craft activities offered on weekends. Vending machines are the only food source, so pack a picnic!

Queens Museum of Art (all ages)

New York City Building, Flushing Meadows–Corona Park, Flushing; (718) 592-9700; www .queensmuseum.org. Open year-round Wed through Sun noon to 6 p.m., Fri in July and Aug noon to 8 p.m.; closed New Year's Day, Thanksgiving, and Christmas. $.

Across the plaza from the twelve-story Unisphere, housed in the New York World's Fair pavilion, and the first home of the United Nations, is this contemporary museum. Although currently in the process of a major 2012 expansion that will double its size to 100,000 square feet, it continues to host multiple exhibitions of cutting-edge artists and site-specific installations, and to display an amazing collection of rare Tiffany lamps. My favorite part is the Panorama of New York. Originally built for the 1964 New York World's Fair, this amazingly accurate miniature metropolis measures 9,335 square feet and has 895,000 Lilliputian-scale buildings crafted from wood and plaster adorning a giant relief map of all five boroughs, complete with regularly departing airplanes. New lighting and sound effects have been added, and you can purchase a "deed" to one of the miniscule buildings. **Free** family art workshops are offered on Sun, as well as family-friendly performances throughout the year.

New York Hall of Science (ages 4 and up)

47-01 111th St., Flushing Meadows–Corona Park, Flushing; (718) 699-0005; www.nyscience .org. Open Apr through June, Mon through Thurs 9:30 a.m. to 2 p.m., Fri 9:30 a.m. to 5 p.m., Sat and Sun 10 a.m. to 6 p.m.; Sept through Mar, Tues through Thurs 9:30 a.m. to 2

p.m., Fri 9:30 a.m. to 5 p.m., Sat and Sun 10 a.m. to 6 p.m.; and July and Aug, Mon through Fri 9:30 a.m. to 5 p.m., Sat and Sun 10 a.m. to 6 p.m.; closed Labor Day, Thanksgiving, and Christmas. $$, golf $.

This is New York City's only hands-on science and technology center, with more than 400 exhibits exploring biology, physics, and chemistry. Understanding Connections, Hidden Kingdoms, Marvelous Molecules, Seeing the Light, and the Search for Life Beyond Earth are only some of the adventures that await. Sports Challenge shows the science behind the sport, with interactive athletic experiences. At Preschool Place, twenty-two multisensory exhibits invite attention, with blocks, magnets, puppets, and music. Outside is the newly designed, doubled-in-size 30,000-square-foot Science Playground, with two dozen playground elements, including massive musical instruments and giant spiderwebs, plus sand pits and foggy forests to climb through for younger folks. Walk around Rocket Park, where legendary exploring machines of the Space Age rest, including the Mercury-Atlas D Rocket and the Saturn VF-1 engine, the most powerful rocket engine ever built. In the shadow of the two titans is the Rocket Park Mini Golf, a course that teaches physics as it challenges a putter's skill at space docking, launch windows, and re-entry angles.

Queens Botanical Garden (all ages)

43-50 Main St., at Dahlia Avenue, Flushing; (718) 886-3800; www.queensbotanical.org. Open Apr through Oct, Tues through Fri 8 a.m. to 6 p.m., Sat and Sun 8 a.m. to 6 p.m.; Nov through Mar, Tues through Sun 8 a.m. to 4:30 p.m.; closed Mon except for legal holidays. Free, donations welcome.

A thirty-nine-acre oasis of flora, featuring formal gardens of roses, tulips, herbs, and candy-colored perennials and annuals awaits visitors, and special bird and bee flower

Also in **the Area**

Forest Park. 1 Forest Park Dr., Woodhaven; (718) 846-2731; www.nycgov parks.org.

Fort Totten Park. 212th Street and Bell Boulevard; (718) 352-1769; www.nyc govparks.org.

Cunningham Park. Horace Harding Expressway and Grand Central Parkway; (718) 217-6452; www.nycgovparks.org.

Kupferberg Center. Queens College Campus, 65-30 Kissena Blvd., Flushing; (718) 793-8080; www.kupferbergcenter.org.

Kingsland Homestead. 14335 37th Ave., Flushing; (718) 939-0647; www .queenshistoricalsociety.org.

beds attract flying fauna, as well. The garden's new visitor center, part of a $24 million improvement plan, has been called the most advanced green building in the city, with solar panels, geothermal heating and cooling, gray water recycling, and compost systems. From mid-July through mid-Nov, a Farmers Market sets up a stand in the parking lot, and classes in composting are offered, worms optional.

Staten Island

Nestled next to New Jersey, the greenest borough of New York is linked to Manhattan by the scenic Staten Island Ferry and connected to Brooklyn by the graceful sweep of the Verrazano-Narrows Bridge.

Snug Harbor Cultural Center
and Botanical Garden (all ages)

1000 Richmond Terrace; (718) 448-2500. Botanical Garden; (718) 273-8200; www.snug-harbor .org. Grounds open daily dawn to dusk; visitor center open daily 9 a.m. to 5 p.m. Noble Maritime Collection; (718) 447-6490; www.noblemaritime.org. Open Thurs through Sun 1 to 5 p.m., closed major holidays; $. Center and grounds free; museum $.

Established in the early nineteenth century by Revolutionary War maritime magnate and possible pirate Robert Richard Randall as a rest home for ancient mariners, this eighty-three-acre complex encompasses twenty-eight historical buildings in various states of preservation. The Noble Maritime Collection is centered on the artwork of marine artist John A. Noble, who crafted a houseboat from salvaged ship parts and lived aboard it in New York Harbor for forty years, documenting the busy port with his paintings. A replica of his houseboat studio has been recreated, as has a typical sailor's 1900 dorm room, a writing room, and a 12,000-square-foot mural of the maritime industry. Surrounding the center is the beautiful **Staten Island Botanical Garden,** a Victorian landscape of lush lawns, ponds, and fragrant gardens. Literate gardeners will want to see the Secret Garden, with its fantastical maze and medieval castle, and the **Chinese Scholar's Garden** was the first one planted in this country. A recent addition is the Tuscan Garden, a classic Florentine oasis of landscaped terraces, topiary, and fountains, with an amphitheater for plays, puppetry, storytelling, and Italian cultural programs. Other family-friendly activities offered are guided garden walks, nature craft projects, doll fashion shows, concerts, and children's theatrical presentations.

Staten Island Museum (all ages)

75 Stuyvesant Place, at Wall Street; (718) 727-1135; www.statenislandmuseum.org. Open year-round Mon through Fri noon to 5 p.m., Sat 10 a.m. to 5 p.m., Sun noon to 5 p.m.; closed major holidays. $.

More than two million objects and artifacts of art, history, and science are housed in one of New York's oldest museums. The international array of decorative arts, paintings, clothing, and crafts is impressive, but it's the 500,000 specimens in the bug collection that will excite the emerging entomologists in your entourage. Hands-on displays and projects are offered at the Family Gallery, along with frequent workshops, programs, and festivals for children The museum is currently renovating one of the front five buildings at the Snug Harbor Cultural Center, which will become the new Staten Island Art Museum in late 2010.

Staten Island Children's Museum (all ages)

1000 Richmond Terrace; (718) 273-2060; www.statenislandkids.org. Open Tues through Sun noon to 5 p.m. when New York City public schools are open, and 10 a.m. to 5 p.m. when the city's public schools are closed, including weekends; closed Thanksgiving, Christmas, and New Year's Day. $.

Head for the award-winning Staten Island Children's Museum, also part of the Center, where the bugs are bigger, and kids can climb inside a giant anthill, examine a honeybee hive, and watch the birth of a butterfly. Block Harbor, a builder's paradise, has hundreds of wooden shapes to shore up, a wonderful waterfall water table with smocks provided, and a number of touchable art exhibits. Be a firefighter at Ladder 11, where you can don the gear, ring the bell, and slide down a fire pole. The newly renovated Portia's Playhouse provides young thespians with props, costumes, and sound effects to present original skits on stage. Outdoors is a Sea of Boats, a play place of maritime merriment, with watercraft, a lighthouse, a crow's nest, and water play activities. Special events include Tot's Time, Kidz Cook classes, and music, art, and storytelling programs.

Staten Island Zoo (all ages)

614 Broadway, between Forest Avenue and Clove Road; (718) 442-3100; www.statenisland zoo.org. Open daily 10 a.m. to 4:45 p.m. Closed Thanksgiving, Christmas, and New Year's Day. Adults $$, children $, free for children under 3.

Eight acres of animals and aquariums attract families at the first educational zoo in America, and the first one to hire a woman veterinarian. More than 250 species are represented, in habitats ranging from tropical forests to the African savanna. The reptile collection is rather extensive and impressive, full of venomous snakes and lizards, including all thirty-two varieties of rattlesnakes known to inhabit the United States. The Children's Zoo has barnyard animals to feed and pony rides for young rustlers. A new Red Panda exhibit has opened recently, and seasonal programs include Breakfast with the Beasts, Wildlife Film Festivals, Careers with Animals, What's Gnu at the Zoo, and an alpaca kissing contest.

Clay Pit Ponds State Park Preserve (all ages)

83 Nielson Ave.; (718) 967-1976; www.nysparks.state.ny.us. Trails open dawn to dusk. Preserve headquarters open 9 a.m. to 5 p.m. Free.

A hundred years ago, the bricks that built New York were made from the abundant clay deposits found here. What remains today is a 260-acre sand and swamp preserve of pitch pines and blackjack oaks, dotted with kettle ponds and spring-fed streams. This unique ecosystem was designated New York City's first state park preserve and provides habitat for box turtles, screech owls, raccoons, fence lizards, and a 170 species of birds.

Recently, a new $1.3 million interpretive center opened, with historical and natural history displays, plus programs year-round on ecology and plant and animal identification, arts and crafts activities, and ranger-led nature hikes. Easy walks for families include the blue-marked Abraham's Pond Trail or the yellow-marked Ellis Swamp Trail, which take you past wetlands, and the green-marked Gericke Trail that winds through a hardwood forest, once home to the Lenape Indians, and includes a secret stop on the Underground Railroad.

Sandy Ground Historical Museum (all ages)

1538 Woodrow Rd.; (718) 317-5796; www.statenislandusa.com. Open spring and summer, Tues through Sun from 1 to 4 p.m., and winter, Tues through Thurs and Sun 1 to 4 p.m. $.

Before the Civil War, the first community established by freed black slaves was founded along the southern shore of Staten Island. A farming and fishing village, it was also an important stop on the Underground Railroad. Archeological artifacts, photographs, rare books, quilts, and film are part of the museum's collection, and special events throughout the year include arts and crafts sessions, a musical heritage series, and quilting workshops.

Alice Austen House Museum & Garden (all ages)

2 Hylan Blvd.; (718) 816-4506; www.aliceausten.org. Open Thurs through Sun noon to 5 p.m.; grounds open daily until dusk. Closed Jan, Feb, and major holidays. $ donation.

Clear Comfort, a charming cottage built in 1690, trimmed in lacy gingerbread and surrounded by rolling lawns and sweeping views of the harbor, was the home of Victorian photographer Alice Austen. From the age of ten, Alice documented nineteenth- and early-twentieth-century life with more than 9,000 glass-plate photographs, of which some 3,500 still exist. The stock market crash of 1929 plunged her into poverty at the age of sixty-three, but she continued to live here until 1945. Forced briefly to live at the local poor house, Alice was finally given recognition for her amazing photographs at a 1951 exhibition of her work at the Richmond Town museum. She passed away eight months later. In the 1960s the house was saved from demolition by concerned citizens, designated a National Historic Landmark, and it is now a museum offering a variety of photography workshops, exhibitions, dance, concerts, and cultural programs.

Historic Richmond Town (all ages)

441 Clarke Ave.; (718) 351-1611; www.historicrichmondtown.org. Open year-round Wed through Sun 1 to 5 p.m., with extended hours June through Aug; closed major holidays. $ admission includes audio tour.

Three hundred years of history are highlighted here, re-created in over thirty-five buildings of a patchwork historic village set on a hundred acres. Rather than freezing a particular moment in time, historical reenactors seek to guide you through time, with demonstrations of rural and colonial crafts, from candle making and campfire cooking to spinning and storytelling. The island's industrial heritage is displayed at the Made on Staten Island exhibit, and a history lesson all kids will love is offered at the TOY! Exhibit, featuring the best loved toys from the mid-nineteenth century through today. Many of Alice Austin's photographs are also on display. Seasonal events are scheduled through-out the year, including Independence Day celebrations, Civil War encampments, harvest festivals, candlelight tours, doll and teddy bear tea parties, Supper with Santa, and the Richmond County Fair. This living museum also manages the Decker Farm, the Billiou-Stillwell-Perine House, and the Judge Jacob Tysen House, each with unique programs and activities. If you're hungry, stop by the cozy Bennett Cafe, open for lunch, plus breakfast on weekends and dinner on Sat.

Garibaldi-Meucci Museum (ages 5 and up)

420 Tompkins Ave., at Chestnut Avenue; (718) 442-1608; www.garibaldimeuccimuseum .org. Open Tues through Sun 1 to 5 p.m. $.

In the mid-1800s, this was the home of Antonio Meucci and Giuseppe Garibaldi, two extraor-dinary men who changed the world. Meucci is now credited with inventing the first tele-phone, long before Alexander Graham Bell, but for lack of the patent fee he lost the rights to his device. Garibaldi, later known as the revolutionary expatriate hero and founder of the nation of Italy, lived here with Meucci and his wife, making candles to pay their bills. Memo-rabilia, medals, and military artifacts document the lives of these remarkable roommates.

Jacques Marais Museum of Tibetan Art (ages 5 and up)

338 Lighthouse Ave., off Richmond Road; (718) 987-3500; www.tibetanmuseum.com. Open Wed through Sun 1 to 5 p.m. $, classes $$.

Housing the largest private collection of Tibetan art in America, this stone temple com-plex is a peaceful place to stroll, with a goldfish pond, a terraced sculpture garden, and scenic water views. Special exhibits may feature photography from remote regions in the Himalayas, pottery collections, or other artwork exploring the traditions and culture of the Tibetan people. Tai Chi and guided meditation classes are offered year-round, and the annual Tibetan Festival is especially colorful.

Blue Heron Park Preserve (all ages)

222 Poillon Ave., between Amboy Road and Hylan Boulevard; (718) 967-3542; www.nycgovparks.org. Nature Center open Tues through Sat 11 a.m. to 4 p.m., Sun noon to 4 p.m. Free.

Once a wasteland filled with over thirty abandoned cars, concerned citizens spent more than four decades trying to protect this unique place. Stop at the visitors center for interesting exhibits and to walk out onto the two observation decks overlooking this restored wetlands. Bird feeders and a mist net are set up to band birds for research, and picnic tables are convenient to bird-watching. The park's namesake, the 4-foot-tall, gray-feathered, yellow-beaked blue heron, is definitely a descendant of dinosaurs. Herons, along with ibis, osprey, turtles, and tree frogs, make their home here, amidst a wealth of wildflowers and white water lilies. Three main trails wind through the park, and the Urban Park Rangers offer guided nature walks, craft classes, storytelling, and seasonal special events.

Staten Island **Sights**

Clove Lake Park. 1150 Clove Lake; (718) 390-8000; cafe (718) 442-7451; ice rink (718) 720-1010 or (718) 720-1014; www.nycgovparks.org.

St. George Theatre. 35 Hyatt St.; (718) 442-2900; www.stgeorgetheatre.com.

CSI Center for the Arts. 2800 Victory Blvd., at the College of Staten Island; (718) 982-ARTS; www.csi.cuny.edu/arts.

Richmond County Bank Ballpark. Richmond Terrace at Wall Street; (718) 720-9265; www.siyanks.com.

Wolfe's Pond Park (all ages)

420 Cornelia Ave., off Hylan Boulevard; (718) 967-3542; www.nycgovparks.org. Open year-round, dawn to dusk; **Free.**

Once a tidal inlet that was filled in with sand by the retreating Wisconsin glacier, these woodlands and rare freshwater pond along Raritan Bay were home to ancestors of Algonquin tribes more than 6,000 years ago, and the area is rumored to be haunted. Now a park of 341 acres, it has two playgrounds, a roller rink, tennis courts, a freshwater wetlands filled with wildlife, a beautiful beach, and horseshoe crabs arriving by the hundreds on the beach every May and June during the new and full moon.

Great Kills Park (all ages)

3270 Hylan Blvd.; (718) 354-4500 and (718) 980-6130; www.nyharborparks.org. and www.statenislandusa.com. Open daily year-round, dawn to dusk. Lifeguards on duty Memorial Day through Labor Day; **Free.**

This 580-acre peninsula park, part of the Gateway National Recreation Area, has both a barrier ocean beach and an inlet harbor and marina. Swimming, fishing, boating, and bird-watching are popular pastimes, and Park Rangers frequently lead nature walks along the Blue Dot Trail, through a diverse ecosystem filled with wildlife. This is the only osprey nesting site on Staten Island, with special platforms provided for them, and in autumn monarch butterflies and dragonflies migrate through the park. At night, the stars are amazing, and amateur astronomy clubs meet here to stargaze.

Miller Field (all ages)

New Dorp Lane; (718) 351-6970; www.nyharborparks.org. Open daily year-round, dawn to dusk. Ranger Station open Wed through Sun 8:30 a.m. to 5 p.m. **Free.**

Another piece of the Gateway National Recreation Area, this was once a wetlands converted to farmland by the Vanderbilt family, then sold to the U.S. government in 1919 to be used as an Army Air Corps base. Active during the early age of aviation, when grass runways were the norm, this was the field Admiral Byrd used to test his new aircraft before flying over the South Pole. An exhibit at the Ranger Station highlights that history, and it's a good place to get information about activities at the 187-acre athletic fields, ball courts, playgrounds, and picnic places. Take a hike through the Swamp White Oak Forest, home to 300 species of birds, or walk down to Midland Beach, where the boardwalk beckons and the concession stands call.

Fort Wadsworth (all ages)

210 New York Ave.; (718) 354-4500; www.nyharborparks.org. and www.nps.gov/gate; Park open daily year-round, dawn to dusk; Visitor center open Wed to Sun 10 a.m. to 5 p.m.; Free.

The guardian of New York's harbor for two centuries, this historic fort was once one of the most important military bases in the country. Now another nugget of the Gateway National Recreation Area, Ranger led tours of Fort Tompkins are offered, with interesting interactive exhibits at the visitor center. Special events include historical military encampments, kayak adventures, and lantern tours, and the panoramic sunset views of the harbor from Battery Weed are often breathtaking. Stretching for nearly 2 miles south along the shore is the boardwalk of South Beach, with ball fields, bocce courts, a playground, a roller rink, and fireworks in summer.

Staten Island Greenbelt (all ages)

700 Rockland Ave.; (718) 667-2165, Nature Center (718) 351-3450; www.sigreenbelt.org. Parks and natural areas open year-round, from dawn to dusk. Center open Apr through Oct, Tues through Sun 10 a.m. to 5 p.m., and Nov through Mar, Wed through Sun 11 a.m. to 5 p.m. Free.

This lush patchwork of woodlands, covering 2,800 acres and laced together by over 30 miles of trails, is three times larger than Central Park. Visit the Greenbelt Nature Center to view educational environmental exhibits and to pick up maps of the four major color-coded foot trails. A family favorite is the Red Trail, an easy-to-moderate 3.8 mile loop that begins and ends at Historic Richmond Town. Within the Greenbelt is High Rock Park, a 90-acre preserve designated a National Environmental Education Landmark by the U.S. Department of the Interior. Special programs and nature adventures are offered at the Greenbelt Nature Center and at High Rock Park, ranging from arts and crafts workshops to owl prowls and Lenape hikes. In the nearby 164-acre Willowbrook Park, a Victorian-style Carousel For All Children spins endangered animals and mythical beasts past panels depicting Staten Island's history. Also within the Greenbelt is the 540-acre La Tourette Park, with a public golf course and a restored nineteenth-century Federal-style brick mansion built near battlegrounds of the Revolutionary War.

The Conference House (all ages)

7455 Hylan Blvd.; (718) 984-6046; www.conferencehouse.org. Open Apr through mid-Dec, Fri through Sun 1 to 4 p.m. $.

Located on 267 acres overlooking Raritan Bay, at the southernmost tip of Staten Island and of the state, this was once a popular Lenape Indian settlement and trading post. In 1680,

British Royal Navy captain Christopher Billopp built the stone manor house, which later became the scene of an unsuccessful peace conference between King George III's representative, Admiral Lord Richard Howe, and Benjamin Franklin and John Adams. Guided tours are available of the Conference House, and there are three other historic houses on the site, although they are currently closed for restoration. Special events are held in season, from reenactments of the 1776 Peace Conference to saltwater fishing classes for kids.

Manhattan

Purchased, or perhaps rented, for $24 in beads from the Algonquin Indians by Peter Minuit in the early seventeenth century, this was the site of New Amsterdam, the only Dutch colony in America. Today folks say this fantasy island heart of New York is the capital of the world, drawing in dreamers, seekers, and pretty much everybody else for a closer look.

Times Square (all ages)

42nd Street and Broadway; Times Square Alliance Information Center located at 1560 Broadway, between 46th and 47th Streets; (212) 768-1560; www.timessquarenyc.org. Open Mon through Fri 9 a.m. to 7 p.m., Sat and Sun 8 a.m. to 8 p.m. Official NYC Information Center-Midtown; 810 Seventh Ave., between 52nd and 53rd Streets; (212) 484-1222; www .nycgo.com.; open Mon through Fri 8:30 a.m. to 6 p.m., Sat and Sun 9 a.m. to 5 p.m. Times Square Information; www.timessquare.com.

It's been said that if you stand in Times Square long enough, you'll run into every person you've ever known in your whole life. This truly is the "Crossroads of the World," and like the rest of the city, it continues to morph. More "Disneyfied" than dangerous these days, it encompasses a 30-square-block neighborhood—from 40th to 53rd Streets and between Eighth Avenue and Avenue of the Americas—and it's the heart of the theater district and the location of more than 250 restaurants. Full-price tickets to more than forty Broadway shows and other attractions can be purchased at the visitor centers and at theater box offices, or you can stand in line in Father Duffy Square, under the big red glass staircase at 47th Street and Broadway at the TKTS ticket booth for deeply discounted day-of-performance shows. Other TKTS ticket booths are located at the South Street Seaport (199 Water Street), and Downtown Brooklyn (1 MetroTech Center).

But much of Times Square's charm is **free,** with 90-foot flashing neon signs, kinetic billboards, and unique street performers. And of course, this is where the big ball drops every New Year's Eve, above 1 Times Sq., attracting more than a million revelers and two tons of confetti. The new ball, by the way, weighs 11,875 pounds and is covered in 2,668 Waterford crystals with more than 32,000 LED lights that can create over 16 million colors and billions of patterns, making it adaptable to a variety of occasions. Recently, a five-block experimental pedestrian plaza was created, with brightly painted tables and chairs scattered about, perfect for impromptu picnics and people-watching. While you're in the area, walk over to the small island between 45th and 46th St., where Broadway and Seventh Avenue intersect. Stand on the metal grate . . . and listen. The mysterious humming noise you hear is an underground art project, or site-specific sound installation, created in 1977 and reinstalled in 2002. Building on the unique sounds created by an unusual tunnel junction, the late artist Max Neuhaus designed a machine that amplified and enhanced natural noise. Most people walk by and miss this place, because there's no sign anywhere, but it's cool to stand in the center and listen to the tones, day or night, and watch the kaleidoscope of colors and culture swirling around you. The crime rates have dropped dramatically in recent years, thanks to increased police patrols, but take common-sense precautions with your family and other valuables, stay off deserted or darkened streets, and you'll have a great time at the center of the universe.

American Museum of Natural History (all ages)

Central Park West at 79th Street; (212) 769-5100; www.amnh.org. Open daily year-round 10 a.m. to 5:45 p.m.; the Rose Center remains open until 8:45 p.m. on the first Fri of the month. Museum is closed Thanksgiving and Christmas. Adults $$$, children $$, with separate admissions for Hayden Planetarium Space Show, IMAX Films, and special temporary exhibitions; ask about combo packages.

Founded in 1869 and housing more than 150 million anthropological artifacts and scientific specimens, this fabulous museum is one of the reasons I can never leave New York. Forty-five exhibition halls explore everything in creation, from world culture to the cosmos, and there are more real dinosaurs here than in Jurassic Park. Since there's too much to see in one visit, stop at the information desk for a map, and to get a schedule of shows, films, workshops, and daily public tours.

If you entered from Central Park West, begin your trek in the Theodore Roosevelt Rotunda, where a rearing barosaurus towers over an attacking allosaurus. That should whet your appetite for the six spectacular fossil halls on the fourth floor, featuring the largest collection of its kind in the world, so head there first. Or, if you prefer to see the dinos later, walk straight ahead toward the herd of charging elephants attempting to exit the Akeley Hall of African Mammals, illuminated by dozens of exquisitely crafted dioramas.

Continue your African safari on the second and third floors, or head back down to the first floor to the North American Mammals, with dramatic dioramas of grizzly bears, bison, and moose. Around the corner, bear right to enter the Hall of Biodiversity, a celebration of Earth's species, and a cautionary tale of extinction. The Spectrum of Life showcases more than 1,500 specimens, from an extinct Dodo Bird to a giant jellyfish, with a video tour of nine ecosystems, plus a re-created 2,500-square-foot Central African Rainforest.

Descend right into the depths of the Milstein Hall of Ocean Life, where you'll be greeted by a replica of a 94-foot-long blue whale floating peacefully through the ultra-marine air. Underwater exhibits surround you, including a dramatically dark diorama of a squid battling a whale, and giant aquatic videos are screened on a wall.

Surface, and again head right into the North American Forests, featuring faux flora perfect for a game of "I Spy," plus a slice of Sequoia to see. Walk through the Warburg Hall of New York State Environment, towards the Discovery Room, a wonderful hands-on interactive, behind-the-scenes look at the museum and its treasures, designed for children ages five to twelve. Ahead is the newly restored Grand Gallery, anchored by a 63-foot Haida war canoe carved from a single cedar tree.

To the right is the incredible Northwest Coast Indians gallery, the oldest exhibit in the museum, with beautiful paintings, models, and masks. On the other end of the canoe is the entrance to the Spitzer Hall of Human Origins, where you can walk past your past, depicted in dioramas dramatizing human evolution. Head into the next room and you'll see a chunk of the largest meteorite ever plucked from the Earth's surface, the 4.5-billion-year-old, 34-ton Ahnighito, part of the 200-ton Cape York meteorite. Take a peek in the mirror on the ceiling at the pile of pennies pitched there by wishful visitors.

Continue around to the right into the glittering Guggenheim Hall of Minerals and the Morgan Memorial Hall of Gems, where the Star of India Sapphire, the Patricia Emerald, and other legendary gems are displayed. On the second floor are the Halls of Asian, African, South American, Central American, and Mexican Peoples, along with a seasonal Butterfly Conservatory. The Hall of Eastern Woodland Indians and the Hall of Pacific Peoples are located on the third floor, along with an incredible Komodo dragon display.

Filling the fourth floor are the dinosaurs—there is no better collection on Earth. Follow the cladogram on the floor, a diagram of evolutionary history, towards a terrifying T rex with 6-inch teeth, a triceratops, an apatosaurus, a massive mammoth, a snarling saber-tooth tiger, a giant sloth, and hundreds of other fascinating fossils, with touch screens and videos in kiosks along the walls.

Depart the dinos, flee the fossils, and go back to the first floor to see the Gottesman Hall of Planet Earth. Rocks of a Richter scale, deep-sea sulfide chimneys, and a floating rear-screen-projection Earth globe are displayed, a wonderful home-planet prelude for the newest portal to the universe, the Rose Center for Earth and Space. Housed inside a 95-foot-high clear cube constructed from nearly an acre of glass, the Rose Center contains a variety of exhibits that explain, explore, and enlighten visitors curious about the cosmos. Begin at the Big Bang Theater's baby universe blast, then follow the spiraling 13-billion-year time line of the Heilbrunn Cosmic

Look **Up!**

Above the building that houses Actor's Equity, at 165 W. 46th St., are four beautiful but grimy statues. A contest was held in the 1920s to chose the top performers of the day, representing drama, comedy, film, and opera. The winners were Ethel Barrymore (Drew's great aunt), Marilyn Miller, Mary Pickford, and Rosa Ponsell, and they've nestled in these nooks ever since.

Boat **Tours**

Sometimes it's easier to get the big picture of the Big Apple from the water. With a breathtaking skyline, twenty-two bridges to sail under, and the Statue of Liberty to marvel at, a mini-voyage around Manhattan is a must. Of course, the best deal in town is still the free Staten Island Ferry ride across New York Harbor and back.

Staten Island Ferry. Whitehall Ferry Terminal (South Ferry); (212) 639-9675; www.nyc.gov/dot.

Circle Line Sightseeing Cruises and *The Beast* Speedboat Rides. Pier 83, West 42nd Street and the Hudson River; (212) 563-3200; www.circleline42 .com; and (212) 924-6262; www.chelseascreamer.com.

World Yacht. Pier 81, West 41st Street at the Hudson River; (212) 630-8100 or (800) 498-4276; www.worldyacht.com.

New York Skyline Cruises (*Bateaux* and *Spirit of New York*). Pier 62, Chelsea Piers, West 23rd Street and the Hudson River; Bateaux (866) 817-3463 and Spirit Cruises (866) 483-3866; www.spiritofnewyork.com.

Classic Harbor Line. Pier 62, Chelsea Piers, West 23rd Street and the Hudson River; (212) 209-3370; www.sail-nyc.com.

Harbor Tours (*Zephyr* Liberty Cruise and the *Shark* Speedboat). Pier 17, South Street Seaport; (866) 989-2542; www.harborexperience.com.

New York Water Taxi. South Street Seaport, and other locations, with hop-on and hop-off options; (212) 742-1969; www.nywatertaxi.com.

New York Waterway. Numerous terminals in New York and New Jersey; (800) 533-3779; www.nywaterway.com.

Manhattan by Sail. North Cove Marina, Battery Park City and South Street Seaport (two schooners and six sloops); (212) 619-0907 or (800) 544-1224; www.manhattanbysail .com.

Statue Cruises. Battery Park; (877) 523-9849; www.statue cruises.com.

NYC Ducks Tour. 49 W. 45th St.; (212) 247-6956; www .coachusa.com.

Pathway past diamond dust and dinosaur teeth into the Cullman Hall of the Universe. Anchored by the legendary Willamette Meteorite, the hall features kinetic models, interactive computer kiosks, video screens with Hubble highlights and NASA news, and a giant glass globe filled with tiny swimming shrimp that explore the possibility of life on other planets.

But the pearl-shaped gem of this museum is the state-of-the-art spherical Hayden Planetarium Space Theater, the largest and most powerful virtual-reality simulator on Earth. At its heart is the Zeiss Mark IX Star Projector and the Digital Dome System, an intergalactic transporter worthy of wrinkling time, as it virtually speeds space travelers to the edge of the observable universe and back home via a black hole. The current presentation, Journey to the Stars, is narrated by Whoopi Goldberg, and previous shows have been narrated by Tom Hanks and Robert Redford. Sonic Vision, a digitally animated alternative music show, is presented every Fri and Sat night. A new attraction is the Field Trip to the Moon, a live virtual presentation complete with a simulated rocket launch and a sunrise in space.

Several IMAX films are screened daily in the completely renovated Lefrak Theater, and special exhibitions, often with live animals, are scheduled throughout the year. There's an excellent cafeteria in the basement, and several terrific gift shops throughout the museum.

Carnegie Hall (ages 7 and up)

154 W. 57th St. at Seventh Avenue; (212) 247-7800; www.carnegiehall.org. Admission depends on the program; $$–$$$$. Public tours are offered Mon through Fri at 11:30 a.m. and 12:30, 2, and 3 p.m., Sat 11:30 a.m. and 12:30 p.m., and Sun 12:30 p.m. $–$$. Rose Museum; open daily during concert season 11 a.m. to 4:30 p.m., closed July through mid-Sept.

Practice, practice, practice. That's the advice usually given to people who ask how to get to "The House That Music Built." If you're not prepared to perform, check the season's schedule of classical and popular music offerings and inquire about the fabulous Family Concerts series and the CarnegieKids programs. By the way, this is where the Beatles made their New York debut in 1964. That and other interesting historical information can be found at the Rose Museum on the second floor, with an amazing archival musical memorabilia collection, plus possibilities to take a backstage tour and see the sights from a performer's perspective.

Cathedral Church of St. John the Divine (all ages)

1047 Amsterdam Ave., at 112th Street; (212) 316-7540 or tours (212) 932-7347; www .stjohndivine.org. Open Mon through Sat 7 a.m. to 6 p.m., Sun 7 a.m. to 7 p.m., grounds and garden open during daylight hours. Free, with admission charged for some special events, tours, and concerts; $–$$$$.

This Gothic- and Romanesque-style work in progress was started in 1892 and when finished, sometime in the future, it will be the largest cathedral in the world. Much larger than Notre Dame, with ceilings more than 100 feet high and a capacity for 10,000 people, this is an awe-inspiring place. Along with regular Episcopalian services, the cathedral sponsors classical, alternative, secular, Universalist, New Age, Native American programs, as well as concerts year-round. Philippe Petit, the man who walked the high wire between the twin towers of the World Trade Center in 1974, is one of the artists-in-residence, as is Paul Winter, who gives seasonal solstice concerts every year. Madeline L'Engle, the writer of the beloved children's book *A Wrinkle in Time* was a volunteer librarian and writer-in-residence for many years, and she is buried here, as are many other notable New Yorkers. My sons' favorite event occurs in Oct, on St. Francis of Assisi's feast day. Animal lovers line the sidewalk by the hundreds, clutching their dogs, cats, hamsters, parakeets, boa constrictors, and even elephants, for the opportunity to walk down the cathedral aisle and have their beasts blessed.

Central Park (all ages)

Between Central Park West and Fifth Avenue, from 59th Street to 110th Street; Central Park Conservancy (212) 360-3444; Dairy Visitors Information Center (212) 794-6564; Chess and Checkers House (212) 794-4064; Belvedere Castle (212) 772-0210; Charles A. Dana Discovery Center (212) 860-1370; North Meadow Recreation Center (212) 348-4867; Urban Park Rangers (212) 427-4040; Central Park Zoo (212) 439-6500; Children's Glade (212) 360-1461; Lasker Rink/Pool (917) 492-3857 or (917) 492-3856; Wollman Rink (212) 439-6900; www.nyc govparks.org or www.centralparknyc.org. Open all year, 6 a.m. to 1 a.m. Free, except for carousel $, zoo adults $$, children $, rowboats $$, and ice rink and Victorian Gardens adults $$–$$$, children $. Free guided walking tours (about one hour).

The most famous park in the country was faceted into a lush emerald jewel from a swampy and desolate diamond in the rough by the architects Frederick Law Olmsted and Calvert Vaux in 1858. Back then, this 843-acre area was in the middle of nowhere, populated by pig farmers and small villages of squatters, Irish immigrants, Native Americans, and free black landowners. Workers took twenty years to carve and sculpt this scenic space, used nearly 20,000 pounds of gunpowder to blast carriage paths and meadows out of Manhattan bedrock, and spread tons of topsoil around half a million trees, shrubs, and flowers. Today more than twenty-five million people come to play here every year, and it's the true heart and soul of the city. With 58 miles of paths, 9,000 benches, 36 bridges, 21 playgrounds, and a wide variety of activities available, you will not be bored—tired, perhaps, but never bored.

Look **Up!**

On the campus of Columbia University, at 116th Street and Broadway is the symbol of the university, the statue of Alma Mater. Based on Minerva, the goddess of wisdom, there is a tiny owl hidden in the folds of her robe. Legends tell of the luck and good fortune bestowed upon those sharp-eyed enough to spot the secret owl.

Begin your exploration at the Dairy Visitors Center, located at 65th Street, mid-park. Once a Victorian refreshment stand for schoolchildren that featured milk from cows grazing in a nearby meadow, this is a good place to pick up a map or schedule of activities, and to ask about walking tours guided by the terrific Urban Park Rangers.

Nearby is the Chess and Checkers House, with **free** use of game pieces, and a restored 1908 carousel sporting fifty-eight brightly painted horses. Not far from the carousel is the bronze statue of the brave Balto, rubbed shiny from people petting him. In winter, swirling skaters whirl around Wollman Rink, enveloped in a steamy fog. In summer the rink becomes the Victorian Gardens Amusement Park, featuring rides, games, concessions, and entertainment for younger folks. Head north towards Sheep Meadow, the place to be on a picnic perfect day. Nearby is the renovated Central Park Zoo, home to more than 450 animals of one hundred species. Walk through an indoor rainforest, home to bats, birds, snakes, poison dart frogs, and an ant colony embedded with tiny video cameras. Outside is a mountain of snow monkeys, plus the polar bears Gus and Ida, an ice palace of penguins, and the newest addition, snow leopards. Don't miss the thrice-daily harbor seal feedings, and if you'd like to feed some animals yourself, head over to the adjacent Tisch Children's Zoo. Surrounded by giant acorns, huge lily pads, dino-size eggshells, and a kid-size spider web, the alpaca, goats, sheep, and pot-bellied pigs jockey for food pellets.

Walking north, you'll pass under the Delacorte Clock, with its whimsically musical bronze animals that chime the hour, then head toward 72nd Street, where the beloved *Alice in Wonderland* statue sits, overlooking the conservatory water often sailed by radio-controlled model boats. Nearby is the statue of Hans Christian Andersen reading from his children's classic *The Ugly Duckling*. Saturdays, June through Sept, **free** storytelling, rain or shine, takes place at the statue. For a schedule, check out www.hcastorycenter.org.

To the west is the Boathouse, a restaurant and snack bar, where rowboats can be rented for a leisurely lake voyage. Further west, at 72nd Street, is Strawberry Fields, the teardrop-shaped garden memorial to slain musician John Lennon, anchored by the black-and-white mosaic *Imagine*.

Directly south about 6 blocks lies the fairy-tale Tavern on the Green restaurant, with trees festooned in thousands of tiny white lights and giant topiaries of animals standing guard. On the north side of the lake is a wilder area favored by bird-watchers, known as the Ramble. Over 275 species of migratory birds have been spotted in the park, as this is a major rest stop on the Atlantic flyway. It's lovely and peaceful to wander through, but it's not a place to linger alone. Perched on a rocky outcrop mid-park at 81st Street is Belvedere Castle, site of the city's weather station and the Henry Luce Nature Observatory. Panoramic views of Turtle Pond and the Great Lawn can be seen from the castle, while the main floor houses hands-on exhibits of local animals, plants, and nature art activities. Discovery Kit backpacks are available to use **free** of charge, and contain binoculars, a guidebook, maps, and sketching materials. The castle is often lighted as a spectacular backdrop to the adjacent Delacorte Theatre's **free** summer productions of Shakespeare in the Park. On the slopes of the castle's hill is the Shakespeare Garden, featuring flowers and plants immortalized by the Bard's words, and the nearby Marionette Theatre presents puppet performances during the school year. At 96th St. are tennis courts and the

North Meadow Recreation Center, offering a variety of outdoor activities, including rock climbing.

On the edge of North Meadow is the seasonal Lasker Pool and Ice Rink. Near the east side at 105th Street is the Conservatory Garden, a trio of formal landscapes, including one inspired by the classic children's book *The Secret Garden.* Cross over to the west side of the park at 103rd Street and enter the new Peter Jay Sharp Children's Glade at the Great Hill. **Free** multicultural performances and art workshops for families are offered from May through Sept, and include storytelling, jazz jams, and puppet shows. Fun family activities are offered at the Charles A Dana Discovery Center, from catch-and-release fishing and craft activities, to the annual Halloween Pumpkin Sail of carved candlelit jack-o'-lanterns on the Harlem Meer at dusk.

Free programs are offered year-round at numerous locations within the park, from alternative concerts at SummerStage to the New York Philharmonic or Metropolitan Opera performances on the Great Lawn, fireworks included. Check the Central Park Conservancy's Web site for current information.

A recent addition are the forty sites throughout the park where cell phone users can dial (646) 862-0997 plus the extension number of the location (1-40), and get a recorded audio tour by a New York celebrity. Some of the participants are Yoko Ono (Strawberry Fields), Whoopi Goldberg (*Alice in Wonderland* statue), Alec Baldwin (Great Lawn), Neil Patrick Harris (Rumsey Playfield), Anne Hathaway (Delacorte Theater), Matthew Broderick (Sheep Meadow) and Martha Stewart (Arthur Ross Pinetum). More locations will be added in the future.

Chelsea Piers Sports and Entertainment Complex

(ages 4 and up)

62 Chelsea Piers, Between 17th and 23rd Streets on the Hudson River; (212) 336-6666; Sky Rink (212) 336-6100; Golf Club (212) 336-6400; www.chelseapiers.com. Open year-round; hours and admission vary with venue.

Built over the piers where *Titanic* would have docked had she made it to New York, this huge, twenty-eight-acre, $120 million play space for all ages offers first-class facilities for just about any sport you can think of. The 80,000-square-foot Field House features indoor soccer and lacrosse surfaces, batting cages, basketball courts, the largest gymnastics arena in New York, the biggest rock-climbing wall in the Northeast, and the longest indoor running track on Earth. Many of the programs are for a series of lessons or league games, but often drop-in play is possible for soccer, basketball, the batting cages, and the Toddler Adventure Center. Sky Rink's indoor ice surfaces stretch out into the Hudson River, across from the open-air Roller Rink. Another pier houses the Golf Club, with a four-tiered, state-of-the-art, 200-yard driving range with fifty-two hitting stalls installed with automatic tee-up systems, a 1,200-square-foot putting green, an indoor putting studio and sand bunker, and two full-swing simulators. Thirty-two lanes lit with disco-Day-Glo lights and videos make the bowling at 300 New York surreal, and the menu is varied. There's also a full-service marina with charter yacht cruises, a health spa, several sports shops, restaurants overlooking the water, and a lovely promenade. One place not open to the public

Theater **Tickets**

TKTS. Three locations: Times Square, under the Red Steps at 47th Street and Broadway; South Street Seaport, 199 Water St.; and in Brooklyn at the MetroTech Center at Jay Street and Myrtle Avenue; (212) 912-9770; www.tdf .org.

Telecharge. (212) 239-6200; www.telecharge.com.

Ticketmaster. (800) 745-3000; www.ticketmaster.com.

Broadway Cares/Equity Fights AIDS. 165 W. 46th St.; (212) 840-0770; www .broadwaycares.org.

The Actors Fund. 729 Seventh Ave.; (212) 221-7300; www.actorsfund.org.

The League of Off Broadway Theatres and Producers. www.offbroadway .com.

TheaterMania. www.theatermania.com.

StubHub. www.stubhub.com.

is Silver Screen Studios on Pier 62, where the popular TV series *Law & Order* has been filmed for two decades. Special seasonal events are scheduled throughout the year, from ice shows to holiday sports camps.

Madison Square Garden (all ages)

4 Penn Plaza, at Seventh Avenue between 31st and 33rd Streets; (212) 465-6080 or (212) 465-6741 or (866) 858-0008; tickets (212) 307-7171; www.thegarden.com. Knicks hot line (212) 465–JUMP or (877) NYK–DUNK; www.nyknicks.com. Rangers fan hot line (212) 465-4459; www.newyorkrangers.com. New York Liberty (212) 564–WNBA; www.nyliberty.com or www.wnba.com. Tours (212) 465-5800. Hours and prices vary with the event. $$.

Outside of Rome's Coliseum, this is possibly the most famous sports arena in the world, and it's the home turf of the New York Knickerbockers ("Knicks"), the New York Rangers, and the women's NBA team the New York Liberty. Although tickets are sometimes tough to get during peak playoff periods, you can almost always get a peek at their locker rooms during the behind-the-scenes tours or book tickets to any of the other events, circuses, and concerts offered throughout the year. Renovations are scheduled for the next three years, to transform this awesome arena into a state-of-the-art amphitheater, with better sightlines, bigger seats, and a HDTV video system.

Children's Museum of Manhattan (all ages)

212 West 83rd St.; (212) 721-1234; www.cmom.org. Open Tues through Sun 10 a.m. to 5 p.m. and most holiday Mondays, but closed Thanksgiving, Christmas, and New Year's Day.

Strollers must be checked. First Friday of every month open late, and admission is free from 5 to 8 p.m. $$.

Five floors of hands-on exhibits and displays make this museum very popular with younger New Yorkers. When you arrive, go to the yellow visitor services desk to sign up for special activities and workshops, as more than eighty are offered each week, from art projects to sing-alongs and storytelling sessions. There's a Block Party going on in the basement, so head there first to build the town towers and train tracks of your own metropolis. On the first floor you may have noticed a giant wooden horse, part of the Gods, Myths and Mortals exhibit exploring the culture and legends of ancient Greece, with hands-on activities and computer games. Have an adventure with Dora and Diego on the second floor, where kids can climb into Boots' Treehouse, crawl through a pyramid, and visit an animal rescue center. Preschoolers will love the pint-size Playworks on the third floor, where they can create a collage or stir up the sand table, and the Little West Side village on the fourth floor, with its colorful grocery store, a miniature mail truck, and a local library. In warmer months, the Sussman Environmental Center opens the City Splash Outdoor Water Play area, with a winding water table, a puddle patch, and aqua explorations. Photography, art, and literature shows change frequently, and a new exhibition, arriving this summer, is titled Toys: The Inside Story, examining the inner workings of our favorite playthings. Stop at the gift shop before you leave, for a nice selection of educational toys, books, pretend play props, puzzles, New York City souvenirs, and science projects.

Jewish Museum (ages 4 and up)

1109 Fifth Avenue at 92nd St.; (212) 423-3200; www.thejewishmuseum.org. Open year-round Sun, Mon, Tues, and Sat 11 a.m. to 5:45 p.m., Thurs 11 a.m. to 8 p.m., Fri 11 a.m. to 4 p.m.; closed on Wed, Thanksgiving, New Year's Day, Martin Luther King Jr. Day, and all major Jewish holidays. Free on Sat, but the children's exhibition, gift shop, and cafe are closed. Adults $$, children under 12 free.

Founded in 1904 and housing a collection of more than 26,000 works of art, artifacts, and objects, this is one of the most important archives of Jewish cultural history in the world. Ask about the kid-friendly audio guide that highlights the museum's collection. Children can discover their inner Indiana Jones at the Archaeology Zone: Discovering Treasures from Playgrounds to Palaces, with a simulated dig and analysis. At the Family Activity Center, visitors can create holiday or historical arts and crafts projects, go on treasure hunts, participate in classes, and enjoy a variety of musical performances year-round. Free family fun is the focus on Sundays Oct to June, with drop-in art workshops, concerts, and storytelling sessions.

Statue of Liberty National Monument (all ages)

Liberty Island, New York Harbor; (212) 269-5755, (212) 363-3200, or (866) STATUE-4; www.nps.gov/stli or www.nps.gov/elis; Castle Clinton (212) 344-7220; Statue Cruises (877) 523-9849; www.statuecruises.com. Open daily, 9 a.m. to 5:15 p.m. Closed Christmas Day. Monument and museum are free, but there's charge for the ferry and the audio tours: adults $$$, children 4 to 12 $, children under 3 free.

Towering 305 feet over New York's harbor, the Statue of Liberty Enlightening the World, a gift from France, has become New York's most famous figure. Designed by sculptor Frederic-Auguste Bartholdi, who used his mother as a model, Lady Liberty has been welcoming visitors since 1886.

Begin your journey by purchasing combination tour tickets for the round-trip ferry ride, statue, and Ellis Island Museum at Castle Clinton National Monument in Battery Park. To enter the Liberty Island museum or statue you must have a Monument Pass, and they are limited. Ask about the new animal character audio guides, available in five languages, designed especially for children ages six to ten, that explain and highlight historical and cultural experiences of the immigrants who came to these shores. Board the nearby Statue Cruises Ferry for a fifteen-minute voyage across New York Harbor, and disembark at the twelve-acre Liberty Island. Stop at the Visitor Information Station for a brochure and to watch a short video about the statue, then walk over to the flagpole for a **free** forty-five-minute ranger-led tour. Kids can become Junior Rangers by completing a fun booklet with indoor and outdoor activities.

Inside the pedestal is a museum housing the original torch, as well as photographs and artifacts of Liberty's construction. While the current torch has been off-limits for a long time, the crown reopened in 2009, and if you are able to climb the 354 steps to the top, you can peer out of the twenty-five tiny windows of the titan's tiara. The stair trek takes an hour or so, and once you're part of the human chain winding up the cramped spiral inside, the words of Emma Lazarus's poem, "Give me your tired, your poor, your huddled masses yearning to breathe free," may take on a new poignancy. High winds in the harbor can cause the statue to sway 3 inches and her torch to sway 6 inches, but she was made to move. (But you would know that if you had seen *Ghostbusters II*.) The seven rays of her crown symbolize the seven seas and continents of the world, the broken chains around her feet represent her as a goddess free from oppression, and the tablet she carries is a law book inscribed in Roman numerals with the date of American Independence, July 4th, 1776.

Head back to the dock and board the ferry for another fifteen-minute ride to Ellis Island. Between 1892 and 1954, more than twenty-two million people, both passengers

The American Merchant **Mariners' Memorial**

In the northwest corner of Battery Park is possibly one of the most poignant public art pieces in Manhattan. It was inspired by a true event during World War II, when a German U-boat torpedoed an undefended American merchant marine ship. Sculpted by artist Marisol from an actual photograph from the Nazi crew, the scene depicted is of the marines attempting to save their drowning friend. The historical marker states, "Left to the perils of the sea, the survivors later perished."

and crew, passed through the portals of this place, seeking a new life in a new land. Reopened in 1990 after a $150 million restoration, the museum helps visitors retrace the steps of their ancestors' journeys, through films, audio tours, and exhibits of treasured personal possessions brought from their homelands. Three floors of the restored main building have been designed as a self-guided museum, but the park offers **free** ranger-led tours, and kids have the opportunity to become Junior Rangers here as well. Databases of all the immigrant manifests are available at the American Family Immigration Center, for folks who'd like to track their family-tree travelers. Outside, overlooking the Manhattan skyline, is the American Immigrant Wall of Honor, an memorial to more than 700,000 members of America's "melting pot."

Empire State Building (all ages)

350 Fifth Ave. at 34th Street; (212) 736-3100; www.esbnyc.com. NY SKYRIDE (212) 279-9777. Observatories are open year-round, 8 a.m. to 2 a.m. Admission to 86th-floor Observatory, adults $$$, children 6 to 12 $$; admission to 102nd floor an additional $$$; NY SKYRIDE (888) 759-7433; www.skyride.com; combo tickets $$$$.

Once the tallest building in the world, and once again the tallest building in New York, this Art Deco skyscraper will always be the most famous. Built during the Depression in only fourteen months, using prefabricated pieces when possible, it towers 1,453 feet, 8\%6 inches into the sky, with observation decks on the 86th and 102nd floors. Take the high-speed elevators to the decks, and on a clear day you can see for miles. Visit at dusk, when the sky glows pink and orange over New Jersey, the lights of the city wink on, and the rivers of tiny cars twinkle along the streets below. For an entirely different aerial experience, older kids and their brave parents may want to hop aboard the NY SKYRIDE, a wild motion-simulator ride past the city's landmarks. There are three separate lines here, for security, tickets, and elevators, and the wait can be long. One option is to buy your tickets at less busy times or online in advance, or purchase the Express Pass, which moves you to the front of each of those lines. If you're curious about the colors that light the Empire State

Multiple **Attraction Passes**

Several companies offer a variety of combination passes for attractions, tours, rides, and museums throughout the boroughs that save money and avoid many long ticket lines. Check the Web sites, decide which attractions best suit your interests, then plan your adventure.

City Pass (six destinations). (888) 330-5008; www.citypass.com.

Explorer Pass (forty attractions). (866) 628-9027; www.smartdestinations .com.

New York Pass (fifty-five attractions). (888) 567-PASS; www.newyorkpass .com.

Red Double-decker **Bus Tours**

There are dozens of tours of the town available, but for kids, nothing beats bouncing around the Big Apple on the top level of a bright blue or red double-decker bus. Currently, two companies offer hop-on, hop-off options, so you can spend more time at favorite attractions and then catch the next bus that comes along.

Gray Line Tours. 777 Eighth Ave.; (212) 445-0848 or (800) 669-0051; www.new yorksightseeing.com.

City Sights NY. 234 W. 42nd St.; (212) 812-2700; www.citysightsny.com.

Building, check out their Web site for a schedule. Red, white, and blue were the first colors used, to celebrate the American Bicentennial in 1976. Blue and white were introduced the following year, when the Yankees won the World Series, as they did again in 2009.

The Cloisters and Fort Tryon Park (all ages)
99 Margaret Corbin Dr., Fort Tryon Park; (212) 923-3700 and (212) 650-2280; www.met museum.org. Open Mar through Oct, Tues through Sun 9:30 a.m. to 5:15 p.m., Nov through Feb, 9:30 a.m. to 4:45 p.m. Closed Mon, Thanksgiving, Christmas, and New Year's Day. Adults $$$, children under 12 free. Fort Tryon Park (212) 568-5323 or (212) 795-1388; www.nycgovparks.org.

For young wizards and fair princesses, this medieval monastery is a time-travel trip to the days of yore. A branch of the Metropolitan Museum of Art reconstructed from parts of five European cloisters, it features the exquisite sixteenth-century Unicorn Tapestries, along with over 5,000 other medieval masterpieces, and authentic medicinal herb gardens. The Trie Café serves snacks in summer, and free gallery workshops for families are offered year-round, usually involving mythical beasts and legendary tales. Every autumn a free fabulous medieval festival surrounds the Cloisters with magicians, minstrels, jugglers, jesters, and jousting knights on horseback. Vendors hawk their wares in the custom and spirit of the Middle Ages, actors roam the grounds in costume and in character, and it's a lot of fun. The Cloisters is nestled inside the sixty-seven acre Fort Tryon Park, scene of an early battle of the Revolutionary War, during which the first woman to fight in the war, Margaret Corbin, was wounded. There are two playgrounds, ball courts, and the charming New Leaf Restaurant & Bar. The restored Heather Garden has thousands of heathers, heaths, and brooms that bloom in summer, and frame the perfect panorama of the picturesque Hudson River.

Fort Washington Park (all ages)
Fort Washington Park, W. 155th St. to W. 179th St., Riverside Drive; (212) 304-2365, (212) 360-2774, or (212) 360-1311; www.nycgovparks.org. Park open year-round, but lighthouse hours vary. Free.

In the shadow of the George Washington Bridge, the 3,500-foot majestic link between New York and New Jersey, is a 160-acre shoreline park that's home to a little red lighthouse, the only one in Manhattan. Made famous by the Hildegarde H. Swift and Lynd Ward classic children's book, *The Little Red Lighthouse and the Great Gray Bridge*, the river beacon was falling apart by 1951 and slated for demolition. Young fans launched a letter-writing campaign, and the power of the pen saved the literary light. Every year families gather to celebrate the book, and a notable New Yorker, recently the popular Dr. Ruth K. Westheimer, entertains everyone with an enthusiastic reading.

Inwood Hill Park   (all ages)

218th Street and Indian Road; (212) 304-2365 and (212) 304-3401; www.nycgovparks.org; park open daily dawn to dusk, nature center open Wed through Sun 10 a.m. to 4 p.m.; free.

This 196-acre, heavily-forested park, sculpted by departing glaciers, was home to prehistoric people long before Peter Minuit bought the borough from the Lenape Indians in 1626. A boulder now marks the spot where the alleged transaction took place, replacing a 280-year-old tulip tree that had witnessed the deal. What does remain is the last remaining salt marsh in Manhattan, now a protected preserve called Shorakapok. Over 150 species of birds fill the forest, and great blue herons, snowy egrets, and belted kingfishers flock to the wetlands. Stop at the Urban Ecology Center for trail and event information, and almost every Wed and Sat, astronomers arrive at dusk to set up telescopes for free star searches.

Bird's-eye **Views**

The four-minute trip across the East River to Roosevelt Island is fast but fun, while braver aerialists may choose a chopper flight.

Roosevelt Island Tram. Tram Plaza located at 59th Street and Second Avenue; (212) 832-4543 and (212) 832-4540; www.ny.com.

Helicopter Flight Services. Heliport Pier 6, South Street and East River; (212) 355-0801; www.heliny.com.

New York Helicopter. Heliport Pier 6, South Street near Broad Street; (212) 361-6060; www.newyorkhelicopter.com.

Liberty Helicopters. VIP Heliport, 30th Street and West Side Highway; (212) 967-2099; www.libertyhelicopters.com.

Manhattan Helicopters. Pier 17, South Street Seaport; (212) 845-9822; www.flymh.com.

Zip Helicopter Tours. Blue Terminal, West 30th Street and Twelfth Avenue; (866) 947-6837; www.zipover.com.

Grand Central Terminal (all ages)

87 E. 42nd St.; (212) 340-2347; www.mnr.org or www.grandcentralterminal.com. Open year-round, daily 5:30 a.m. to 1:30 a.m. Free.

After a $585 million renovation, this Beaux Arts titan of travel terminals gleams again, from the fiber-optic stars in the ceiling's constellations to the gold-plated, melon-shaped chandeliers. See if you can see the tiny brown square in the corner of the cerulean ceiling. That was the color of the ceiling for many years, before the renovation, and was left there to show the difference before and after. By the way, the zodiac depicted in gold leaf is backwards, because the painter was using a medieval manuscript that showed the stars as seen from outer space, not Earth. Sitting atop the terminal is the sculpture *Transportation,* depicted by the figures of Minerva, Mercury, and Hercules, weighing a titanic 1,500 tons. If you're hungry, you can dine fancy at five upscale restaurants or food-court-style at twenty casual cuisine kiosks on the lower level, or perhaps pack a picnic prepared from the bounty of a dozen gourmet food purveyors at the Grand Central Market. There are over fifty specialty shops scattered throughout the concourses, and a wonderful Holiday Crafts Fair and laser light show in Dec. While you're downstairs, wander over to the Whispering Gallery, in front of the Grand Central Oyster Bar & Restaurant. Stand facing one corner, have a family member stand facing the diagonal corner, and whisper something to the wall—you will be able to hear each other clearly all the way across the room. Cool!

Intrepid Sea-Air-Space Museum (ages 6 and up)

Twelfth Avenue at 46th Street on Pier 86; (212) 245-0072; www.intrepidmuseum.org. Open Apr through Sept, Mon through Fri 10 a.m. to 5 p.m., Sat, Sun, and holidays until 6 p.m.; Oct through Mar, Tues through Sun 10 a.m. to 5 p.m., with some Mon openings; Closed Thanksgiving and Christmas. $$$$, under 3 free, plus $$ for simulator rides and $ for audio tours in 7 languages.

A veteran of World War II, Vietnam, and a prime recovery vessel for NASA, this massive aircraft carrier has been reborn as a terrific museum, housing exhibits of naval, aeronautic, and space exploration history. The *Intrepid* recently returned from a two-year $120 million renovation and restoration. Test your piloting skills inside the G-Force Encounter simulator, survive six minutes of sensory overload inside the Transporter FX, or transcend time and space aboard the new 4-D Motion Ride Theater. Rent an audio tour for a total immersion trip, as veteran narrators guide you to suggested stopping points. Military memorabilia, astronaut artifacts, and interactive exhibits make history pretty interesting. New areas are open to the public for the first time, including the forecastle and the berthing quarters. On deck are over thirty aircraft, with names like *Tomcat, Tiger, Demon, Cobra, Cougar,* and *Fury,* as well as the legendary *Blackbird.* On the pier is the supersonic British Airways *Concorde,* and moored at the dock is the Cold War USS *Growler,* the only nuclear missile submarine open to the public anywhere in the world. Special activities for families include *Intrepid* Investigators, with behind-the-scenes tours and take-home projects, ship sleepovers, and a drop-off camp, SOSI, open during school holidays and vacations.

Look **Up!**

Climbing the canopy of the Graybar Building next to Grand Central Terminal are three determined rats attempting to scale three support rods resembling mooring lines of ships.

Lincoln Center for the Performing Arts (ages 4 and up)

165 W. 65th St.; (212) 875-5456, (212) 875-5000 or CenterCharge (212) 721-6500; www .new.lincolncenter.org. Seasonal schedule, with hours and admissions depending upon performance.

Possibly the finest performing arts complex in the country, this multi-arts center is the home of twelve resident organizations that present thousands of performances in twenty-two different venues on its sixteen-acre campus. Among the temples to talent are the legendary Metropolitan Opera House, the New York City Opera, the New York City Ballet, the New York Philharmonic, Lincoln Center Theater, the Film Society of Lincoln Center, Jazz at Lincoln Center, the Chamber Music Society of Lincoln Center, and the Lincoln Center for the Performing Arts, which presents the Great Performers series, the Mostly Mozart Festival, and Midsummer's Night Swing. The famous Juilliard School and the School of American Ballet are also part of this amazing place. The Performing Arts branch of the New York Public Library is located here as well, and houses the most extensive collection of research materials on theater, dance, and music in the world. A new addition is the David Rubenstein Atrium, on Broadway between 62nd and 63rd Streets, and it's a good place to plan your entertainment. While tickets for all the venues are available at full price at the Atrium, as well as at their individual box offices, there are also opportunities to purchase discount tickets to day-of performances at the Zucker Box Office. There's a nice cafe, **free** Wi-Fi, two vertical gardens, and **free** concerts and performances every Thurs night.

Metropolitan Museum of Art (all ages)

1000 Fifth Avenue, at 82nd Street; (212) 535-7710; www.metmuseum.org. Open Tues, Wed, Thurs, and Sun 9:30 a.m. to 5:30 p.m., Fri and Sat until 9 p.m. Closed Mon, except holiday Mondays, and Thanksgiving, Christmas, and New Year's Day. Recommended admission, adults $$$, children under 12 **free** with adult. Guided and recorded tours $.

Housing more than two million international works of art from prehistory to present day, this is the country's finest and most comprehensive art museum. With so much to see, it can be overwhelming, but if you let your child be your tour guide, go with the flow, and leave before you're worn out, you'll have a great time. First stop should be the Children's Gift Shop, where you'll find a wonderful children's introductory guide to this place called Inside the Museum, by Joy Richardson. Or let your children pick out an assortment of postcards of favorite or intriguing works of art, and together embark on a treasure hunt to find the originals.

Among the riches are the European paintings, including eighteen Rembrandts, thirty-seven Monets, and five Vermeers. A recent $45 million purchase is Duccio's *Madonna and Child*, a fourteenth-century 8-inch-by-8-inch painting. Pick up a map at the entrance and plot a path past family favorites. The mummies mustn't be missed, and wishes can be made at the Temple of Dendur, for the price of a pitched penny. Charge into the Arms and Armor Gallery, to view an amazing collection of chain mail, swords, helmets, and guns, from every continent and century. Dozens of European and American period rooms, filled with decorative arts and exquisite furnishings are scattered throughout the museum, many mentioned in the classic children's book, *From the Mixed-up Files of Mrs. Basil E. Frankweiler*. The recently renovated Greek and Roman Galleries draw from more than 35,000 works, and the American Wing has Tiffany stained-glass panels. The Costume Institute cares for a closet of over 80,000 outfits and accessories, and seasonal shows are themed by designers or historical importance. The modern art collection contains more than 10,000 works, from Picasso to Pollock, and the bulk of the museum's medieval collection is displayed here, while the rest is exhibited at the Cloisters uptown. The rooftop sculpture garden has a variety of outdoor exhibitions, but it's the view overlooking Central Park that makes it special. In winter, the museum decorates a huge Christmas tree with beautiful angels, and concerts of holiday music are presented. **Free** programs for children include "How Did They Do That?," Art Evenings, and Family Orientations for special exhibitions.

Bike the **Boroughs**

If your family is ready to roll, biking can be a blast. Thanks to Mayor Bloomberg, we have more bike lanes than ever, and greenways are growing around and through the boroughs. If you want to stay out of traffic, stick to Central Park, with over 6 miles of bike paths, or travel through the perimeter parks along the rivers. The two companies below offer bicycle rentals and guided themed tours, and they have kid-size bikes and helmets, too. For more information check the city Web site at www.nyc.gov/bikes.

Central Park Bike Tours and Rentals. 203 W. 58th St.; (212) 541-8759; www.centralparkbiketours.com.

Bike and Roll. 557 Twelfth Ave., Pier 84, Hudson River Park; (212) 260-0400; www.bikeandroll.com. (They also have other locations at Battery Park, Governors Island, and South Street Seaport, so you can hop-on, hop-off at a different locations.)

Suggested **Reading**

My New York, by Kathy Jakobsen

Hillary and the Lions, by Frank Desaix

Eloise, by Kay Thompson

The Nighttime Chauffeur, by Carly Simon

How to Take Your Grandmother to the Museum, by Lois Wyse and Molly Rose Goldman

You Can't Take a Balloon into the Metropolitan Museum, by J. P. Weitzman and R. P. Glasser

The Cricket in Times Square, by George Selden

Stuart Little, by E. B. White

All-of-a-Kind Family, by Sydney Taylor

A Tree Grows in Brooklyn, by Betsy Smith

Journey Around New York from A to Z, by Martha and Heather Z. Schock

Tar Beach, by Faith Ringgold

The Little Red Lighthouse and the Great Gray Bridge, by Hildegarde H. Swift

The Saturdays, by Elizabeth Enright

From the Mixed-Up Files of Mrs. Basil E. Frankweiler, by E. L. Konigsburg

Micawber, by John Lithgow

Hey Kid, Want to Buy A Bridge?, by Jon Scieska

The Old Pirate of Central Park, by Robert Priest

Next Stop Grand Central, by Maira Kalman

Central Park Serenade, by Laura Godwin

Milly and Macy's Parade, by Shana Corey

Lyle, Lyle, Crocodile, by Bernard Waber

New York, New York, by Laura Krauss Melmed

New York's Bravest, by Mary Pope Osborne

Pale Male, by Janet Schulman

Morris-Jumel Mansion (ages 7 and up)

65 Jumel Terrace; (212) 923-8008; www.morrisjumel.org and www.nycgovparks.org. Open Wed through Sun 10 a.m. to 4 p.m. Closed major holidays $.

Built in 1765, this Georgian-style manor served as the Revolutionary War headquarters of Gen. George Washington, and it is the oldest colonial mansion in Manhattan. It's also reportedly New York's most famous haunted house. **Free** family workshops are offered in sundial construction, storytelling, and colonial tea parties, as well as seasonal baroque and jazz concerts.

National Museum of the American Indian (all ages)

George Gustav Heye Center, Alexander Hamilton U.S. Custom House, 1 Bowling Green; (212) 514-3700; www.nmai.si.edu. Open daily year-round 10 a.m. to 5 p.m., Thurs to 8 p.m. Closed Christmas. **Free.**

In 1897, New Yorker George Gustav Heye bought a Navajo deer-hide shirt in Arizona. That was the beginning of his passion for building a collection of Native American archeological artifacts that eventually numbered over 700,000 items. Unfortunately, it was difficult to display so many things in New York, so in 1989 the museum became the sixteenth addition to the Smithsonian Institution, with the majority of the artifacts transferred to Washington, D.C., and a smaller branch based inside a beautiful Beaux Arts custom house. Demonstrations of beadwork, basket weaving, quillwork, and doll making are offered throughout the year, as well as traditional dance performances, concerts, and film screenings.

New-York Historical Society (ages 7 and up)

170 Central Park West; (212) 873-3400; www.nyhistory.org. Open Tues, Wed, Thurs, and Sat 10 a.m. to 6 p.m., Fri 10 a.m. to 8 p.m., Sun 11 a.m. to 5:45 p.m.; closed Mon and Thanksgiving and Christmas; Adults $$, children under 12 **free.**

For nearly two centuries this museum has been the archival heart of New York, housing an interesting and eclectic collection of art and artifacts of the Empire State. Among the more than a million treasures are an original copy of the Declaration of Independence, 435 original watercolors of American birds by John James Audubon, and more than a hundred Louis Comfort Tiffany stained-glass lamps. Special events for families include creative-writing workshops, book signings and talks with local authors, and themed scavenger hunts.

New York Public Library (all ages)

455 Fifth Avenue at 42nd Street; (917) 275-6975; www.nypl.org. Open Mon, Thurs, Fri, and Sat 10 a.m. to 6 p.m., Tues and Wed 10 a.m. to 9 p.m., and Sun 1 to 5 p.m. **Free.**

Guarded by the literary lions Patience and Fortitude, this Beaux Arts building houses one of the finest research libraries in the world, with forty miles of books beneath its Bryant Park location. Barrel-vaulted ceilings and cool marble staircases lead to the breathtaking Rose Reading Room. Nearly as long as a football field and 52 feet high, the Rose Reading Room is truly one of the great public spaces, with polished oak tables, glowing brass lamps, Tintoretto-type clouds on a gilded ceiling, and **free** access to the thoughts, ideas, and dreams of great minds and master spirits. Access has improved considerably with the wiring of laptop computer and multimedia workstations into the tables, which can connect with the library's electronic collections, databases, and the Internet. While adults can't check out any of the materials at this research branch, children can at the new Children's Center, a lending library for kids under twelve, with books, CDs, DVDs, eight PC stations with Internet access, and a flat-screen TV for video games. Special events including storytelling, musical and theatrical performances, and opportunities to meet authors and illustrators. New neighbors, given to the library in 1987, are the original Winnie-the-Pooh and his friends Kanga, Piglet, Eeyore, and Tigger, the inspirations for the beloved stories created for Christopher Robin.

Rockefeller Center (all ages)

45 Rockefeller Plaza (visitor center); (212) 632-3975 or (212) 632-4041; www.rockefeller center.com. Radio City Music Hall (212) 307-7171; www.radiocity.com. NBC Studios (212) 664-7174; www.nbc.com. Top of the Rock, 30 Rockefeller Center; (212) 698-2000; www .topoftherocknyc.com. Open year-round. Visitor center open weekdays 10 a.m. to 5 p.m. Top of the Rock open 8 a.m. to midnight. Tour and Top of the Rock, $$$$. Ice Rink (212) 332-7654; www.therinkatrockcenter.com. Show admission varies with performance.

An Art Deco dream city within a city of nineteen buildings on twenty-two acres, this complex was developed by the visionary millionaire John D. Rockefeller Jr. during the Great Depression. Most famous of these structures is Radio City Music Hall, home of the awesome Rockettes and of the "Mighty Wurlitzer" organ, whose booming notes are noted by subway travelers below. The music hall, housing the biggest indoor stage in the world, offers behind-the-scenes tours daily. Nearby are the Channel Gardens, floral fountains sandwiched between the British and French buildings. Stroll down to the golden Prometheus statue that hovers over a seasonal outdoor cafe in summer or a popular winter ice rink in winter The buildings are all connected by underground concourses, lined with over a hundred stores, more than forty places to dine, and seven subway lines below them. There's even a post office so you can mail those postcards! Behind-the-scenes tours are also available at NBC Studios, but not of shows in production. For the best view in town, head to 30 Rockefeller Plaza, and take a 70-floor elevator ride to the Top of the Rock Observation Deck for panoramic views of Central Park and the city skyline. If you're here in Dec, don't miss the world's most famous Christmas Tree, usually a donated 75-foot Norway Spruce garlanded with 5 miles of lights. A week or so later, Tuba Christmas takes to the ice, and hundreds of tuba players give an amazing **free** holiday concert in the recessed rink.

More **Manhattan Museums**

Cooper-Hewitt National Design Museum. 2 E. 91st St.; (212) 849-8400; www .cooperhewitt.org.

National Academy of Design. 1083 Fifth Ave.; (212) 369- 4880; www.national academy.org.

The Morgan Library & Museum. 225 Madison Ave.; (212) 685-0008; www.the morgan.org.

The Skyscraper Museum. 39 Battery Pl.; (212) 968-1691; www.skyscraper.org.

Neue Gallerie. 1048 Fifth Ave.; (212) 628-6200; www.neuegalerie.org.

Ukrainian Institute of America. 2 E. 79th St.; (212) 288-8660; www.ukrainian institute.org.

The Ukrainian Museum. 222 E. 6th St.; (212) 228-0110; www.ukrainian museum.org.

The Asia Society Museum. 725 Park Ave.; (212) 288-6400; www.asiasociety .org.

International Center of Photography Museum. 1133 Avenue of the Americas; (212) 857-0000; www.icp.org.

Museum of Jewish Heritage. 36 Battery Pl.; (646) 437-4200; www.mjhnyc.org.

Museum of Comic and Cartoon Art. 594 Broadway, Suite 401; (212) 254-3511; www.moccany.org.

Ground Zero Museum Workshop. 420 W. 14th St.; (212) 209-3370; www .groundzeromuseumworkshop.com.

Madame Tussauds Wax Museum. 234 W. 42nd St.; (800) 246-8872; www.nyc wax.com.

Ripley's Believe It Or Not!. 234 W. 42nd St.; (212) 398-3133; www.ripleysnew york.com.

Theodore Roosevelt Birthplace (ages 7 and up)

28 E. 20th St.; (212) 260-1616; www.nps.gov/thrb. Open Tues through Sat 9 a.m. to 5 p.m. **Free.**

This reconstructed childhood home of our twenty-sixth president houses the largest collection of artifacts and memorabilia about his life in the world and is a National Historic

Site. Although the original house was demolished in 1916, this re-created brownstone has five period rooms filled with original furnishings, including Teddy's crib.

Sony Wonder Technology Lab (ages 4 and up)

550 Madison Ave., between 55th and 56th Streets; (212) 833-8100; www.sonywondertech lab.com. Open Tues through Sat 10 a.m. to 5 p.m., Sun noon to 5 p.m. Free.

Four floors of cutting-edge communication, industrial, and entertainment technology await visitors at this fascinating electronic play place. Using a personally customized photo ID card, kids can experiment with robots, video games, virtual surgery, animation, movies, music, color, dance, and even a high-definition television production studio, and then get a certificate of their accomplishments printed out at the end. Sometimes there's a bit of a wait, but once inside there are plenty of open stations and a helpful staff to guide you.

South Street Seaport (all ages)

12 Fulton St.; (212) 748-8786; www.southstreetseaportmuseum.org and www.southstreet seaport.com. Open year-round Jan through Mar, Fri through Sun 10 a.m. to 5 p.m., Mon 10 a.m. to 5 p.m.; and Apr through Dec, Tues through Sun 10 a.m. to 6 p.m., closed Mon; ships open noon to 4 p.m.; $, children under 5 free; harbor sails, adults $$$$, children $$$. Little Airplane Studios, 207 Front St.; (212) 965-8999; www.littleairplane.com.

Once scores of sleek clipper ships docked at this busy nineteenth-century port. As the city grew, many of the ships moved to the Hudson River, the area fell into disrepair, and by the 1960s the buildings were slated for demolition. A group of concerned citizens was committed to preserving this part of New York's nautical heritage, and after a $268 million renovation, the twelve-block cobblestoned historic district morphed into a maritime park and marketplace, with shops, restaurants, and activities year-round. In 1998 Congress designated the South Street Seaport Museum as America's National Maritime Museum, so stop there first to get information about special family workshops, events, and harbor sails aboard the *Pioneer*, the *W.O. Decker*, and sometimes even a tugboat. Housed in the restored Schermerhorn Row, the museum has several galleries with displays of nautical memorabilia, paintings, scrimshaw, ship models, and photographs. Around the corner at 211 Water St. is Bowne & Company, a restored nineteenth-century print shop and a good place to get customized stationary.

New York **Trivia**

The New York Public Library has over 40,000 restaurant menus dating back to the 1850s. It also has Charles Dickens's favorite ivory letter opener, with a handle made from the paw of his beloved cat Bob. Other curiosities include Truman Capote's cigarette case, Virginia Woolf's cane, Elizabeth Barrett Browning's slippers, and hair from the heads of Walt Whitman, Mary Shelley, and Wild Bill Hickok.

Outside at the docks is the country's largest fleet of privately maintained historic vessels. Some are permanently moored at the museum pier, and the *Peking* and the *Ambrose* are open for tours. The *Peking* is one of the largest sailing vessels ever built, so climb aboard, explore the living quarters below, and see amazing film footage of *Peking* rounding Cape Horn. Watch woodcarvers craft figureheads for ships, and builders build boats in bottles at the Maritime Crafts Center at Pier 15, under the bow of the tall ship *Wavertree*.

Also at the Seaport, but separate from the museum, is a new attraction, Little Airplane Studios. Tours of a real working preschool television production company are offered every Tues and Thurs, plus one Sat a month, and there's a cool cafe with live performances by the hottest kids' artists. Indie rock concerts for all ages occur both outside and inside year-round, buskers and singers roam the pier, and an eclectic mix of theatrical productions and workshops are offered through Seaport Semester. Seasonal activities include fireworks, festivals, a Singing Christmas Tree, and story time with a sea-worthy Santa.

Forbes Magazine Galleries (all ages)

62 Fifth Ave., at 12th Street; (212) 206-5548; www.forbesgalleris.com. Open Tues, Wed, Fri, and Sat 10 a.m. to 4 p.m. Thurs is reserved for group tours; closed Sun and Mon and major holidays. Free.

Media magnate Malcolm Forbes amassed an amazing collection of over 10,000 toy soldiers, 500 toy boats, antique Monopoly games, historical documents, photographs, trophies, and an incredible vintage jewelry collection. While the toys aren't touchable, they are displayed in detailed formations. Don't miss the chance to peek in the diorama window of a young boy, home sick, playing with his soldiers on his coverlet, as described in Robert Louis Stevenson's poem "The Land of Counterpane." The fabulous Fabergé Egg Collection is no longer here, unfortunately, but the toys are worth the trip.

Riverside Church (ages 4 and up)

490 Riverside Dr., at 122nd Street; (212) 870-6700; www.theriversidechurchny.org. Free.

This interdenominational progressive church, modeled after the thirteenth-century Gothic cathedral in Chartres, France, is the tallest in the country, and houses the largest carillon in the world. Dr. Martin Luther King Jr., Nelson Mandela, Fidel Castro, Kofi Annan and other world leaders have spoken from the pulpit. Inside the 392-foot tower is the 20-ton Bourdon hour bell, plus seventy-four bronze bells, totaling over one hundred tons of heavy-metal music. Although access to the tower is no longer available to the public, **free** tours of the church are offered every Sun after services, and include visits to the chapels, the nave, and the twenty-two-pipe organ console. Carillon concerts occur before and after those services, as well as in late afternoon, and are best appreciated when sitting in nearby Riverside Park, overlooking the Hudson River. The Riverside

Bowling the Borough **of Manhattan**

Bowlmor Lanes. 110 University Pl.; (212) 255-8188; www.bowlmor.com.

Leisure Time Bowl. 625 Eighth Ave.; (212) 268-6906; www.leisuretimebowl
.com.

Lucky Strike Lanes. 624-660 W. 42nd St.; (646) 829-0170; www.bowllucky
strike.com.

300 New York. Pier 60, at 23rd Street and West Side Highway, in Chelsea
Piers; (212) 835-2695; www.threehundred.com.

Harlem Lanes. 2116 Adam Clayton Powell Blvd.; (212) 678-2695; www.harlem
lanes.net.

Theatre in residence offers year-round entertainment, with over 120 dance, music, and
drama performances annually, and family arts festivals and park picnics are offered in
season.

United Nations (ages 7 and older)

First Avenue, at 46th Street; (212) 963-8687; www.un.org. Call (212) 963-1234 in the morning for session agenda. For tours in other languages, call (212) 963-7539. Guided tours conducted Mon through Fri from 9:45 a.m. to 4:45 p.m.; closed major international holidays
and when General Assembly is in session. Children under 5 not allowed on tours; adults
$$$, children $$; exhibits **free.**

Technically, this eighteen-acre complex is not part of New York or the United States
but is an international zone with its own security force, fire department, and post
office. Founded in 1945, the 191 member nations meet to promote world peace and
self-determination and to provide humanitarian, economic, and social aid to the world.
Tours in twenty languages start in the lobby of the General Assembly building, and
the international guides, who come from more than thirty countries are briefed each
morning on world events. Gifts from nations are scattered throughout, from a Chagall
stained-glass window to the Japanese Peace Bell, cast from coins collected by children
from over sixty countries. Take a moment to look at the poignant exhibit of artifacts
from the nuclear bombing of Hiroshima and Nagasaki. For security reasons, visitors are
no longer allowed access to the Conference Building or the Security Council Chamber,
but you will get to see the General Assembly Hall, where world leaders and diplomats
discuss global issues, although you can no longer eavesdrop with headsets during sessions. In the basement is a terrific international gift shop, with crafts from all over the
world, plus wonderful UNICEF cards that you can send postmarked from this unique
international zone.

Hudson River Park (all ages)

353 West St., at West Houston, Pier 40; (212) 627-2020; www.hudsonriverpark.org. Park and piers open daily year-round from dawn to 1 a.m., playgrounds close at dusk, bike path open daily twenty-four hours. Free.

Trimming the Hudson River with an emerald ruffle from 59th street to the tip of Manhattan at Battery Park, this new 550-acre greenbelt rose from the ashes of the abandoned Westway Project. A 5–mile bike and running path links piers, parks, and playgrounds, and skirts the edges of Hell's Kitchen, Chelsea, Greenwich Village, and Tribeca. Although Chelsea Piers is the largest gem in this necklace of play places, there are plenty of other activities to pursue. Pier 84 offers **free** catch-and-release fishing from Big City Fishing, along with an introduction to the ecology of the Hudson River Park's Estuarine Sanctuary, and bikes may also be rented at the kiosk. **Free** kayaking may be attempted at Piers 40, 66, and 96, lessons included. There are currently three creative spray-ground playgrounds spread out along the water. Six piers are under construction at present, so several new activities are in the development stages. Plans for Pier 26 include a miniature golf course, a playground, boathouse, an estuarium, and a cafe. The Tribeca Film Festival will establish a permanent outdoor venue on Pier 57, along with an outdoor public marketplace for artisans, and Pier 62 has a carousel coming its way. Several of the piers are popular with sunbathers in warmer months, especially during the Take Me To The River Festival, a great summer series of **free** concerts, dances, boxing matches, and River Flicks movies for kids. The southern tip of the park melds into Battery Park, and offers spectacular views from the esplanade of New York's harbor and the Statue of Liberty, especially at sunset.

Museum of Modern Art (all ages)

11 West 53rd St.; (212) 708-9400; www.moma.org. Open Sun, Mon, Wed, Thurs, and Sat 10:30 a.m. to 5:30 p.m., Fri 10:30 a.m. to 8 p.m.; closed Tues and major holidays; adults $$$$, children 16 and under free.

With over 150,000 paintings, prints, and sculptures, along with about 22,000 films and four million film stills, this museum houses probably the best collection of Western modern masterpieces of art in the world. *The Starry Night* by Vincent van Gogh, *Christina's World* by Andrew Wyeth, and Monet's *Water Lilies* are but a sample of the sights to see, along with works by Warhol, Hopper, Picasso, Kahlo, Pollock, Rousseau, and Dali. The architecture and design galleries display objects from teapots to helicopters, and classic, rare, and family films are screened daily. The museum has a good introduction to the collection for kids on its Web site, with Destination: Modern Art for five- to eight-year-olds and Red Studio for teenagers. Gallery talks for children are offered according to age, from

New York **Trivia**

The lowest point in New York is on the Atlantic coast, sea level (1,850 miles of ocean coastline).

four to fourteen, with drop-in programs Tours for Fours and A Closer Look for Kids, and a preregister series Tours for Tweens. Special exhibitions are scheduled throughout the year, a recent one focusing on filmmaker Tim Burton. Outside is the Abby Aldrich Rockefeller Sculpture Garden, adjacent to the upscale restaurant, The Modern. Casual gourmet cuisine can be found at Cafe 2 and Terrace 5, serving soups, sandwiches, salads, pastas, and desserts. **Free** audio programs with Wi-Fi, accessible on your iPhone or iPod Touch, are available for all ages, and interactive digital kiosks are scattered throughout the galleries, with exhibit information. The museum bookstore is next door, and across the street is the MOMA Design Store, a great gift shop.

High Line Park (all ages)

Gansevoort Street to 34th Street, between Tenth and Eleventh Avenues; (212) 500-6035; www.thehighline.org. Open 7 a.m. to 10 p.m. **Free.**

Constructed in the 1930s to elevate dangerous freight trains above the city streets, this abandoned railway was transformed into the city's newest park in 2009. When completed, it will run 1½ miles through the neighborhoods of Chelsea and Clinton, to Gansevoort Market. Naturalized landscaping, inspired by the self-seeded flora that sprang up from the old tracks, includes 210 species of sturdy shrubs, grasses, flowers, and trees, and the views of the Hudson through the aging buildings are unique. The Standard Hotel, built by the owner of the Chateau Marmont in LA, sits astride the High Line at West 13th Street, and has a trendy restaurant. Site-specific art is displayed along the Line, ranging from paintings to performance pieces. Access to the park is available at Gansevoort Street, 18th Street, and 20th Street, with stairs and elevators at 14th and 16th Streets.

Governors Island (all ages)

New York Harbor; (212) 440-2200; www.govisland.com. Open May through Oct, 10 a.m. to 5 p.m. **Free** **ferries depart Battery Maritime Building at 10 South St., next to the Staten Island Ferry.** **Free.**

Eight hundred yards from the tip of Manhattan is an island the Native Americans called Pagganck, or Nut Island, because of the forests of oak, chestnut, and hickory trees that blanketed the land. In 1637 it was purchased by the Dutch from the Manahatas for a couple of axes, a string of beads, and assorted nails. In 1784 it was renamed Governors Island by the British, and became a military base for the next two centuries, until it was decommissioned in 1995. In 2003 the U.S. government sold the island to New York for one dollar, with the promise that it would be used for public benefit. Opened in 2004, today the park offers car-free biking, **free** art exhibitions and performances, an artist-designed miniature golf course, an archeological dig, a sustainable farm, Civil War encampments, cultural festivals, film screenings, scavenger hunts, arts and crafts activities, ecology talks, and ranger-led walks. Development is continuing, with plans for a 2.2-mile Great Promenade along the water, and a new 40-acre landscaped park.

Fun **Stores**

New York is a shopper's paradise, with more than 10,000 shops selling anything and everything you could imagine. For kids, however, it's the toy stores that are tops, and there is no shortage of those. Below is a list of some of my favorite places to track down unique toys.

West Side Kids. 498 Amsterdam Ave.; (212) 496-7282.

Kidding Around. 60 W. 15th St.; (212) 645-6337; www.kiddingaround.us.

Dinosaur Hill. 306 E. 9th St.; (212) 473-5850;www.dinosaurhill.com.

Kidrobot. 118 Prince St.; (212) 966-6688; www.kidrobot.com.

Boomerang Toys. 119 W. Broadway; (212) 226-7650; www.boomerangtoys .com.

Toy Tokyo. 121 Second Ave., No. F; (212) 673-5424; www.toytokyo.com.

Mary Arnold Toys. 1010 Lexington Ave.; (212) 744-8510; www.maryarnold toys.com.

Bank Street Bookstore. 2879 Broadway; (212) 678-1654; www.bankstreet books.com.

Forbidden Planet. 8440 Broadway; (212) 473-1576; www.fpnyc.com.

FAO Schwarz Toy Store. 767 Fifth Ave.; (212) 644-9400; www.fao.com.

Toys "R" Us. 1514 Broadway; (646) 366-8800; www.toysrustimessquare.com.

Nintendo World Store. 10 Rockefeller Plaza; (646) 459-0800; www.nintendo worldstore.com.

Build-A-Bear Workshop. 565 Fifth Ave.; (212) 871-7080; www.buildabear .com.

American Girl Place. 609 Fifth Ave.; (877) 247-5223; www.americangirl.com.

The World of Disney Store. 711 Fifth Ave.; (212) 702-0702; www.worldof disney.com.

Tannen's Magic. 45 W. 34th St.; (212) 929- 4500; www.tannens.com.

NBA Store. 666 Fifth Ave.; (212) 515-6221; www.store.nba.com.

Children's Museum of the Arts (ages 2 to 10)

182 Lafayette St.; (212) 274-0986; www.cmany.org. Open Wed, Fri, Sat, and Sun noon to 5 p.m., Thurs noon to 6 p.m.; pay what you wish Thurs 4 to 6 p.m. $$ or $$$$ for family Wee-Arts Class.

As the city's only hands-on art museum for children, this is a great place to explore art unrestricted. Two floors of activities are available for expression, and guided workshops are offered in paint, paper, clay, and fabric. The Open Art Studio has materials for self-guided arts and crafts projects. For inspiration, the museum curates a collection of over 2,000 paintings and works of art made by children from more than fifty countries. On the lower level is a massive multicolored ball pond to thrash around in, an active alternative to the quiet Book Nook, which is filled with colorful children's books to read.

Museum of the City of New York (all ages)

1220 Fifth Ave. at 103rd Street; (212) 534-1672; www.mcny.org. Open Tues through Sun 10 a.m. to 5 p.m.; closed Mon, except holiday Mondays, and Thanksgiving, Christmas, and New Year's Day. $, children 12 and under free.

With more than a million objects and images of New York's past, this is an interest-ing place. Displays about the city's maritime heritage, firefighting history, and period rooms are informative, but what will really impress your kids is the amazing collection of over 10,000 antique toys, including several unique dollhouses. My favorite is the 1920s Stettheimer Doll House, with real miniature paintings, sculptures, and books by famous artists of the time. Almost 27,000 articles of clothing make up the costume collection, and there are at least 2,500 works of art, including paintings, prints, and decorative objects, about New York and New Yorkers. The Theater Collection has thousands of show posters, playbills, and production folders pertaining to the New York theater world, as well as over 5,000 costumes and props, including Peter Pan's shadow from the Mary Martin Broadway production. Special events occur year round, and may include cultural festivals, movies, and craft projects.

Museum of Arts & Design (ages 7 and up)

2 Columbus Circle; (212) 956-3535; www.madmuseum.org. Open Tues, Wed, Fri, Sat, and Sun 11 a.m. to 6 p.m., Thurs 11 a.m. to 9 p.m. closed Mon and major holidays. $$$, chil-dren 12 and under free. $$ for Studio Sundays.

Originally called the American Craft Museum, the newly-named MAD moved to its new home on Columbus Circle in 2008. Exhibitions celebrate a variety of materials and pro-cesses used in creating crafts, art, architecture, fashion, technology, and interior design. The permanent collection has over 2,000 objects, and new exhibitions are presented throughout the year. An ongoing show, Perma-nently MAD, displays about 250 of the museum's favorite works. Free guided gallery tours are given daily. Demonstrations are given in the Open Studio on the sixth floor, and Studio Sundays offer opportunities for families to transformation their creative ideas into mixed media works of art to take home.

FDNY Fire Zone (ages 5 and up)

34 West 51st St.; (212) 698-4520; www.fdnyfirezone.org. Open Mon through Sat 9 a.m. to 7 p.m., Sun 11 a.m. to 5 p.m.; closed major holidays. $.

This state-of-the-art fire-safety learning center gives visitors an up-close and personal experience in respecting the power of fire, and what to do in an emergency. Hands-on exhibits and a multimedia Simulated Fire scene are followed by an exit through a smoke-filled hallway, to the Empowerment Zone, where families are given information and materials necessary for making their home safer.

New York City Fire Museum (all ages)

278 Spring St.; (212) 691-1303; www.nycfiremuseum.org. Open Tues through Sat 10 a.m. to 5 p.m., Sun 10 a.m. to 4 p.m.; closed Mon and major holidays. $.

Located in a renovated 1904 firehouse, this two-story museum houses the largest collection of fire-related art and artifacts in the country, from colonial times to the present. From fire engines to fire equipment and gear, this is a great place to appreciate New York's bravest.

New York City Police Museum (all ages)

100 Old Slip; (212) 480-3100; www.nycpolicemuseum.org. Open Mon through Sat, 10 a.m. to 5 p.m. $, under 2 free.

The history of the world's largest and most famous police force is highlighted at this interesting museum. Vehicles used by New York's finest, along with vintage communication equipment and uniforms are displayed on the first floor. Upstairs there's an authentic jail cell and some weapons of notorious criminals, such as Al Capone's machine gun, and on the third floor is an exhibit that explores how 9/11 affected the New York Police Department. At the opposite end of the floor is the Hall of Heroes, a tribute to all the police officers killed in the line of duty since 1845, with the badge of every fallen officer displayed. The slang name for a policeman in the nineteenth century was cop, because their badges were made of copper. Special programs for families include Junior Detective Day, with hands-on activities and a mystery to solve, and holiday parties.

The Guggenheim Museum (all ages)

1071 Fifth Ave. at 89th Street; (212) 423-3500; www.guggenheim.org. Open Sun through Wed 10 a.m. to 5:45 p.m., Fri 10 a.m. to 7:45 p.m.; closed Thurs, Thanksgiving, Christmas Eve, Christmas Day; open New Year's Eve 10 a.m. to 5:45 p.m., New Year's Day 11 a.m. to 6 p.m. Adults $$$, children under 12 free.

A public collection of several private collections, from late nineteenth-century Impressionists to twenty-first-century conceptual artworks, are displayed in this Frank Lloyd Wright–designed, spiral-shaped architectural landmark. Paintings by Picasso, Kandinsky, van Gogh, Gauguin, Chagall, Renoir, Manet, Monet, and Matisse line the walls of the circular rotunda and the galleries jutting out from the sides. The artwork is amazing, but even if your kids aren't impressed with the Impressionists, they will be by the helical ramp, winding around a huge rotunda for four floors. New temporary exhibitions are opened frequently, and guided family programs include interactive gallery tours, workshops, art and drama activities, storytelling, and seasonal Family Days.

The Whitney Museum (all ages)

945 Madison Ave. at 75th Street; (212) 570-3600; www.whitney.org. Open Wed, Sat, and Sun 11 a.m. to 6 p.m., Fri 1 to 9 p.m.; closed Thanksgiving, Christmas, and New Year's Day. Adults $$$, 18 and under free. Fri is pay what you wish 6 to 9 p.m.

More than 2,800 American artists are represented with over 18,000 paintings, sculptures, drawings, photographs, films, and new media at this museum, with a focus on twentieth-century work. The film and video collection has experimental, independent, and vintage works that are screened daily, and the Whitney Live performance series showcases eclectic artists. Family programs include Stroller Tours, given before the museum is open to the public, Whitney Wees, for ages four and five, Family Fun Art Workshops and the Tours at Two for ages six to ten, and Artist's Choice Workshops for ages eight to twelve. Special events for kids are offered throughout the year, and range from interactive gallery tours, hands-on art making, punk rock concerts, and the annual free WhitneyKids at the Circus, a celebration of Calder's *Circus*.

The New Museum (all ages)

235 Bowery; (212) 219-1222; www.newmuseum.org. Open Wed, Sat, and Sun noon to 6 p.m., Thurs and Fri noon to 9 p.m.; closed Mon and Tues, and Thanksgiving, Christmas, and New Year's Day. Adults $$$, 18 and under free.

This seven-story structure, opened in 2007, curates an ever-changing collection of cutting-edge contemporary art crafted in a variety of media, from performance pieces to political commentary creations. The free First Saturdays for Families is a hands-on program for kids ages five to fifteen, with gallery tours and art activities.

The Rubin Museum of Art (all ages)

150 West 17th St.; (212) 620-5000; www.rmanyc.org. Open Mon and Thurs 11 a.m. to 5 p.m., Wed 11 a.m. to 7 p.m., Fri 11 a.m. to 10 p.m., and Sat and Sun 11 a.m. to 6 p.m.; closed Christmas, Thanksgiving, and New Year's Day. Adults $$, under 12 free.

The most comprehensive collection of Himalayan art in the West is displayed at this new museum, opened in 2004. The exhibit "What Is It?" is a good guide through the landscape of this art world, and changing exhibitions explore mandalas, mythology, religion, and the cosmos, with paintings, sculptures, textiles, and photographs. Programs range from concerts by Tuvan throat singers, to film screenings and talks with filmmakers and writers. Family Workshops are offered every Sat for folks over five, and those under five can enjoy art, movement, and storytelling sessions during the week. Family Days and festivals are held throughout the year, with interactive performances, demonstrations, scavenger hunts, and art activities.

Look **Up!**

There's a wizard sitting atop a clock at 470 Park Ave., who waves his wand every hour, as his apprentice swings a hammer to strike the hours and the "Queen of Silk" emerges from her cocoon to listen.

Riverside Park and Grant National Memorial (all ages)

Hudson River, from 72nd Street to 158th Street; (212) 408-0264; 79th Street Boat Basin (212) 496-2105; Boat Basin Café (212) 496-5542; www.nycgovparks.org and www.nps.gov. Park open dawn to dusk, Memorial open daily 9 a.m. to 5 p.m.; closed Thanksgiving Day, Christmas, and New Year's Day. Free.

Stretching serpentine for 4 miles along the Hudson River, between 72nd Street to 158th Street, this is the city's prettiest riverfront park. It was landscaped by Frederick Law Olmstead, the same man who helped design Central Park, and it offers panoramic views of the river. At the 72nd Street entrance there's a wonderful sculpture of humanitarian and First Lady Eleanor Roosevelt. Twenty-two recreational facilities, including basketball, handball, tennis, and volleyball courts, plus football, softball, and soccer fields, a community garden, and numerous playgrounds are scattered along this greenbelt. Across from the 110-slip marina at the 79th Street Boat Basin there's a wonderful outdoor cafe, very popular at sunset. Further north, at 122nd Street, is the General Grant National Memorial, the largest mausoleum in North America, and the final resting place of Grant and his wife, Julia. Free guided tours of the monument are offered several times daily, and special events include candlelight tours of the crypt, and General Grant's Birthday Celebration, with a Civil War encampment and costumed reenactors.

National Track and Field Hall of Fame (ages 6 and up)

216 Fort Washington Ave., between 168th Street and 169th Street; (212) 923-1803; www .usatf.org. Open mid-Nov to mid-Apr, Tues through Sun 10 a.m. to 5 p.m., and mid-Apr to mid-Nov, Tues through Fri 10 a.m. to 5 p.m. $.

Located inside a former armory since 2002, three floors of interactive exhibits hit the historical highlights of track and field, the technology of the sports, and the accomplishments of the 229 people currently enshrined. Next door is a 65,000-square-foot arena that's home to the largest indoor collegiate and high school invitational events in the world.

Riverbank State Park (all ages)

679 Riverside Dr.; (212) 694-3600; www.nysparks.state.ny.us. Open year-round 6 a.m. to 11 p.m.; fees for different facilities, $. Call ahead to confirm changes to hours, activities available, and possible closures due to pending state budget cuts.

This 28-acre multilevel landscaped recreational facility was built on top of a waste treatment plant, and it's the only park of its kind on this side of the planet. Five large buildings house an Olympic-size pool, a seasonal roller- and ice-skating rink, an 800-seat theater, a

2,500-seat athletic complex, and restaurant. Outside are a lap pool, a wading pool, plus tennis, basketball, and handball courts, a running track, a soccer field, picnic areas, a colorful carousel, and two playgrounds.

Paley Center for Media (all ages)

25 West 52nd St.; (212) 621-6800 and (212) 621-6600; www.paleycenter.org. Open Wed, Fri, Sat and Sun noon to 6 p.m., Thurs noon to 8 p.m.; closed Mon and Tues, New Year's Day, Independence Day, Thanksgiving, and Christmas. $$, $ for children under 14.

Almost 150,000 television and radio programs and advertisements are available for viewing at private consoles at the former Museum of Television and Radio. Go early in the day, as time slots fill up fast, and order up programs from a computer database, then view them on monitors. For kids nine and older, the Re-creating Radio Workshop offers the opportunity to produce a vintage radio program, with scripts, sound effects, and music, then take home a copy of the completed show. *She Made It* is a collection of programming created by women in radio, television, and film, with inductees into a hall of fame every year, including icons Donna de Varona, Dr. Ruth Westheimer, Christiane Amanpour, Candice Bergen, Martha Stewart, Ellen DeGeneres, and Oprah Winfrey. Several galleries exhibit an array of artifacts and art relating to radio, TV, and film, and screenings are scheduled daily, drawn from the center's collections.

American Folk Art Museum (all ages)

45 West 53rd St.; (212) 265-1040; branch location, 2 Lincoln Square, (212) 977-7170; www .folkartmuseum.org. Open Tues through Sun, 10:30 a.m. to 5:30 p.m., Fri 11 a.m. to 7:30 p.m.; closed Mon. $$, under 12 free.

Folk Art is the creative expression of contemporary self-taught artists. Preserving, conserving, and interpreting this "outsider art" is the mission of the museum, whose collection has grown to include international objects along with American pieces, from the eighteenth century to the present. Paintings, pottery, quilts, furniture, trade signs, toys, weathervanes, and whirligigs are displayed in the galleries of the main museum, and at the branch opposite Lincoln Center. The Contemporary Center presents lectures, symposia, and special events year-round. **Free** family guides are available at the front desk, and the Family and Folk Art program is offered the first Sat of every month, with interactive gallery tours and hand-on art activities.

El Museo del Barrio (all ages)

1230 Fifth Ave. at 104th Street; (212) 831-7272; www.elmuseo.org. Open Wed through Sun 11 a.m. to 5 p.m., closed Mon, Tues, New Year's Day, Fourth of July, Thanksgiving, and Christmas. $, under 12 free; free for everyone every third Sat.

Created during the Civil Rights Movement, when parents, teachers, and activists demanded that children receive a culturally diverse education, this museum celebrates the city's Caribbean, Latino, and Latin American heritage. Drawing from a collection of more than 6,500 paintings, prints, photographs, sculptures, and musical instruments, the museum offers changing exhibitions focusing on a particular artist or style of art. Gallery tours are offered in English and Spanish, and special events for families include a Holiday Posada and Parranda Party, and the annual Three Kings Day Parade through the streets of El Barrio, complete with camels.

Federal Hall National Memorial (ages 6 and up)
26 Wall St.; (212) 825-6990; www.nps.gov. Open year round Mon through Fri 9 a.m. to 5 p.m., and open seven days a week in Aug; closed all Federal holidays. Free.

This beautiful Greek Revival building was built on the site where George Washington took the oath of office to become the country's first president. Although the original building burned down, the current structure became a customs house, then a treasury, and now a museum. The Bible Washington used at the inauguration is on display inside, along with information about the ceremony. Kids can be sworn in, too, as Junior Rangers, upon completing a fun activity booklet. Self-guided and ranger-led tours are available, and there's a great visitors center with information about other city attractions, and maps of the ten National Parks of the New York Harbor. Alexander Hamilton's home, Hamilton Grange, is currently being relocated and restored, so many of the exhibits from that museum are on display here for now. Special events are scheduled year-round, and range from the

The Vendy **Awards**

Every corner has a food cart, but how do you know which ones are good? For several years street vendors have valued winning the Vendy Award, sort of the Oscar for street food excellence. Many of the movable feasts have Twitter and Web sites to let foodie fans know where they'll be on a given day. Check the Vendy Web site at www.streetvendor.org for links. The recent competitors included:

Biryani Cart (Indian). 46th Street and Sixth Avenue, Manhattan.

The King of Falafel (Middle Eastern). 30th Street and Broadway, Astoria, Queens.

Rickshaw Dumpling Bar (Asian). Various locations; www.rickshawdumplings .com.

Jamaican Dutchy (Jamaican). 51st Street and Seventh Avenue, Manhattan.

Country Boys (Mexican). Red Hook Ball Fields, Brooklyn.

Good For You BBQ (BBQ). Wall Street between Front and South Street, Manhattan.

Cupcake Stop (desserts). Various locations; www.cupcakestop.com.

Schnitzel & Things (German). Various locations; www.schnitzelandthings.com.

president's birthday celebration, to reenactors bringing history to life during Women's History Month and African American History Month.

Lower East Side Tenement Museum (ages 5 and up)

108 Orchard St.; (212) 431-0233; www.tenement.org. Open every day 10 a.m. to 6 p.m., except Thanksgiving, Christmas Day, and New Year's Day. $$$.

Founded in 1992, this museum rose from the ruins of an abandoned tenement that was home to almost 7,000 working class people, and it's a time-travel trip through the lives of nineteenth- and twentieth-century American immigrants. Tours are tailored to age and interest, last about an hour, and offer opportunities to visit Jewish, Irish, and Russian apartments, hosted by costumed reenactors. A favorite tour for kids is the Confino Family Living History Program, where Victoria, a young Sephardic girl from 1916, answers questions about adjusting to a new life in New York. Currently six apartments have been restored, and a nearby visitor center is being opened at 103 Orchard St. soon. Special events include Tenement Talks, a series of lectures and readings by local authors.

The Studio Museum in Harlem (all ages)

144 West 125th St.; (212) 864-4500; www.studiomuseum.org. Open Wed through Fri noon to 6 p.m., Sat 10 a.m. to 6 p.m., Sun noon to 6 p.m.; closed Mon, Tues, and major holidays. $, under 12 free, and free to everyone on Sun.

Created as a center of art and music expression for local, national, and international black artists, this museum offers a variety of exhibits drawing from its permanent collection, and showcases emerging cutting-edge artists.

Special free programs with hands-on activities for families with kids ages five to ten are offered year-round but require advanced registration.

Museum of Chinese in America (ages 5 and up)

215 Centre St.; (212) 619-4785; www.mocanyc.org. Open Mon and Fri 11 a.m. to 5 p.m., Thurs 11 a.m. to 9 p.m., Sat and Sun 10 a.m. to 5 p.m.; closed on Thanksgiving, Christmas Eve, Christmas, New Year's Eve, New Year's Day. Adults $, children under 12 free, everybody free on Thurs.

Recently moved to a bigger, brighter space, this stunning building, designed by artist Maya Lin, houses the heritage of the Chinese-American experience. Exhibits explore traditions, struggles, and accomplishments of the Chinese immigrants, through priceless artifacts, papers, photographs, and oral histories. Family programs include calligraphy workshops, concerts, book readings, and interactive games.

New York **Trivia**

Besides the Big Apple, other New York City nicknames include the Big Onion, the Big Smear, and, of course, Gotham.

Dyckman Farmhouse Museum (all ages)

4881 Broadway, at 204th Street; (212) 304-9422; www.dyckmanfarmhouse.org. Open Wed to Sat 11 a.m. to 4 p.m., Sun noon to 4 p.m. Closed Mon and Tues. $, under 10 free.

This charming 1784 Dutch Colonial farmhouse was restored in 1916, and donated to the city by the Dyckman family as a museum. Inside are artifacts and articles of the era, and outside is a small symbolic garden recently landscaped with historically correct flowers. Special activities throughout the year range from back porch concerts to educational craft activities.

Tribute WTC Visitor Center (ages 10 and up)

120 Liberty St.; (212) 393-9160 and (866) 737-1184; www.tributewtc.org. Open Mon, Wed, Thurs, Fri and Sat 10 a.m. to 6 p.m., Tues noon to 6 p.m., and Sun noon to 5 p.m. $$.

On Sept 11, 2001, nineteen Al-Qaeda terrorists hijacked four commercial jets and crashed two of them into the Twin Towers of the World Trade Center. Two thousand nine hundred and ninety-five people from more than ninety countries died that day downtown, and the city changed forever. A museum and memorial is currently under construction and will be located on the plaza at the new World Trade Center, but in the interim visitors can stop at the Tribute Center and explore five galleries filled with mementos, personal memories, and artifacts of that day. Walking tours are offered around the construction site, guided by local residents, recovery workers, and volunteers who personally were involved. The new museum, officially titled the National September 11 Memorial & Museum at the World Trade Center, will be surrounded by an acre of 400 swamp white oak and sweetgum trees that will turn brilliant shades of red and gold every autumn anniversary.

Where to Eat

New York City has more than 20,000 restaurants, featuring every ethnic cuisine in every price range and nearly 3,000 pizzerias. If the weather permits, pack a picnic with deli delights and head for the nearest park. There are restaurants on every block and a pizza parlor on almost every corner. Below are some of my family's favorite places:

America. 9 E. 18th St., Manhattan; (212) 505-2110.

Applewood. 501 11th St., Park Slope, Brooklyn; (718) 788-1810; www.applewoodny .com.

Beacon. 25 W. 56th St., Manhattan; (212) 332-0500; www.beaconnyc.com.

Performing for **Young Audiences**

Along with the many family-friendly theater, dance, and music offerings at the bigger venues, there are many performing arts places that tailor their shows for younger audiences. For a current schedule, contact the theaters directly via phone or Web, visit NYCkidsARTS (www .nyckidsarts.org), or check out local listings in *TimeOutKids* magazine.

New Victory Theater. 209 W. 42nd St.; (646) 223-3010; www.newvictory.org.

The Duke on 42nd Street. 229 W. 42nd St.; (646) 223-3010; www.newvictory.org.

The New 42nd Street Studios. 229 W. 42nd St.; www .newvictory.org.

Galli's Fairytale Theater. 38 W. 38th St.; (212) 352-3101; www.galli-group.com.

Manhattan Children's Theatre. 52 White St.; (212) 352-3101; www.manhattan childrenstheatre.org.

Symphony Space. 2537 Broadway; (212) 864-5400; www.symphonyspace.org.

TADA! Youth Theater. 15 W. 28th St.; (212) 252-1619; www.tadatheater.com.

Theatreworks/USA. Lucille Lortel Theatre, 121 Christopher St.; (212) 647-1100; www.theatreworksusa.org.

Players Theatre. 115 MacDougal St.; (212) 352-3101; www.literallyalive.com.

DR2 Theatre. 103 E. 15th St.; (212) 375-1110; www.dr2theater.com.

New World Stages. 340 W. 50th St.; (212) 239-6200; www.gazillionbubble show.com.

The Little Orchestra Society. 330 W. 42nd St.; (212) 971-9500; www.little orchestra.org.

Vital Theatre Company. 2162 Broadway; (212) 579-0528; www.vitaltheatre .org.

Joyce Dance Theater. 175 Eighth Ave.; (212) 691-9740; www.joyce.org.

Bubby's Pie Company. 120 Hudson St., Manhattan; (212) 219-0666; www.bubbys.com.

The Burrito Bar. 585 Forest Ave., Staten Island; (718) 815-9200; www.theburritobar.com.

Buttermilk Channel. 524 Court St., Carroll Gardens, Brooklyn; (718) 852-8490; www.buttermilkchannelnyc.com.

EJ's Luncheonette. 447 Amsterdam Ave., Manhattan; (212) 873-3444.

The Farm on Adderley. 1108 Cortelyou Rd., Ditmas Park, Brooklyn; (718) 287-3101; www.thefarmonadderley.com.

Fatty Crab. 2170 Broadway, Manhattan; (212) 496-2722; www.fattycrab.com.

Grilled Cheese NYC. 168 Ludlow St., Manhattan; (212) 717-1122.

John's Pizzeria. 278 Bleecker St., Manhattan; (212) 243-1680.

Katz's Delicatessen. 205 E. Houston St., Manhattan; (212) 254-2246.

Kelley & Ping. 127 Greene St., Manhattan; (212) 228-1212; www.eatrice.com.

Landmarc. 10 Columbus Circle, Time Warner Center, Manhattan; (212 823-6123; www.landmarc-restaurant.com.

Mama Mexico. 2672 Broadway, Manhattan; (212) 864-2323.

Max. 181 Duane St., Manhattan; (212) 966-5939; www.max-ny.com.

Mike's Deli. 2344 Arthur Ave., the Bronx; (718) 295-5033; www.arthuravenue.com.

Peanut Butter and Co. 240 Sullivan St., Manhattan; (212) 677-3995.

Philip Marie. 569 Hudson St., Manhattan; (212) 242-6200; www.philipmarie.com.

Pinch & S'MAC. 474 Columbus Ave., Manhattan; (646) 438-9494.

The Pink Teacup. 42 Grove St., Manhattan; (212) 807-6755; www.thepinkteacup.com.

Popover's Café. 551 Amsterdam Ave., Manhattan; (595-8555.

Rack & Soul. 258 W. 109th St., Manhattan; (212) 222-4800; www.rackandsoul.com.

Rice. 227 Mott St., Manhattan; (212) 226-5775.

Serendipity 3. 225 E. 60th St., Manhattan; (212) 838-3531; www.serendipity3.com.

Sushi Samba 7. 87 Seventh Ave. South, Manhattan; (212) 691-7885; www.sushisamba.com.

Tom's Restaurant. 782 Washington Ave., Prospect Heights, Brooklyn; (718) 636-9738.

Vynl. 1491 Second Avenue, Manhattan; (212) 249-6080; www.vynl-nyc.com.

Zenon Taverna. 34-10 31st Ave., Astoria, Queens; (718) 956-0133; www.zenontaverna.com.

Where to Stay

There are hundreds of hotels in New York, but they're often heavily booked during peak tourist times, so make reservations in advance. Although accommodations are usually expensive, here are fifteen family-friendly favorites, many offering amenities and welcome kits for kids, and often they can stay free with an adult. NYC & Company at www.nycgo.com can provide many more suggestions.

Affinia 50. 155 E. 50th St.; (212) 751-5710 or (800) 637-8483; www.affinia.com.

Casablanca Hotel. 147 W. 43rd St.; (212) 869-1212; www.casblancahotel.com.

Theme **Restaurants**

Personally, I think New York is one giant theme park, but for pockets of pop themes in Manhattan, here's a list:

Carnival (boardwalk). 110 University Pl.; (212) 255-8188; www.carnivalnyc .com.

Ninja New York (ninja village). 25 Hudson St.; (212) 274-8500; www.ninjanew york.com.

Jekyll & Hyde Club (spooky). 1409 Avenue of the Americas; (212) 541-9505; www.jekyllandhydeclub.com.

Hard Rock Cafe (rock 'n' roll). 1501 Broadway; (212) 343-3355; www.hard rock.com.

Planet Hollywood (movies). 1540 Broadway; (212) 333-7827; www.planet hollywood.com.

Brooklyn Diner (1950s diner). 212 W. 57th St.; (212) 977-1957; www.brooklyn diner.com.

Mars 2112 (space). 1633 Broadway; (212) 582-2112; www.mars2112.com.

Ellen's Stardust Diner (1950s subway). 1650 Broadway; (212) 956-5151; www .ellensstardustdiner.com.

ESPN-Zone (sports). 1472 Broadway; (212) 921-3776; www.espnzone.com.

Mickey Mantle's Restaurant (baseball). 42 Central Park South; (212) 688-7777; www.mickeymantles.com.

Cowgirl Hall of Fame (western). 519 Hudson St.; (212) 633-1133; www.cow girlnyc.com.

Doubletree Guest Suites. 1568 Broadway; (212) 719-1600 or (800) 222-8733; www .doubletree1.hilton.com.

Embassy Suites Hotel New York. 102 North End Ave.; (212) 945-0100 or (800) 362-2779; www.newyorkcity.embassysuites.com.

Hotel on Rivington. 107 Rivington St.; (212) 475-2600 or (800) 915-1537; www.hotel onrivington.com.

Inn on 23rd. 131 W. 23rd St.; (212) 463-0330; www.innon23rd.com.

The Iroquois. 49 W. 44th St.; (212) 840-3080 or (800) 332-7220; www.iroquoisny .com.

Le Parker Meridien. 118 W. 57th St.; (212) 245-5000 or (800) 543-4300; www.parker meredien.com.

Mandarin Oriental. 80 Columbus Circle; (212) 805-8800; www.mandarinoriental.com.

Marriott Marquis. 1535 Broadway; (212) 398-1900 or (800) 843-4898; www.marriott .com.

New York Palace Hotel. 455 Madison Ave.; (212) 888-7000 or (800) 697-2522; www .newyorkpalace.com.

Omni Berkshire Place. 21 E. 52nd St.; (212) 753-5800 or (800) 843-6664; www.omni hotels.com.

Ritz-Carlton New York, Battery Park. 2 West St.; (212) 344-0800; www.ritzcarlton .com.

Tribeca Grand. 2 Avenue of the Americas; (212) 519-6600 or (800) 965-3000; www .tribecagrand.com.

Westin New York at Times Square. 270 W. 43rd St.; (212) 201-2700 or (866) 837-4183; www.westinny.com.

For More Information
NYC & Company. 810 Seventh Ave.; (212) 484-1222; www.nycgo.com.

New York City Department of Parks and Recreation. 830 Fifth Ave.; (212) NEW-YORK or 311 in the city; www.nycgovparks .org.

Times Square Visitor Center. 1560 Broadway; (212) 768-1560; www.timessquarebid .org.

Grand Central Partnership. 6 E. 42nd St.; (212) 883-2420 and (212) 818-1777; www .grandcentralpartnership.org.

34th St. Partnership Visitor Info Center. Penn Station, 250 W. 34th St.; (212) 967-3433; www.nycvisit.com.

The Bronx Tourism Council. 851 Grand Concourse; (718) 590-3518; www.ilivethe bronx.com.

Brooklyn Tourism and Visitors Center. 209 Joralemon St.; (718) 802-3846; www.visit brooklyn.org.

Brooklyn Tourism. www.brooklyntourism .org.

Queens Tourism Council. 120-55 Queens Blvd., Kew Gardens; (718) 263-0546; www .discoverqueens.info.

Staten Island Tourism. 120 Borough Hall, Staten Island; (718) 816-2000; www.staten islandusa.com.

New York State. www.iloveny.com.

New York City Government. www.nyc .gov.

Time Out New York Kids. www.newyork kids.timeout.com.

Hudson River Valley Region

Designated a National Heritage Area by Congress in 1996, the Hudson River valley has enchanted authors and artists for more than three centuries. Its breathtaking scenery cradles a treasure trove of history and culture, and its lore and legends capture the imaginations of young and old alike. Travel back in time as you soar above the lush, rolling hills in a World War I biplane, stroll through the fabulous mansions of millionaires, or speculate on the whereabouts of the buried treasures of Rip Van Winkle and Captain Kidd. Whether your family is interested in castles or country fairs, petroglyphs or planetariums, there is something for everyone here. Long after your visit is over, the Hudson will weave magic in your memories of the adventures shared with your children along these shores.

DRIVING TIPS

West of the Hudson, many of the towns along the river are accessible from US 9W or the Palisades Interstate Parkway. Heading southwest from there, use I-84, or NY 17 if heading northwest. Storm King Highway (NY 218) has dramatic views. Seven Lakes Parkway runs through the heart of Harriman, and along the Delaware River near Sparrowbush on NY 97 is a wonderfully winding road seen in a lot of car commercials. On the eastern side of the river, US 9 is the main artery along the riverbank, but you'll want to check out at least part of the Taconic State Parkway, which runs through some of the prettiest scenery of the valley.

Tarrytown

On US 9, north of the Tappan Zee Bridge.

Washington Irving said the name of this town came from the local Dutch farmers' tendency to "tarry" at the taverns. Once a small market town and rural port located at one of the Hudson River's widest points, Tarrytown today is a bustling commuter village with several attractions that'll make you want to tarry, too.

HUDSON RIVER VALLEY REGION

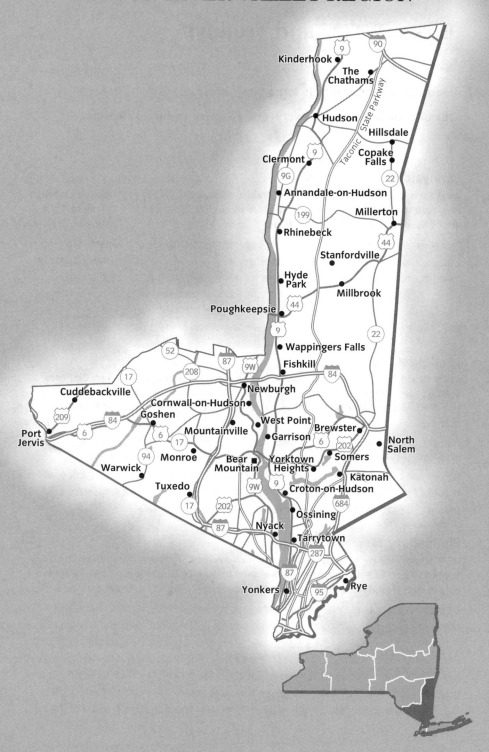

Boats, Trains, **and Trolleys**

NY Waterway. (800) 53–FERRY or (800) 533-3779; www.nywaterway.com.

Metro North Railroad train tours. (800) 638-7646; www.mta.info.

Historic River Towns Trolley. (914) 271-2238; www.hudsonriver.com.

Sunnyside (ages 5 and up)

West Sunnyside Lane, off US 9; (914) 631-8200; www.hudsonvalley.org. Open Apr through Nov, Wed to Mon 10 a.m. to 6 p.m.; and Nov through Dec, Sat and Sun 10 a.m. to 4 p.m. Adults \$\$, children 5 through 17 \$, under 5 free.

Perhaps the most magical of the Hudson River estates, Sunnyside was home to Washington Irving, author of *Rip Van Winkle*. Costumed guides give tours of the charming cottage and grounds, and children are loaned "Irving's Traveling Totes" containing nineteenth-century games, a picture book, and a scavenger hunt. Colonial crafts and skills are demonstrated daily, and autumn harvest celebrations culminate with dramatic readings of Irving's *The Legend of Sleepy Hollow*, complete with the galloping arrival of the "headless horseman."

Lyndhurst (ages 5 and up)

635 S. Broadway; (914) 631-4481; www.lyndhurst.org. Open mid-Apr through Oct, Tues through Sun and holiday Mondays 10 a.m. to 5 p.m.; open weekends only Nov 1 through mid-Apr and holiday Mondays 10 a.m. to 4 p.m. Adults \$\$, children 6 to 16 \$, under 6 free.

An 1838 Gothic Revival mansion, Lyndhurst was once the home of the notoriously wealthy financier Jay Gould. Many original furnishings are still here, recalling an era of robber barons and pre–income tax wealth. The arboretum includes a historic rose garden, a children's playhouse, and a picnic-perfect landscaped lawn overlooking the river. Light snacks and picnic lunches are available at the Carriage House Cafe.

Philipsburg Manor (ages 5 and up)

US 9, Sleepy Hollow; (914) 631-8200; www.hudsonvalley.org. Open Apr through Oct, Wed to Mon 10 a.m. to 5 p.m., and Nov to Dec, Wed to Mon 10 a.m. to 4 p.m.; open weekends only in Mar; closed Jan and Feb. Adults \$\$, children 5 through 17 \$, under 5 free.

Carefully restored to its seventeenth-century roots as a farm and gristmill, Philipsburg Manor offers children a chance to check out colonial life firsthand. Help the miller grind grain at the water-powered mill, visit the farm animals, or plan a picnic on the plantation grounds. Because the Philipse family had one of the largest slaveholdings in the area, new emphasis has recently been put on the little-known but powerful story of slavery in the North. Up until the mid-1700s, New York had the largest urban slave population in the northern colonies. But unlike slaves in the South, many in this area were skilled artisans in a variety of trades, from millers and translators to blacksmiths and expert river pilots, giving them some nego-tiating rights. Across the street from the estate is the Old Dutch Church, believed to be the oldest in New York State. Legend has it that the ghost of a headless Hessian soldier haunts the site, which inspired Washington Irving to write *The Legend of Sleepy Hollow.*

Old Croton Aqueduct State Trailway (all ages)

Many entrances to the trail between Yonkers and Ossining; (914) 693-4117. For a detailed trail map, send SASE plus $5.75 to Friends of Old Croton Aqueduct, 15 Walnut St., Dobbs Ferry, NY 10522. Free.

Running parallel to the Hudson River is a popular, more-than-150-year-old hiking trail perfect for families. This 26-mile-long linear park is the result of New York City's need for clean water, and the Croton watershed became the chosen source. Considered one of the greatest engineering feats of the nineteenth century, it provides a wide, level, and grassy path that meanders past nineteenth-century estates and historic churches of eleven communities.

Where to Eat

Blue Hill at Stone Barns. 630 Bedford Rd., Pocantico Hills; (914) 366-9600; www.stonebarnscenter.org. Local seasonal cuisine harvested from surrounding eighty-acre farm, and a nonprofit educational center. $$$

Horsefeathers. 94 N. Broadway; (914) 631-6606. Hearty home-style fare, great burgers with sweet potato fries, and a kids' menu. $$

Santa Fe. 5 Main St.; (914) 332-4452. South-western and Mexican cuisine, including taco baskets, fajitas, and homemade desserts, plus a children's menu. $–$$

Where to Stay

Castle on the Hudson. 400 Benedict Ave.; (914) 631-1980; www.castleonthehudson.com. Sleep like a prince or princess in an authentic century-old Scotch-Irish-Welsh-Norman castle. $$$$

Courtyard by Marriott. 475 White Plains Rd.; (914) 631-1122 or (800) 589-8720; www.marriott.com/hpngr. One hundred and thirty-nine rooms, restaurant, and indoor pool. $$–$$$

Hampton Inn. 200 Tarrytown Rd., NY 119, Elmsford; (914) 592-5680; www.hamptoninnwhiteplains.com. One hundred and fifty-six rooms, outdoor pool, and continental break-fast. $$–$$$

Also in **the Area**

Rockefeller State Park Preserve. NY 117, Tarrytown 10591; (914) 631-1470; www.nysparks.com/parks. Just off NY 117, about 1 mile north of Philipsburg Manor.

The Tarrytown Music Hall. 13 Main St., Tarrytown 10591; (914) 631-3390; www.tarrytownmusichall.org.

State Parks **in the Area**

Dotting the western shores along the Hudson River and the Palisades are several terrific parks. While not as large or well known as the vast Bear Mountain and Harriman State Parks, each offers a variety of scenery and recreational facilities to please everyone. Call ahead to confirm changes to hours, activities available, and possible closures due to pending state budget cuts.

Tallman Mountain State Park. US 9W, Palisades; (845) 359-0544; www.nys parks.com/parks.

Nyack Beach State Park. 698 N. Broadway, Upper Nyack; (845) 268-3020; www.nysparks.com/parks.

Hook Mountain State Park. US 9W, Upper Nyack; (845) 268-3020; www.nynj tc.org.

Blauvelt State Park. Highland Avenue, Greenbush Road, Blauvelt; (845) 359-0544; www.nysparks.com/parks (undeveloped).

Rockland Lake State Park. US 9W between Congers and Valley Cottage, Congers; (845) 268-3020; www.nysparks.com/parks.

High Tor State Park. 415 S. Mountain Rd., New City; (845) 634-8074; www .nysparks.com/parks.

Buttermilk Falls. 199 Greenbush Rd., West Nyack; (845) 364-2670.

Tackamack Town North and South Park. Clausland Mountain Road (CR 28), Orangetown; (845) 359-6503.

Clausland Mountain County Park. Clausland Mountain Road (CR 28) Orange-town; (845) 364-2670; www.nynjtc.org.

Kakiat County Park. US 202, opposite Viola School, Montebello; (845) 364-2670; www.nynjtc.org.

Kennedy Dells County Park. Park entrance off Main Street, near County Court House, New City; (845) 364-2670; www.nynjtc.org.

Monsey Glen Park. Saddle River Road, Monsey; (845) 364-2670; www.nynjtc.org.

Mount Ivy Environmental County Park. US 202 and Palisades Interstate Parkway, Pomona; (845) 364-2670; www.nynjtc.org.

Mountainview County Nature Park. Strawberry Hill Lane, West Nyack; (845) 364-2670; www.nynjtc.org.

Nyack

Cross the Hudson River via the Tappan Zee Bridge (I-87 and I-287) onto US 9W.

Originally from the area now called Brooklyn, the Native American Nyacks lived here until the Dutch came in the mid-seventeenth century. Memorial Park, down by the river's edge, has wonderful views of the Hudson, and tucked into the steep hills behind you are the spectacular homes of resident artists and celebrities.

Helen Hayes Performing Arts Center (all ages)

117 Main St.; (845) 358-6333; www.helenhayespac.org. Open year-round. Call for schedule and ticket prices.

This lovely 600-seat center offers a variety of excellent entertainment, including adult and children's theater, magic shows, concerts, dance programs, and lectures.

Where to Eat

The Cheesecake Factory. 1612 Palisades Center Dr., West Nyack; (845) 727-1000. Lots of family-friendly food and of course terrific cheesecake. $

Strawberry Place. 72 South Broadway; (845) 358-9511. Great waffles with fruit plus create-your-own omelets. $

Temptations. 80½ Main St.; (845) 353-3355; www.temptationscafe.com. Family friendly with a kids' menu plus terrific ice cream and desserts. $

Where to Stay

Best Western, Nyack on Hudson. 26 NY 59; (845) 358-8100 or (800) 358-8010; www.bestwesternnewyork.com. Restaurant, cable TV with free movies, and Internet; children 17 and under are free with adult. $–$$

Nyack Motor Lodge. 110 N. NY 303, West Nyack; (845) 358-4100. Open twenty-four hours, and it's across the street from the Palisades Shopping Center. $

Tuxedo

Take I-87 west.

The name of the town is believed to come from the Native American word *P'tauk-seet-tough,* which means "place of the bears." Later it was used to describe the attire worn by men of high society from the wealthy enclave of nearby Tuxedo Park.

New York Renaissance Faire (all ages)

600 NY 17A; (845) 351-5174; www.renfair.com. Open rain or shine weekends Aug to mid-Sept 10 a.m. to 7 p.m. Adults $$$, children 5 to 12 $$, under 5 free. Free parking available, preferred parking $.

Spend a day with a knight, or rescue a damsel in distress . . . it's all part of the fun at this annual festival, the largest of its kind on the East Coast. Spread over sixty-five acres, this re-creation of a sixteenth-century country fair appears on summer weekends like Briga-doon, complete with jousting knights, magicians, mimes, jugglers, acrobats, and a king or queen or two plus craft demonstrations from glassblowing to blacksmithing. For younger kids, there are puppet shows, pony rides, and a petting zoo.

Sterling Forest State Park (all ages)

116 Old Forge Rd.; (845) 351-5907 or (845) 351-5910; www.nysparks.com/parks. Open year-round (avoid hiking during hunting season). Free.

In 1998 New York acquired 15,280 acres of rugged woodland 40 miles northwest of New York City, expanding the park to a total of 17,953 acres. Home to bobcats and bears and dotted with sparkling lakes, Sterling Forest supported a flourishing iron industry in the nineteenth century and years later hosted tulip festivals amid its botanical gardens. Seven miles of the Appalachian Trail wind through here, as well as several other scenic strolls, including walks through the Doris Duke Wildlife Sanctuary. Stop by the information center near the south end of Sterling Lake for current trail conditions.

Tuxedo Ridge at Sterling Forest ski center (all ages)

581 NY 17A West; (845) 351-1122 or (800) 843-4414; ski school (845) 351-5727; conditions (845) 351-4788. Open daily mid-Dec to mid-Mar, 10 a.m. to 5 p.m., weekends and holidays 9 a.m. to 5 p.m. Night skiing until 10 p.m. Wed through Sat, 9 p.m. Sun through Tues, Jan and Feb. Adults $$$$, children $$$.

Thirty-five acres of terrain, eight groomed trails, four double chairlifts, a snowboarding area, lessons, and snowmaking capabilities.

Monroe

North on I-87 to NY 17M.

South of Schunemunk Mountain lies the town of Monroe, birthplace of the notorious Revolutionary War outlaw Claudius Smith and suspected site of his as yet unfound treasure trove.

Horsing **Around**

Nickel-O-Farm. 369 Strawtown Rd., West Nyack; (845) 358-8006; www.nickelo farms.com.

Diamond Double Ranch. 269 N. Main St., New City; (845) 638-0271.

Country Lee Farm. 346 Old Route 202, Pomona; (845) 354-0133.

Minetto's Stonehedge Farm. 220 Spook Rock Rd., Suffern; (845) 357-8887.

Also in **the Area**

94 Pitch & Putt. 94 Hudson Rd., Washingtonville; (845) 496-6418.

Arrow Park. 1061 Orange Turnpike, CR 19, Monroe; (845) 783-2044.

Museum Village at Old Smith's Clove (all ages)
1010 NY 17M; (845) 782-8247 or (845) 782-8248; www.museumvillage.org. Open Apr
through June and Sept through Nov, weekdays 10 a.m. to 2 p.m.; July and Aug, Tues
through Sun 11 a.m. to 6 p.m.; closed Mon and major holidays. Adults $$, children 4 to 15
$, under 4 **free.**

Travel back to the nineteenth century at this thirty-five-acre living-history museum. Laid
out like a typical crossroads village, forty exhibit and demonstration buildings house
more than a quarter million historical artifacts of preindustrial America. Costumed guides
answer your questions as you stroll around the village green watching weavers, potters,
printers, blacksmiths, and bakers busy at work.

Goosepond Mountain State Park (all ages)
NY 17M, Chester; (845) 786-2701 (Palisades Interstate Park); www.nysparks.com/parks.
Open year-round dawn to dusk. **Free.**

Undeveloped and wild, the 1,558-acre park's marshes and meadows attract an enormous
volume and variety of birds. While most of the trails are not well marked, the two-hour
round-trip hike along Lazy Hill Road is pretty easy. Ancient artifacts, including arrowheads
and pottery shards dating back to 3500 B.C., have been found in the rock shelters on the
mountain and are displayed at Bear Mountain's Trailside Museum. Some say those rock
shelters may also have been the hideout of the infamous Claudius Smith and his gang.

Where to Eat
The Barnsider Tavern. 1372 Kings Hwy.,
Sugar Loaf; (845) 469-9810; www.barnsider
.net. Chicken fingers, burgers, hot dogs, fries,
and dessert. $–$$

Warwick

Head south on NY 5 onto NY 17A west.

The town of Warwick encompasses several nearby villages, including Greenwood
Lake, Florida, and Pine Island. The Appalachian Trail passes near here, the hamlets are full
of quaint antiques and craft shops, and the valley is famous for its juicy apples and flavor-
ful onions.

Farms and Markets **in Warwick**

Warwick Valley Farmers Market. South Street Parking Lot; (845) 986-2720. www.warwickinfo.net. Open Sun, 9 a.m. to 2 p.m.

Applewood Orchards. 82 Four Corners Rd., CR 13; (845) 986-1684; www .applewoodorchards.com.

Masker Orchards. Ball Road; (845) 986-1058; www.maskers.com.

Wright Family Farm. 325 Kings Hwy.; (845) 986-1345; www.wrightfamilyfarm .com.

Pennings Orchard Farm Market. 169 NY 94; (845) 986-7080; www.pennings farmmarket.com.

Ochs Orchards. 4 Ochs Lane, NY 94; (845) 986-1591.

Greenwood Lake (all ages)
Parallel to NY 210 (Jersey Avenue); (845) 477-9215; www.villageofgreenwoodlake.org. Pontoon boat tours of the lake are available at Long Pond Marina, 634 Jersey Ave.; (845) 477-8425. Departures every hour on weekends 9 a.m. to 5 p.m. Memorial Day through Labor Day.

Created when a dam was built to power a nearby ironworks, this 7.3-mile lake is a popular summer resort. Go fishing, boating, skiing, or hiking—there's no shortage of water sports here. For landlubbers, walk a bit of the Appalachian Trail for its scenic vistas of the lake, or check out the 1-mile Mountain Spring Trail off NY 210, south of the village.

Also in **the Area**

Warwick Drive-in. 5 Warick Turnpike (CR 21) just off NY 94; (845) 986-4440; http://webusers.warwick.net/~u1006131/driveinmovie. First-run films, open every night. Cinema under the stars! A vanishing bit of America, the drive-in is a classic family adventure.

Mount Peter Ski Area. 51 Old Mount Peter Rd., off NY 17A; (845) 986-4940 or (845) 986-4992; www.mtpeter.com. Skiing and snowboarding in winter and hawk-watching in spring and fall.

Horse Fun **in Warwick**

Borderland Farm. 340 S. NY 94; (845) 986-1704or (845) 986-9433; www.border landfarm.net. Offering lessons and trail rides to children of all abilities. Reservations required.

Crystal Water Farm. 35 Union Corners Rd.; (845) 986-0100; www.crystalwater farm.com. Horseback rides and lessons.

Whisper Wind Farm. 39 Foley Rd.; (845) 986-0588; www.warwickinfo.net/ whisperwindfarm/index.html.

Where to Eat

Pioneer Restaurant. 49 Oakland Ave.; (845) 986-6500. Great burgers, prime rib, seasonal soups, and homemade apple dumplings. $$

Ye Jolly Onion Inn. 625 Glenwood Rd., Pine Island; (845) 258-4277. The onions of Orange County are the star here. Children's menu. $$$

Where to Stay

Black Bear Campground. 197 Wheeler Rd., Florida; (845) 651-7717; www.blackbear campground.com. Campsites, playground, pool, mini-golf and arcade, fishing pond, hayrides, nature trails, and summer children's arts and crafts program. $

Warwick Motel. 1 Overlook Dr.; (845) 986-4822 or (888) 8–WARWICK; www.warwick motel.com. Swimming pool; complimentary continental breakfast. School playground across the street. $

Goshen

Take NY 17A north.

The countryside surrounding Goshen is dotted with many farms, for the black dirt of Orange County is a highly organic soil called "muck," the deposits left by glacial lakes. This area is second only to the Everglades in its concentration of muck, which may be why more than half the crop of New York's most successful vegetable—the onion—is grown here. Pick up a self-guided walking-tour map of the town at the chamber of commerce kiosk at Park Place.

New York **Trivia**

New York, the thirtieth-largest state, has a land area of 42,224 square miles.

Harness Racing Museum and Hall of Fame (ages 6 and up)

240 Main St.; (845) 294-6330; www.harnessmuseum.com. Open Mon through Fri 9 a.m. to 5 p.m., Sat and Sun 10 a.m. to 5 p.m. closed Thanksgiving, Christmas, Easter, and New Year's Day. **Free.**

Housed in the former Good Time Stables, this museum immortalizes the history of America's pre-baseball passion for trotters and pacers. Visit the Hall of the Immortals with its dozens of small statuettes of famous trainers and drivers, and check out the life-size displays of legendary horses. A 3-D interactive simulator lets you feel what it's like to drive a harnessed horse, judge a race, or visit a breeding farm. Walk next door to Park Place and the Goshen Historic Track, the only sporting arena designated a National Historic Landmark, to watch harness horses training here almost daily, and there's usually a blacksmith at work as well. Ask about behind-the-scenes tours of the track. Racing season runs July 4 through Labor Day (no betting allowed).

Hill-Hold (all ages)

NY 416, Campbell Hall; (845) 291-2404. Open mid-May through early Oct, Wed through Sun 10 a.m. to 4:30 p.m. Closed Memorial Day and Labor Day. $.

Tour this historic eighteenth-century working farm, complete with a one-room schoolhouse, fragrant herb gardens, and friendly farm fauna.

Also in **the Area**

Orange Heritage Trail. 182 Greenwich Ave., Goshen; (845) 294-8886; www .orangecountygov.com. A 11.5- mile paved "rail trail," good for skates or strollers.

Silent Farm Stables. 35 Axworthy Lane, Goshen; (845) 294-0846; www.silent farm.com, English & western riding lessons, indoor and outdoor.

The Castle Family Fun Center. 109 Brookside Ave. NY 17M, Chester; (845) 469-2116; www.thecastlefuncenter.com. Mini-golf, go-karts, batting cages, arcade, roller-skating, laser tag, and rock climbing.

Where to Eat

Goshen Plaza Diner. 1 Clowes Ave.; (845) 294-7800. Great Goshen cuisine, plus a nice kids' menu. $–$$

Catherine's. 153 West Main St.; (845) 294-8707. Chicken, steak, and pasta specialties. $$$–$$$$

Where to Stay

Comfort Inn & Suites. 20 Hatfield Lane; (845) 291-1282. Seasonal outdoor pool, free wireless Internet access, and free Belgian waffles. $$$

Port Jervis

Take NY 17 north, then I-84 west.

Stephen Crane wrote his famous Civil War novel, *The Red Badge of Courage,* here, but for many, Port Jervis is a doorway to the Delaware. Rent a canoe and paddle on down the lazy river. Landlubbers may opt to walk the 5-mile self-guided Delaware River Heritage Trail through town, from Fort Decker (127 Main St.) to the Tri-State Rock.

New Hope Farms (all ages)

517 Neversink Dr.; (845) 856-8384. Open daily year-round. Many events are free. Call for lesson prices and schedule of events.

This is one of the largest equestrian centers in the country, offering lessons at all levels, as well as many events throughout the year.

Gillinder Glass (ages 7 and up)

Corner of Erie and Liberty Streets; (845) 856-5375; www.gillinderglassstore.com. Open year-round except for July. Tours are conducted Mon through Fri at 10:15 a.m., 12:30, and 1:30 p.m. There are some weekend tours throughout the year. Closed holidays. Store: Mon through Fri 9:30 a.m. to 5:30 p.m., Sat 9:30 a.m. to 4 p.m., Sun noon to 4 p.m. $.

Watch hot molten masses of glass be formed into crystalline creations at one of the country's oldest glass factories.

Raft, Canoe, and **Tube Rentals**

Silver Canoe Raft Rentals. 37 South Maple Ave., Port Jervis; (800) 724-8342 or (845) 856-7055; www.silvercanoe.com.

Whitewater Willie's. 37 S. Maple Ave., Port Jervis; (800) 724-8342 or (845) 856-7055; www.whitewaterwillies.com.

West End Beach (all ages)

Ferry Street to Water Street; (845) 858-4045. Open daily mid June through late Aug 11a.m. to 7 p.m. Free.

Folks come here to enjoy the swimming, fishing, playground, and softball field.

Where to Eat

Cornucopia Restaurant & Inn. 176 US 209; (845) 856-5361. German and continental cuisine, $$

Flo-Jean. US 6 and US 209; (845) 856-6600. Steaks, seafood, and homemade desserts, plus a children's menu, outdoor deck dining overlooking the Delaware River, and an antique doll and toy collection. $$$

Where to Stay

The Erie Hotel and Restaurant. 9 Jersey Ave.; (845) 858-4100. Late nineteenth-century hotel, newly renovated, with American cuisine restaurant, outdoor patio, and a kids' menu. $$–$

Cuddebackville

Head north on US 209.

In the early nineteenth century, the D&H Canal was built through here, linking the Delaware and Hudson Rivers with a 108-mile-long waterway with which to transport coal from the Pennsylvania mines and bluestone from the Catskills, both destined for New York City. While much smaller than the Erie Canal, it was designed by the same man, and the D&H was considered an engineering wonder.

Delaware and Hudson Canal Park (all ages)

26 Hoag Rd., off US 209; (845) 754-8870 or (845) 457-4900. Museum open Apr through Oct, Fri through Sun noon to 4 p.m. and by appointment; park open daily dawn to dusk. $, children under 6 free.

This 300-acre county park encompasses about a mile of the D&H Canal, a National Historic Landmark. Among the century-old buildings on the grounds is the **Neversink Valley Area Museum.** Housed in the home of a former blacksmith, the museum offers exhibits about the history and people who lived and worked along the canal. Guided towpath walks offered on Sun are fun and informative, and special seasonal events and activities for families are offered throughout the year, from nature walks and maple sugaring to ghost stories and silent-film festivals.

Where to Eat

O'dell's Country Pizza. 1015 US 209; (845) 754-7422. Best pizza in town. $

Where to Stay

Oakland Valley Campground. 399 Oakland Valley Rd.; (800) 832-2254; www

.oaklandvalleycampground.com. Riverfront campsites and RV hookups, fishing, hiking, horseshoes, volleyball, badminton, Ping-Pong, a video arcade, bingo, bonfires, laundry, and hot showers. $

American Family Campground. 110 Guymard Turnpike, Godeffroy; (845) 754-8388;

www.americanfamilycampground.com. Campsites; RV hookups; Wi-Fi; swimming pool; recreation hall; arcade; hayrides; crafts; bingo; driving range; softball, basketball, volleyball, badminton and tetherball; horseshoes; tube, paddleboat, and bike rentals; campfires; hot showers; and sing-alongs. $

Newburgh

Take US 209 north, then head east on NY 17K.

Newburgh was once a prosperous whaling center that evolved into a manufacturing town. Today the area has several Revolutionary War sites of interest to older children, as well as festivals, special events, and farmers' markets that will appeal to everyone.

Washington's Headquarters State Historic Park (ages 7 and up)

84 Liberty St.; (845) 562-1195. **Open mid-Apr through Oct, Mon, Wed, Thurs, Fri, and Sat 10 a.m. to 5 p.m., Sun 1 to 5 p.m. $, children under 5 free.**

This was George's and sometimes Martha's home during the final months of the Revolutionary War. Designated as the nation's first historic site, the Dutch-style farmhouse

Seven Stables of Stallions
in Northern Orange County

Denman Farm. 219 Red Mills Rd., Pine Bush; (845) 744-7791.

Juckas Stables. NY 302, Pine Bush; (845) 361-1429; www.juckasstables.com.

J&E Ranch. 100 Union School Rd., Montgomery; (845) 361-4433.

Gardnertown Farms. 822 Gardnertown Farm Rd., Newburgh; (845) 564-6658; www.gardnertownfarms.com.

Schunnemunk Shadow Stables. NY 94, Purdy's Lane, New Windsor; (845) 534-0365; www.centerlinestudios.com/schunnemunk.

Shadow Brook Farm. 89 Camp Orange Rd., Middletown; (845) 692-5046 or (914) 443-2431.

Dorian Equestrian Center. 173 Sarah Wells Trail, Campbell Hall; (845) 496-2858; www.dorianequestriancenter.com.

Farm Markets and **Farm Animals**

Overlook Farm Market. US 9W, Newburgh; (845) 562-5780 or (800) 291-9137; www.overlookfarmmarket.com. Pick-your-own apples and pumpkins, hay maze, fishing, and petting zoo.

Manza Family Farm. 730 NY 211, Montgomery; (845) 692-4363. Pumpkin picking, hay maze, hayrides, farm animals, and cut-your-own Christmas trees. Santa and his reindeer visit on Dec weekends.

Maples Farm. 749 NY 17M, Middletown; (845) 344-0330; www.maplesfarm .com. Pumpkin picking, hayrides, hay maze, barnyard animals, and cut-your-own Christmas tree.

Rock Ridge Alpaca Farm. 229 Gibson Hill Rd., Chester; (845) 469-6196; www .rockridgealpacas.com. Working alpaca farm.

Rogowski Farm. 327–329 Glenwood Rd., Pine Island; (845) 258-4574; www .rogowskifarm.com. Over 200 varieties of vegetables, small fruits, and unusual herbs, plus farm tours and a tomato festival.

Bellvale Farms. 75 Bellvale Lakes Rd., Warwick; (845) 988-5414 or (845) 988-1818; www.bellvalefarms.com. A 200-year-old family farm demonstrating milking techniques.

Peacock Hill Farms. 337 Pressler Rd., Newburgh; (845) 564-0010. Eco-friendly educational farm with over 300 animals, petting zoo, butterfly house, pony rides, gold mining, and catch-and-release fishing.

Hodgson Farms. 2290 Albany Post Rd., Walden; (845) 778-1432; www.hodgson farm.com. Pick-your-own strawberries, blueberries, and raspberries. October Fall Festival includes hayrides to pumpkin field, three-acre corn maze, straw maze, petting zoo, haunted house, and magic show.

Lawrence Farms Orchards. 39 Colandrea Rd., Newburgh; (845) 562-4268; www.lawrencefarmsorchards.com. Apples, cherries, grapes, peaches, pears, strawberries, pumpkins, and vegetables. New England village for children with farmyard animals and horse-drawn carriage rides.

Pierson Bicentennial Farm. 1448 NY 211 West, Middletown; (845) 386-1882. A 214-year-old family farm with raspberry and pumpkin picking, hayrides, mazes, animals, sheep-shearing demonstrations, and an Indian tepee.

Pine Hill Farm. 3298-3316 NY 94, Chester; (845) 325-1115. Historic 1782 family farm with heirloom tomatoes, organic raspberries, and pumpkin picking.

owned by the Hasbrouck family gave Washington and his aides a good vantage point from which to monitor British troops still encamped in New York City. Adjacent to the house is a museum with videos and exhibits of eighteenth-century military life, along with some of Washington's personal possessions.

Newburgh Landing (all ages)

City Park, on Front Street, Hudson River; (845) 569-4022; (845) 569-7300 for event schedule. Hudson River Adventures, 26 Front St., *Pride of the Hudson;* (845) 220-2120; www.pride ofthehudson.com. Departures Wed through Sun, May through Oct. Call for schedule. $$$, children under 3 free.

This park is the site of numerous special events and festivals designed for children. On Tues and Fri from 10 a.m. to 6 p.m., the Farmers' Market offers an opportunity to stock up on the wide variety of foods grown in the area, and you can also cruise the river aboard the Pride of the Hudson.

Gomez Mill House (all ages)

11 Mill House Rd., Marlboro; (845) 236-3126; www.gomez.org. Summer hours Wed through Sun 10 a.m. to 4 p.m. $.

This is the oldest standing Jewish dwelling in North America, the oldest house in Orange County, and the site of an ancient Native American ceremonial ground. Besides the house tours, special programs are offered to children, from gardening to archaeology digs.

Where to Eat

Commodore Chocolatier. 482 Broadway; (845) 561-3960. Legendary homemade ice cream and chocolates. $

Torches on the Hudson. 120 Front St.; (845) 568-0100. Eclectic American cuisine, a 6,000-gallon saltwater aquarium, floor-to-ceiling windows overlooking the river, and a kids' menu. $$$

Where to Stay

Howard Johnson Inn. 95 NY 17K; (845) 564-4000 or (800) 446-4656; www.hojo.com. Outdoor pool, Wi-Fi, restaurant, refrigerator in some rooms, complimentary continental breakfast, and cribs/roll-away beds available. $–$$

Ramada Inn. 1289 NY 300; (845) 564-4500 or (800) 228-2828. Forty luxury suites, some with Jacuzzis; restaurant; outdoor pool; gym; Internet and cable TV; and complimentary continental breakfast. $$–$$$

Cornwall-on-Hudson

Head south on US 9W.

Hudson Highlands Nature Museum (all ages)

Two locations: The Outdoor Discovery Center, 100 Muser Dr., across from 174 Angola Rd., Cornwall; (845) 534-5506; and the Wildlife Education Center, 25 Boulevard, Cornwall-on-Hudson; (845) 534-7781; www.museumhudsonhighlands.org. The Wildlife Education Center is open year-round Fri through Sun noon to 4 p.m. The Outdoor Discovery Center office is open Tues through Fri 8:30 a.m. to 5 p.m., and trails open daily from dawn to dusk. $.

This is one of the oldest environmental education centers in the country, founded by a group of teenagers in 1959 who wanted to display their small collection of plants, animals, and rocks. Natural-history dioramas of regional habitats prepare families for exploring the nature trails on the seventy-acre grounds. Special activities are scheduled throughout the year, from storytelling and dance programs to birdhouse building and raptor watching.

The museum also operates the nearby Outdoor Discovery Center at the former Kenridge Farm, a wildlife sanctuary that offers programs celebrating the cultural, historical, and natural diversity of the area, along with miles of trails to explore. Check with the museum for current programs, especially the award-winning Discovery Quests. There are single- and multiday programs geared for young children as well as parent/child events.

New Windsor Cantonment (all ages)

374 Temple Hill Rd. (NY 300, right side of the road), Vails Gate; (845) 561-1765; www.nys parks.com/sites. Open year-round Mon, Wed, Thurs, Fri, and Sat 10 a.m. to 5 p.m., Sun 1 to

New York **Trivia**

The longest distance from north to south in the state is 310 miles.

Hudson Valley **Lighthouses**

The Little Red Lighthouse. Fort Washington Park, at 181st Street, New York City; (212) 304-2365

883 Lighthouse at Sleepy Hollow. Kingsland Point Park, Palmer Avenue, US 9, Sleepy Hollow; (914) 366-5109.

Esopus Meadows Lighthouse. Port Ewen; www.esopusmeadowslighthouse .org.

Hudson Athens Lighthouse. 2 First St., Riverfront Park, Hudson; (518) 828-5294.

Stony Point Lighthouse. Battlefield Road, Stony Point; (845) 786-2521.

Rondout Lighthouse. Rondout Creek, Kingston; (845) 338-0071; www.hrmm .org/rondout/light.htm.

Saugerties Lighthouse. Lighthouse Drive, Saugerties; (845) 247-0656; www .saugertieslighthouse.com.

5 p.m. Closed Tues, Thanksgiving, Christmas, and New Year's Day. $, children 4 and under **free.** Call ahead to confirm changes to hours, activities available, and possible closures due to pending state budget cuts.

While Washington was settled in at the Hasbrouck house, his 7,000 troops, along with about 500 women and children, waited out the last months of an eight-year war in log huts, struggling to survive a bitter winter. Today costumed guides demonstrate colonial life—blacksmithing, cooking, or playing musical instruments. The two-story visitor center is run by the state and offers historical exhibits, including the National Purple Heart Hall of Honor, featuring the original Purple Heart medal. Cannons and muskets are fired in an artillery demonstration almost every day.

The Last Encampment of the Continental Army (all ages)

19 Causeway Rd., NY 300, left side of the road, Vails Gate; (845) 561-5073; www.national templehill.org. Park open daily during daylight hours; visitor center open Thurs through Sun noon to 4:30 p.m. **Free,** donations accepted.

Across the road from the New Windsor Cantonment, this 167-acre site has preserved some of the authentic military huts from the Revolutionary War campground. Walk the Freedom Appreciation Trail, a newer addition, or explore the self-guided Nature Trail and tower.

Also in the Area

Kowawese Unique Area at Plum Point. US 9W, across from Anthony's Pier 9, New Windsor; (845) 615-3830; www.orangecountygov.com.

Algonquin Powder Mill Park. Powder Mill Road and NY 52, Newburgh; (845) 562-8413.

Where to Eat

Painter's Restaurant and Inn. 266 Hudson St., Cornwall-on-Hudson; (845) 534-2109; www.painters-restaurant.com. Wonderful eclectic cuisine of sandwiches, pasta, salads, and more, a special kids' menu, and the rooms at the Inn are decorated with Hudson River murals. $$

Fiddlestix Cafe. 319 Main St., Cornwall; (845) 534-3866. Creative breakfast and lunch place with homemade desserts. $$

Where to Stay

Cadet Motel. 2582 US 9W, Cornwall; (845) 534-4595. Small and tidy rooms.

Mountainville

Take NY 32 south.

Storm King Art Center (all ages)

Old Pleasant Hill Road, just off NY 32 North; (845) 534-3115; www.stormking.org. Open Apr through Oct, Wed through Sun 10 a.m. to 5:30 p.m.; Nov 1 through 15, Wed through Sun 10 a.m. to 5 p.m.; May through early Sept, Sat 11 a.m. to 8 p.m. $$, **free** for children under 5.

It would be hard to find a better place to introduce your children to modern art. The largest sculpture park in the country, this breathtaking 500-acre park and outdoor museum has more than 120 sculptures nestled among rolling foothills and landscaped gardens, backed by the spectacular Shawangunk Mountains. It's an opportunity for everyone in the family to see the works of master sculptors—from Calder and Moore to Nevelson and Noguchi. Pick up a map at the gate and explore! Pack a picnic lunch or eat at the small cafe, which is open on weekends. Call about special events for families.

Storm King **Mountain**

America's environmental consciousness was born at Storm King in 1963, when Franny Reese and other concerned citizens began a seventeen-year battle to save the majestic mountain from becoming the site of a massive hydroelectric power plant. Today that spirit of grass-roots environmentalism continues, as people pressure industrial polluters to clean up toxic PCBs dumped in the Hudson River. Franny passed away in 2003, but New York's newest state park, located in Highland, has been named Franny Reese State Park in her honor. For more information about area environmental issues, activities, and trails, contact:

Scenic Hudson. (845) 473-4440; www.scenichudson.org.

The Riverkeeper. (845) 424-4149 or (800) 21–RIVER; www.riverkeeper.org.

Clearwater. (845) 454-7673 or (800) 67-SLOOP; www.clearwater.org.

Where to Eat

Mario's Restaurant. 503 NY 32, Highland Mills; (845)928-2805; www.mariosny.com. Italian cuisine including pasta, chicken, steak, and a children's menu. $$

The Savory Grill. 923 NY 32, Highland Mills; (845) 928-6145; www.savorygrill.net. Steak, scampi, chicken, salmon, vegetarian specialties, plus a children's menu. $$$

Where to Stay

The Storm King Lodge. 100 Pleasant Hill Rd.; (845) 534-9421. Lovely bed-and-breakfast with gardens, outdoor pool, fireplaces, and a veranda overlooking mountain views. $$$

West Point

Head north on NY 32, then south on US 9W.

Occupying a strategic bluff overlooking a bend in the Hudson River, West Point was an important American fortification during the Revolutionary War. It was here that Washington ordered a 150-ton iron chain strung across the river in an attempt to block British ships from sailing up the Hudson. This was also the fort that a disgruntled Benedict Arnold tried to betray to the British.

United States Military Academy (ages 10 and up)
NY 218, Highland Falls; (845) 938-2638 or (845) 938-3614; www.usma.edu. Tours (845) 446-4724; www.westpointtours.com. Museum (845) 938-3590; www.usma.edu/museum. USMA

New York **Firsts**

First school in America (1663)

First cattle ranch in America (1747)

First capital of the United States (1789)

First steamboat (1807)

First telegraph (1831)

First chess tournament in the United States (1843)

First pizzeria in the United States (1895)

First motion picture (1896)

First toilet paper in the United States (1857)

First Eagle Scout in the United States (1912)

First presentation of 3-D films (1915)

First potato chip (1925)

First solar-powered battery (1954)

visitor center, Building 2107, near Thayer Gate, is open daily year-round 9 a.m. to 4:45 p.m. Museum open daily 10:30 a.m. to 4:15 p.m. Closed New Year's Day, Thanksgiving, and Christmas. Free. Constitution Island Association (845) 446-8676; www.constitutionisland .org. Take boat from West Point's South Dock June through Sept. Tours depart 1 and 2 p.m. every Wed and Thurs. Reservations recommended. $$, children under 5 $.

As cadets, Robert E. Lee, Ulysses S. Grant, Douglas MacArthur, and Norman Schwarzkopf marched here, as did astronauts Buzz Aldrin, Frank Borman, Edward White, and Michael Collins. Tradition and a strong sense of duty, honor, and country are evident everywhere, from the **Cadet Chapel,** with its spectacular stained-glass windows and the largest church organ in the world, to exciting football games and precision parades. Visit the **West Point Museum,** where dioramas depict famous battles, galleries highlight the history of war and the academy, and rotating exhibits drawn from more than 15,000 artifacts may include Napoleon's sword, Hitler's pistol, or MacArthur's bathrobe. Stop at Trophy Point, where some of the 300-pound links of "Washington's watch chain" rest. Nearby are **Battle Monument** and **Fort Putnam,** a partially restored Revolutionary fortification overlooking West Point. For an interesting side trip, take the boat from West Point's South Dock to nearby Constitution Island and explore the Victorian Warner House (temporarily closed for restoration) and gardens.

Hudson Highlands Cruises (all ages)

South Dock, West Point, and Haverstraw Marina; (845) 534-7245; www.commanderboat .com. Open May through Oct, weekdays and last Sat of the month. Reservations required. Departs Haverstraw Marina 10 a.m. Departs West Point 12:30 p.m. $$$–$$$$.

Enjoy a narrated Hudson River cruise aboard the historic M/V Commander.

Where to Eat

West Point Pizza & Restaurant. 282 Main St., Highland Falls; (845) 446-5544; www .westpointpizza.com. Great pizza, pasta, chicken parmigiana, hot and cold subs, cheesesteaks, and cheesecakes. $

Where to Stay

Thayer Hotel. 674 Thayer Rd.; (800) 247-5047 or (845) 446-4731; www.thethayerhotel .com. One hundred and fifty-one luxury rooms and suites, including double-bed rooms for families of five; concierge services; plus a lovely restaurant overlooking the Hudson that serves a spectacular Sunday brunch. $$$$

Bear Mountain

Head south on US 9W.

Bear Mountain State Park (all ages)

US 9W; (845) 786-2701; www.nysparks.state.ny.us. Trails open daily year-round, Trailside Museum open on weekends 10 a.m. to 4:30 p.m.; pool opens in summer Mon through Fri 10 a.m. to 6 p.m., weekends and holidays 9:30 a.m. to 7 p.m. $ per car; separate admission for pool, ice rink, and museum.

Covering more than 5,000 acres of the Hudson Highlands and adjacent to Harriman State Park in the south, Bear Mountain offers breathtaking views of the Hudson River and, on a clear day, the skyline of Manhattan. Cruise by car to the summit along Perkins Memorial Drive and enjoy the panorama, or visit the Trailsides Museum and Wildlife Center, a refuge for rescued animals of the area. The newest animals in the park are of the carousel kind; forty-two hand-carved creatures representing Hudson Valley wildlife circle daily in summer aboard the Bear Mountain merry-go-round. The Appalachian Trail runs through the park, and the nature trails in the area are some of the oldest in the country. Check at the Park Visitor Center for maps and current special events schedules.

Harriman State Park (all ages)

Access via I-87 or NY 17, Palisades Interstate Parkway, Palisades Interstate Park; (845) 786-2701, or Park Visitor Center (845) 786-5003. Sebago Cabins (845) 351-2360; Beaver Pond Campgrounds (845) 947-2792; reservations (800) 456-2267; www.nysparks.state.us/parks. Open daily year-round; hours vary with the seasons and the area. $$ per car. Call ahead to confirm changes to hours, activities available, and possible closures due to pending state budget cuts.

This scenic and historic 46,000-acre preserve, less than an hour's drive from New York City, was created in 1910 from land and cash donated by Mary Harriman and other conservation-minded people. Before the Harriman family intervened, the area was meant to be the new home of the notorious Sing Sing Prison, but today the park offers families the freedom to explore more than 225 miles of hiking trails, three beaches, multiple campgrounds, cabins, lots of wildlife, and thirty-one lakes and reservoirs in which to swim, fish, or paddle a boat. The surrounding mountains, once more than 12,000 feet high like the Rockies, have eroded to expose Precambrian bedrock, making this one of the oldest land masses in North America.

Lake Sebago is a favorite spot for families with small children because of the shady picnic areas and the playground located near the sandy beach. Lake Welch has one of the largest inland beaches in America, but it can get pretty busy on the weekends, as it's near the Beaver Pond Campground. Rowboat rentals (no gasoline motors allowed) and snacks are available at both lakes in season. Lake Tiorati also has a nice sandy beach and quite a few largemouth bass.

A nature museum is near Lake Kanawauke, and the Silver Mine area has trails and picnic grounds. A number of recreational and educational programs are offered throughout the park, from campfire talks to river walks. There are trails to tempt everyone here, including a segment of the Appalachian Trail, but some of the more popular hikes for families with young children are along the 3-mile-loop trail to Pine Swamp Mine and the 4-mile-loop trail to Pine Meadow Lake. Stop by the Park Visitor Center (located on the Palisades Interstate Parkway) for maps, fishing licenses, and current activities schedules.

Where to Eat

Mount Fuji. 296 NY 17, Hillburn (exit 15A off I-87, then 1 mile north on NY 17); (845) 357-4270; www.mtfujirestaurants.com. This is a great steakhouse, Japanese-style, and they've recently added comedy murder mystery shows on select dates throughout the year. $$

Where to Stay

Bear Mountain Inn. US 9W South and Palisades Interstate Parkway; (845) 786-2731; www.visitbearmountain.com. Built in 1914, this lovely stone and wood lodge has a restaurant, picnic areas, outdoor swimming pool, ice-skating, boat rentals, and 12-foot fireplaces in the lobby. $$

Garrison

Cross the Hudson River via the Bear Mountain Bridge, then head north on NY 9D.

When location scouts for *Hello, Dolly!* wanted to re-create nineteenth-century Yonkers, Garrison got the part. This picturesque village has a lovely waterfront park, Garrison Landing, that offers panoramic views of the Hudson from a gazebo featured in the movie; the Garrison Depot Theatre; the Garrison Art Center (845) 424-3960; www.garrisonartcenter .org; and numerous children's activities throughout the summer.

Henry **Hudson**

In 1609, while searching for the fabled northwest passage to the Orient, Henry Hudson sailed his ship *Half Moon* up the river that bears his name. He got as far as Albany before realizing he couldn't get there from here and turned back. He returned in 1611 only to navigate his ship into Hudson Bay, where it became icebound. Hungry, cold, and having serious doubts about their captain's abilities, the crew mutinied. Hudson, his young son, and eight other loyal crew members were put into a small boat in the vast Canadian bay and never seen again. If you're feeling luckier than Hudson, take a time traveler's mini-voyage by sailing on a full-scale replica of the *Half Moon*. Contact the New Netherland Museum at www.halfmoon.mus.ny.us for a current schedule.

Boscobel (ages 4 and up)

1601 NY 9D; (845) 265-3638; www.boscobel.org. Hudson Valley Shakespeare Festival (845) 265-9575 and (845) 265-7858; www.hvshakespeare.org. Open Nov and Dec, Wed through Mon 9:30 a.m. to 4 p.m.; Apr through Oct, Wed through Mon 9:30 a.m. to 5 p.m. Closed Jan, Feb, Mar, Thanksgiving, and Christmas. Guided tours every fifteen minutes. House and grounds $$$ $$, children under 6 **free.**

Perched on a bluff overlooking the Hudson River, this elegant nineteenth-century Federal mansion once sold for $35 and was scheduled for demolition. Fortunately, concerned citizens raised money to purchase the house and move it to its present location. Restored to its original glory, Boscobel is full of graceful period furnishings. The gardens will captivate the kids, with colorful tulips, fragrant roses, pungent herbs, and an orangerie filled with orchids. In summer the Hudson Valley Shakespeare Festival takes up residence.

Constitution Marsh Audubon Center and Sanctuary (all ages)

127 Warren Landing Rd.; (845) 265-2601; www.constitutionmarsh.org. Grounds are open daily year-round 9 a.m. to 5 p.m.; nature center closed Mon. **Free.**

This 207-acre freshwater tidal marsh, managed by the National Audubon Society, is teeming with wildlife, from snapping turtles and muskrats to more than 194 species of birds. Stop at the visitor center for directions and to view the 500-gallon aquarium, then follow a short and easy self-guided nature trail to Jim's Walk, a 700-foot boardwalk overlooking the marsh, or follow the path to nearby Indian Brook Falls and wade in the pond at its base. For children over 7 and parents, guided canoe trips are offered daily at high tide.

Manitoga/The Russel Wright Design Center (all ages)

584 NY 9D; (845) 424-3812; www.russelwrightcenter.org. Open May through Oct weekdays 9 a.m. to 4 p.m., weekends 10 a.m. to 6 p.m. Tours of the house and grounds are offered most weekdays at 11 a.m. and Sat and Sun at 11 a.m. and 1:30 p.m. with reservations. Adults $$$, children $. Self-guided nature hikes $.

Also in **the Area**

Hudson Highlands State Park. NY 9D, Beacon; (845) 225-7207; www
.nysparks.com/parks.

William Clough Nature Preserve. Farm Market Road, Patterson; (845) 878-
6500; www.pattersonny.org.

Patterson Environmental Park. South Street, Patterson; (845) 878-6500; www
.pattersonny.org. (situated inside the Great Swamp)

Michael Ciaiola Conservation Area. Haviland Hollow Road, Patterson; (845)
225-3650; www.putnamcountyny.com.

Manitoga is an Algonquin word meaning "Place of the Great Spirit," and legendary industrial designer Russel Wright created this center with the intention of bringing the spirits
of people and nature together. There are 4 miles of paths lacing through the seventy-five-
acre landscape, with links to the Appalachian Trail. The environmental education center
offers guided nature walks, seasonal family programs, summer camp programs for kids,
and a full-size Native American wigwam. Call in advance to arrange a visit to Wright's cliff
home, Dragon Rock, a glass-walled wonder of inspirational architecture.

Clarence Fahnestock State Park (all ages)

1498 NY 301, Carmel; (845) 225-7207 or (800) 456-2267 (campsites); www.nysparks.state.ny
.us/parks. Taconic Outdoor Education Center, 75 Mountain Laurel Lane, Cold Spring; (845) 265-
3773. Open daily year-round sunrise to sunset. Canopus Beach opens weekends beginning
Memorial Day weekend, then open daily the fourth week of June through Labor Day week-
end. Campground open daily from the third Fri in Apr through the second Sun in Dec. $$. Call
ahead to confirm changes to hours, activities available, and possible closures due to pend-
ing state budget cuts.

This scenic highlands area once supported numerous farms
and a thriving iron industry. Today the popular park comprises
more than 10,000 acres of woodlands, streams, and stocked
fishing ponds and is laced with a network of easy to moderate
hiking trails suitable for families with young children. A favorite hike
is the 1.5-mile Pelton Pond Nature Trail. The park's crown jewel is
Canopus Lake, with its sandy beach, concession stand, showers, row-
boat rentals, and picnic area. Fishing by boat is allowed (with permit) at
Stillwater and Canopus Lakes and in the four ponds, where bass, perch,
pickerel, and rainbow trout can be caught by crafty anglers. In winter,
Fahnestock Winter Park opens its 15 kilometers of groomed cross-country
skiing trails, sled areas, and ponds for ice-skating and ice fishing. The **Nature
Center,** located at the campground, offers guided nature walks, crafts, and

interpretive programs; overnight visitors can enjoy family film nights. The larger **Taconic Outdoor Education Center,** west of the main park area, has environmental programs and workshops for all ages, from bird and animal identification to orienteering and star searches (night hikes). Seasonal programs include Winterfest (Feb), Sap to Syrup (Mar), and an Outdoor Rec Fest (May).

Where to Eat

The Stadium. 1308 US 9; (845) 734-4000. Featured on the History Channel, this family sports bar has some incredible memorabilia, such as Babe Ruth's Yankee contract, the first Heisman Trophy, Mickey Mantle's Triple Crown Award, several Super Bowl trophies, and Derek Jeter's autographed rookie cleats. The food ranges from burgers to salads, pasta, seafood, steaks, plus a Little Leaguer's menu. $–$$

Tavern Restaurant. 955 NY 9D; (845) 424-3254; www.highlandscountryclub.net/tavern .html. Located within the Highlands Country Club, this excellent gourmet restaurant has a terrific Sunday Family Night meal as well as a Date Night on Thurs during which your children are fed their own special meal, then entertained by a child-care professional with arts and crafts, games, and a movie, while you get to enjoy a relaxing romantic dinner with your partner. $$$$

Where to Stay

The Bird & Bottle Inn. 1123 Old Albany Post Rd. (US 9); (845) 424-2333; www.thebird andbottleinn.com. Once a stagecoach stop known as Warren's Tavern, this historic inn boasts eighteenth-century furnishings, working fireplaces, and a wonderful restaurant. $$$

Fishkill

Head north on US 9.

The Dutch word for creek is *kill;* hence this town was named for the creek that runs through it. Important strategically during the Revolutionary War, it was briefly the capital for our rebellious young government.

Van Wyck Homestead (ages 9 and up)

504 US 9; (845) 896-9560; www.fishkillridge.org. Open June through Oct, Sat and Sun 1 to 4 p.m. or by appointment. $.

This Dutch Colonial country farmhouse was built in 1732 by Cornelius Van Wyck and was used as a headquarters, supply depot, and courtroom during the Revolutionary War. Costumed guides conduct tours of the homestead, with its museum of eighteenth-century artifacts, and colonial crafts and skills may be demonstrated during special events.

Splash Down Beach (all ages)

16 Old Route 9; (845) 897-9600; www.splashdownbeach.com. Open from end of May through Labor Day. Hours vary weekly. $$$–$$$$.

This small water theme park is a fun way to cool off after a hot hike or a history lesson. Younger folks won't mind being marooned in Ship Wreck Lagoon or chillin' in the Coconut

Pool. Older children will enjoy three big waterslides, water balloon wars, and the 700-foot-long Crocodile Creek Action River. There's also mini-golf, mini-basketball, pirate-themed magic shows, a picnic area, and a snack bar.

Mount Gulian Historic Site (ages 7 and up)
145 Sterling St., Beacon; (845) 831-8172. Open Apr through Oct, Wed, Thurs, Fri, and Sun 1 to 5 p.m. $.

A fourteen-acre restored Dutch Colonial homestead, built in 1730, that was the Revolutionary War headquarters of Gen. Baron Von Steuben.

Dia: Beacon (age 8 and up)
3 Beekman St., Beacon; (845) 440-0100; www.diabeacon.org. Open mid-Apr to mid-Oct, Thurs through Mon 11 a.m. to 6 p.m.; mid-Oct to early Nov, Thurs through Mon 11 a.m. to 4 p.m.; mid-Nov through mid-Apr, Fri through Mon 11 a.m. to 4 p.m. Closed major holidays. $$.

Formerly a 240,000-square-foot Nabisco box-printing plant, this museum opened in 2003 with exhibitions of works by Andy Warhol, Richard Serra, Agnes Martin, and other modern artists. Exhibits are always changing, and public programs include gallery tours and talks, concerts, and Merce Cunningham Dance Company performances.

Where to Eat

Copper. 1111 Main St.; (845) 896-1000. Pastas, seafood, eclectic specials, and terrific homemade desserts. $$–$$$

Hudson's Ribs and Fish. 1099 US 9; (845) 297-5002; www.hudsonsribsandfish.com. Great barbecue, fresh seafood delivered daily, and homemade popovers with strawberry butter. $$

Where to Stay

Residence Inn by Marriott. 14 Schuyler Blvd., US 9, at I-84, exit 13; (845) 896-5210; www.residenceinn.com. All rooms have fully equipped kitchens, Wi-Fi, and complimentary grocery shopping service. $$$–$$$$

Snow Valley Campground. 111 US 9; (845) 897-5700. Sixty-acre campground with forty tent sites and forty RV hookup; laundry room, hot showers, phone and cable hookup available, plus a nice lake with children's beach. $

Also in **the Area**

Sylvan Lake Beach Park. 18 McDonnells Lane, Hopewell Junction; (845) 221-9889; www.dutchesscountycampground.com.

Fishkill Ridge. NY 52, Fishkill; (845) 473-4440; www.scenichudson.org.

Mount Beacon. NY 9D and Howland Avenue, Beacon; (845) 473-4440; www.scenichudson.org.

Wappingers Falls

Head north from Fishkill on US 9.

For thousands of years this area was the homeland of the Paleo Indians, and later the Wappingers, long before the Europeans arrived. In 1683 the Wappinger tribal leaders agreed to "sell" (for about $1,200 in guns, rum, and tobacco) to Francis Rombout and his partners Stephanus Van Cortlandt and Gulian Verplanck all the land that Rombout could see. The Wappingers meant, naturally, all the land one could see from ground level and were dismayed when Rombout climbed to the top of nearby South Beacon Mountain and "saw" about 85,000 acres.

Stony Kill Farm Environmental Center (all ages)

79 Farmstead Lane; (845) 831-8780; www.dec.ny.gov/education/1833.html. Open daily year-round dawn to dusk. Visitor center open weekdays 8:30 a.m. to 4:45 p.m., Sat 9:30 a.m. to 4:30 p.m., Sun 1 to 4:30 p.m. Barns open Sat only, 11 a.m. to 1 p.m., May through Sept, weather permitting. Free (fee for materials and some activities).

Once part of a large seventeenth-century estate, today it's a facility of over 1000 acres of farmland, fields, and meadows, and a fun place for families to learn about the ecology, agriculture, and natural history of the area. The nineteenth-century barns house beef cattle, pigs, sheep, and chickens. The stone Verplanck Manor House offers interpretive exhibits, but just about everything else is outdoors. There are five different self-guided trails here, including an ADA-accessible Woodland Trail, all of them 2½ miles long or less and easy for children to explore. Family activities and workshops range from building bird feeders to snowshoe hikes to hayrides.

Hudson Valley Renegades (ages 5 and up)

Dutchess Stadium, 1500 NY 9D; (845) 838-0094 or (800) 585-1329 for tickets; www.hvrenegades.com. $–$$$.

Take everyone out to the ball game! This Class A minor-league club, affiliated with the Tampa Bay Rays, plays from mid-June to Sept.

Fun Central (all ages)

1630 NY 9; (845) 297-1010; www.fun-central.com. Open year-round Mon, Tues, Wed, and Thurs 3:30 to 8 p.m., Fri 3:30 to 10:30 p.m., Sat 11 a.m. to10:30 p.m., and Sun noon to 8 p.m. Individual prices for each activity, with economical family ticket packages available. $–$$.

Rain or shine, this popular family amusement park offers activities from batting cages and bumper boats to arcade games, miniature golf, a virtual-reality indoor roller coaster, and a do-it-yourself gemstone mining operation.

Where to Eat

Planet Wings. 1546 US 9; (845) 298-9464; www.planetwings.com. Build your own burgers; Philly cheesesteaks; and bean, beef, or chicken burritos. Also choose from among twenty-four flavors of buffalo wings and shrimp. $

Poughkeepsie

Continue north on US 9.

Once a thriving nineteenth-century industrial center, Poughkeepsie has several restored historic districts (Academy Street, Garfield Place, and Union Street) that are fun to walk through. Vassar College was founded here in 1861 as a college for women, a concept so radical for the mid-nineteenth century that the main building of the campus was reputedly designed so that if women were found to be uneducable, it could be converted into a brewery.

Mid-Hudson Children's Museum (all ages)

75 N. Water St.; (845) 471-0589; www.mhcm.org. Open Tues through Fri 9:30 a.m. to 5 p.m. and weekends 11 a.m. to 5 p.m. Open Mon in summer. $$.

Two floors of hands-on science,art, and virtual-reality exhibits ranging from a costume corner and a computer center to a giant bubble machine and a kid-operated radio station, with a variety of special programs for newborns to twelve-year-old explorers offered year-round.

Locust Grove, the Samuel Morse Historic Site (ages 6 and up)

2683 South Rd., US 9; (845) 454-4500; www.lgny.org. Open daily 10 a.m. to 5 p.m. Mar through Dec; for Dec hours please check the Calendar of Events at the Web site. Adults $$, children 6 to 18 $–$$.

Gardens & Grounds are open year-round, 8 a.m. to dusk. **Free.** This nineteenth-century summer home of telegraph and Morse code inventor Samuel Morse is an octagonal Tuscan villa chock-full of antiques, art, and historical memorabilia as well as changing exhibits of toys, dolls, and costumes. Morse considered painting his primary career and regarded his inventions as simply a way of paying the bills. Special events include concerts, art exhibitions, antique car shows, and a Civil War Encampment in May. Extensive gardens surround the estate, and the 145-acre **Young Memorial Wildlife Sanctuary** next door offers short hiking trails.

Bardavon Opera House and Children's Theatre
(age levels depend on shows offered)

35 Market St.; (845) 473-5288; www.bardavon.org. Performances Sept through June; tours year-round. Box office open Mon through Fri 11 a.m. to 5 p.m.; (845) 339-6088. Performance times, offerings, and tickets vary; call for current information. $$$.

The cultural gem of Poughkeepsie, this performing arts center offers a variety of concerts, puppet shows, ballets, magic shows, and plays for a wide range of ages. Because the emphasis is on learning through entertainment, there are usually opportunities for children to go backstage after the show and meet the performers, and it's a terrific place to introduce your family to the magic of theater.

Hudson Valley Fairs and Festivals

Fairs

Chatham. Columbia County Fair; www.columbiafair.com.

Rhinebeck. Dutchess County Fair; www.dutchessfair.com.

Middletown. Orange County Fair; www.orangecountyfair.com.

Festivals

Poughkeepsie. Clearwater Festival; www.clearwaterfestival.org.

Katonah. Caramoor International Music Festival; www.caramoor.org.

Cold Spring. Hudson Valley Shakespeare Festival; www.hvshakespeare.org.

Hunter. Hunter Valley Beer and Food Festival; www.tapnewyork.com.

The *Clearwater* (all ages)

112 Market St.; (845) 454-7673; www.clearwater.org. **Educational hands-on sailing from mid-Apr to mid-Nov aboard the sloop *Clearwater*, with some limited availability aboard her sister tall ship, the schooner *Mystic Whaler*; to book passage, call (800) 67-SLOOP, ext. 107. $$–$$$$.**

This volunteer-built sloop has been sailing the Hudson since 1969, spreading its message of environmental consciousness and sharing love of the river with families everywhere. By the way, 2009 marked the fortieth anniversary of the launch of *Clearwater,* the ninetieth birthday celebration of folk singer legend Pete Seeger (and Hudson River hero), and the 400th anniversary of Henry Hudson's voyage up the Hudson.

Where to Eat

Aloy's Garden Restaurant. 157 Garden St.; (845) 473-8400. Italian-American specialties, burgers, subs, pizza, and kids' menu. $$

River Station. 1 Water St.; (845) 452-9207; www.riverstationrest.com. Oldest restaurant in town, with nice river views, serving pasta, steak, and seafood, five kinds of chowder, plus a children's menu. $$$–$$$$

Where to Stay

Inn at the Falls. 50 Red Oaks Mill Rd.; (845) 462-5770 or (800) 344-1466; www.innatthefalls.com. Under new management, this elegant thirty-six room bed-and-breakfast offers free wireless Internet, CD & DVD players, cable/satellite TV, and a game room. $$–$$$$

Residence Inn Poughkeepsie. 2525 South Rd.; (845) 463-4343 or (800) 943-6717; www.marriott.com. Large studios, one- and two-bedroom suites with pullout sofas in living room, fully equipped kitchens, free high-speed Internet, heated indoor pool and spa, Sport Court, billiards room, free hot breakfast buffet, and year-round barbecues. $$$$

Also in **the Area**

Mid-Hudson Civic Center–McCann Ice Arena. 14 Civic Center Plaza; (845) 454-5800; midhudsonciviccenter.com.

Overlook Golf & Recreation Center. 39 DeGarmo Rd.; (845) 471-8515; www .overlookgolfcenter.com.

The River Rose Tours & Cruises. Poughkeepsie Dock; (845) 562-1067; www .riverrosecruises.com.

Hyde Park

Continue north on US 9.

Named after Edward Hyde, Lord Cornbury, an English governor and cousin of Queen Anne, Hyde Park is perhaps best known for the country estates of the Vanderbilts and Roosevelts. That's just as well, for Lord Cornbury, aside from his inclinations toward bribes, bad debts, and booze, had the habit of wearing extravagant women's dresses, much to the annoyance of the colonists.

Franklin D. Roosevelt Home National Historic Site (ages 7 and up) 🏛

4079 Albany Post Rd. (US 9); (845) 486-7770 or (800) FDR–VISIT; www.nps.gov/hofr; www .fdrlibrary.marist.edu. Open daily year-round 9 a.m. to 5 p.m. Closed New Year's, Thanksgiving, and Christmas. $$, children 15 years and under are free. Grounds are open from sunrise to sunset and are free.

Springwood was the birthplace and lifelong residence of FDR, a former governor of New York and our thirty-second president. It is where he and Eleanor raised their five children, and it is a good place to introduce families to the man who guided America through the Great Depression and World War II. Begin your tour at the Henry A. Wallace Visitor and Education Center, where you'll get tickets for the museum, library, and house, which are filled with personal and historical memorabilia. Don't forget to get your **free** *Junior Secret Service Handbook* for seven- to twelve-year-old spysters; then check out the interactive video game that gives kids the chance to make some of the decisions Roosevelt had to make during the war. The grounds surrounding the "Summer White House" are lovely, particularly the rose garden in June, and a nature study center sits on the slightly steep path leading down to the Hudson River.

Eleanor Roosevelt National Historic Site (ages 7 and up)

NY 9G, directly east of FDR home; (845) 229-9115; www.nps.gov/elro. Guided tours Thurs through Mon 9 a.m. to 5 p.m. May to Oct; grounds open daily year-round sunrise to sunset. Closed Thanksgiving Day, Christmas Day, and New Year's Day. Guided tours $$, children under 16 free, grounds free.

Eleanor Roosevelt considered Val-Kill to be her only real home. Built as a weekend retreat from the pressures of political life and her domineering mother-in-law, it is striking in its simplicity. Eleanor entertained many heads of state here as well as children from a nearby reform school. After her husband's death, she was enlisted by President Harry Truman as a United Nations delegate, and it was here that Eleanor drafted the Universal Declaration of Human Rights.

Vanderbilt Mansion (ages 10 and up)

US 9, (2 miles north of the FDR National Historic Site); (845) 229-7770; www.nps.gov/ vama. Open 9 a.m. to 5 p.m. daily year-round, closed major holidays. House admission $$, children under 17 free. Grounds open daily year-round from sunrise to sunset and are free.

This fifty-four-room Beaux Arts country palace is filled with European antiques, tapestries, and paintings and cost more than $2.5 million when completed in 1899—at a time when the average annual income was less than $500. The landscaped grounds include

Suggested **Reading**

River of Dreams: The Story of the Hudson River, by Hudson Talbott

Hudson: The Story of a River, by Robert Baron and Thomas Locker

The Legend of Sleepy Hollow, by Washington Irving

Rip Van Winkle, by Washington Irving

Beyond the Sea of Ice: The Voyages of Henry Hudson, by Joan Elizabeth Goodman

The Book of Alfar: A Tale of the Hudson Highland, by Peter W. Hassinger

The Bad Man of the Hudson, by Dorothea Boyd Wolfe

The Lost Treasure of Captain Kidd, by Peter Lourie

Eleanor Roosevelt: A Life of Discovery, by Russell Freeman

Robert Fulton: From Submarine to Steamboat, by Steven Kroll

The Gold Bug, by Edgar Allan Poe

Hyde Park **Parks**

Hackett Hill. East Market Street; (845) 229-8086; www.hydeparkny.us.

Pinewoods Park. Pinewoods Road; (845) 229-8086; www.hydeparkny.us.

Riverfront Park. West Market Street; (845) 229-8086; www.hydeparkny.us.

formal Italian gardens dotted with fountains and statues, sprawling lawns on which to run around, lots of hiking trails winding through the woods, and lovely views of the Hudson River. Pick up a map (at any of the mansions) of the Hyde Park Trail, and explore an 8.5-mile network of easy, well-marked paths that follow the Hudson River between the Vanderbilt and Roosevelt homes.

Where to Eat

Culinary Institute of America. NY 9; (845) 471-6608; www.ciachef.edu. Legendary chef school with four different award-winning restaurants (American Bounty, Escoffier, Ristorante Caterina de' Medici, and St. Andrew's Café) plus the Apple Pie Bakery Café is awesome! $$$

Twist. 4290 Albany Post Road; (845) 229-7094; www.letstwist.com. Casual eclectic American restaurant with a unique, well, twist . . . plus a fun kid's menu. $$$–$$$$

Where to Stay

Golden Manor Motel. US 9, across the road from the FDR home; (845) 229-2157; www.goldenmanorhydepark.com. Free continental breakfast, cable TV, outdoor pool. Some rooms have kitchens, and the motel is next door to a good restaurant. $

The Roosevelt Inn. 4360 Albany Post Rd. (US 9); (845) 229-2443; www.rooseveltinnof hydepark.com. Within walking distance of the Vanderbilt Mansion, this inn offers rustic and deluxe rooms and a nice coffee shop. $–$$$

Rhinebeck

Continue north on US 9.

German immigrants followed the Dutch and English to this area, naming the town in honor of their beloved Rhine River. Today Rhinebeck is a charming village of interesting shops and picturesque Victorian houses, including the oldest inn in America, the Beekman Arms. And yes, George Washington really did sleep here.

Old Rhinebeck Aerodrome (all ages)

42 Stone Church Rd., a right turn off US 9; (845) 752-3200; www.oldrhinebeck.org. Open mid-June through mid-Oct, daily 10 a.m. to 5 p.m. Biplane rides begin at 10 a.m., air show begins at 2 p.m. (No air shows on weekdays.) Weekend admission: adults, teens (ages 13

to 17), and seniors $$$; juniors (ages 6 to 12) and Scouts in uniform $; children 5 and under free. Weekday admission $. Biplane ride $65 per person.

This thrilling aviation museum, which celebrated its fiftieth season in 2009, features dramatic dogfights and spectacular stunts performed by fearless and funny pilots in pre– and post–World War I aircraft. Saturday shows focus on the early history of flight, and on Sunday families can cheer the aerobatic antics of Sir Percy Goodfellow as he battles Der Black Baron. After the show, stroll the grounds and marvel at the amazing collection of antique aircraft and automobiles amassed by museum founder and avid collector Cole Palen, then take to the air aboard a 1929 open-cockpit biplane.

Where to Eat

Foster's Coach House Tavern. 6411 Montgomery St.; (845) 876-8052; www.fosterscoachhouse.com. This is a fun equestrian-themed restaurant serving steak, seafood, sandwiches, salads; kids' menu. $$

Gigi Trattoria. 6422 Montgomery St., US 9; (845) 876-0543; www.gigitrattoria.com. "Hudson Valley Mediterranean" cuisine, made with locally grown organic produce, affiliated with the Gigi Market at the Grieg Farm in Red Hook (845) 758-1999). $$–$$$

Where to Stay

Beekman Arms and Delamater Inn. 6387 Mill St.; (845) 876-7077. The historic Beekman Arms, built in 1766, has a variety of accommodations in four buildings (each room comes with a decanter of sherry), while the Delamater Inn has fifty rooms and suites and seven separate guesthouses, most with fireplaces. Complimentary continental breakfast is included, and the Tavern Restaurant on the grounds is excellent. $$$$

Interlake Farm Campground. 428 Lake Dr.; (845) 266-5387; www.interlakervpark.com. Ducks, lake and pond fishing, boating, playground, recreation hall, heated swimming pool, kiddie pool, Laundromat, camp store, cable TV, and wireless Internet. They also offer trailer rentals, fully furnished, as well as planned activities for families. $–$$

Whistle Wood Farm. 52 Pells Rd.; (845) 876-6838; www.whistlewood.com. Working horse farm and bed-and-breakfast. $$$–$$$$

Also in **the Area**

Ferncliff Forest. Mt. Rusten Road and River Road, north of Rhinebeck; (845) 876-3196.

Poets' Walk Park. River Road near Kingston-Rhinecliff Bridge, Red Hook; (845) 473-4440; www.scenichudson.org and www.hvnet.com.

Greig Farm. 223 Pitcher Lane, Red Hook; (845) 758-1234; www.greigfarm.com.

The Southlands Foundation. 5771 US 9S; (845) 876-4862; www.southlands.org.

Annandale-on-Hudson and Clermont

Take NY 9G north, then US 9.

Montgomery Place (all ages)

River Road, CR 103, Annandale-on-Hudson; (914) 631-8200; www.hudsonvalley.org. Open Apr through Oct, Wed through Mon 10 a.m. to 5 p.m.; weekends Nov through mid-Dec, 10 a.m. to 5 p.m. Closed Jan through Mar and Thanksgiving. Adults $$, children 5 to 17 $, under 5 free, grounds pass $.

Another of the sites operated by Historic Hudson Valley, this exquisite Federal-style mansion has lovely views of the river and easy trails past 434 acres of manicured gardens, woods, waterfalls, and orchards. Special seasonal activities are scheduled for families. Currently, Montgomery Place is undergoing extensive restoration, and the site is temporarily closed to the general public. The opening date has not been announced yet, so please call before visiting.

Clermont (all ages)

1 Clermont Ave. (off NY 9G), Germantown; (518) 537-4240; www.friendsofclermont.org. House is open Apr 1 through Oct 31, Tues through Sun, plus Monday holidays 11 a.m. to 5 p.m. Open weekends only Nov 1 through Dec 31, 11 a.m. to 4 p.m.; grounds open year-round 8:30 a.m. to sunset. $, children under 5 free.

Home to the illustrious Livingston family for seven generations, Clermont is a restored Georgian-style mansion perched on a breathtaking bluff overlooking the Hudson. Special activities for families, from wildlife watching to sheep shearing, occur almost every weekend.

Lake Taghkanic State Park (all ages)

1528 NY 82, Ancram; (518) 851-3631; campground (800) 456-2267; www.nysparks.com/ parks. Park open daily year-round 8 a.m. to 9 p.m. during camping season and sunrise to sunset the rest of the year; campground open May through Oct. Parking fee $.

The *Clermont*

In 1686 a royal charter granted Robert Livingston a 162,000-acre tract of land in what later became the southern third of Columbia County. His great-grandson, Robert R. Livingston, signed the Declaration of Independence, administered the oath of office to George Washington, negotiated the Louisiana Purchase, and helped finance Robert Fulton's steamboat, the *Clermont*.

This popular park, centered around a lake and nestled among rolling hills and woodlands, has two beaches (East and West Swimming Beaches), several playgrounds, small-boat rentals, concession stands, campgrounds, cabins and cottages, a recreation hall, ball fields, shady picnic areas, fishing, a nature center, and 8 miles of trails for hiking and biking. In winter, equipment rental is available for ice-skating and cross-country skiing. Please note that currently the East Swimming Beach and Bathhouse is closed, but the newly renovated West Swimming Beach and Bathhouse will be open weekends only from Memorial Day, then daily in June through Labor Day weekend.

Where to Eat

West Taghkanic Diner. NY 82, (West Taghkanic) Ancram, off Taconic State Parkway; (518) 851-7117; www.taghkanicdiner.com. Classic 1953 diner serving breakfast and dinner all day long. $–$$

Where to Stay

Brook N Wood Family Campground. 1947 CR 8, Elizaville; (518) 537-6896 or (888) 544-3201; www.brooknwood.com. Open late Apr through Oct. Campsites, cabins, RV rentals and hookups, a country store, playground, pool, recreation hall, hot showers, and cottage playhouse. $

Taghkanic Motel. 1011 NY 82, Ancram (West Taghkanic), off Taconic State Parkway; (518) 851-9006; www.taghkanicmotel.com. Walking distance to Taghkanic Lake State Park, and across the street from the Taghkanic Diner. $

Hudson

Continue north on NY 9G.

In the mid-1700s, Nantucket whalers and other fishermen settled in this area, building Hudson into an efficient shipping center that twenty-five schooners called home port. In 1797 the town came within one vote of becoming the state's capital, but by the mid-1800s, the whaling industry was declining, as were the whales. Today a stroll through town reveals a wonderful variety of nineteenth-century New England–style architecture. Warren Street is lined with nearly seventy inviting antiques shops, and 1 block over, Columbia Street (formerly Diamond Street) had the dubious distinction of being the oldest red-light district in the country. Walk down to Front Street and enjoy the river vistas from the Parade or Promenade Hill Park.

American Museum of Firefighting (all ages)

117 Harry Howard Ave.; (877) 347-3687www.fasnyfiremuseum.com. Open daily year-round 10 a.m. to 5 p.m. Closed major holidays. Family rate $$, adults and children 12 and older $, under 12 free.

For the fledgling firefighters in your family, this is a fascinating place. The collection, the largest of its kind in the world, includes more than seventy antique and unusual fire engines from 1725 to the present day, as well as firefighting equipment, artwork, and memorabilia from three centuries. The McCadam Cheese Fire Safety and Prevention Discovery Room has several kid-friendly interactive, educational craft stations, and the McCadem Safety Station Puppet Theater presents shows on weekends. Five fire trucks have been designated official play stations, and come complete with kid-size firefighters' gear to wear. Special events throughout the year include Dalmatian Day and culminate with the New York State Firefighters Competition and Field Day in July.

Olana (all ages)

NY 9G, 1 mile south of Rip Van Winkle Bridge; (518) 828-0135; www.olana.org. Guided tours only. See Web site for seasonal hours and fees to tour the house or to visit the Evelyn and Maurice Sharp Gallery. Grounds open daily 8 a.m. to sunset year-round. $.

Envisioned as a Persian palace by Hudson River School painter Frederick Edwin Church, Olana is his spectacular effort to create a romantic, 3-D landscape work of art. The gilded and tiled mansion was the result of his love of exotic lands. From mixing the vivid paints for the walls himself and filling the rooms with exquisite objects to landscaping the 250-acre grounds overlooking the Hudson River, Church created his vision. Numerous programs are offered year-round at the Wagon House Education Center, encouraging and inspiring artistic vision for everybody in the family. Toddlers are treated to storytelling and finger painting on Sat; family tours are scheduled throughout the year; and self-guided activities, including backpacks and maps that are loaned out, are offered Thurs through Sun for adventurous artists and intrepid explorers.

Where to Eat

Hudson Park Restaurant. 3521 US 9; (518) 851-2228; www.hudsonparkbaseball .com. This baseball-themed restaurant serves stadium fare, including many varieties of hot dogs, and has big-screen TVs, an arcade, and daily trivia games. It is also the future home of the Teenage American Baseball Tournament. $–$$

Swoon Kitchenbar. 340 Warren St.; (518) 822-8938; www.swoonkitchenbar.com. Open Thurs through Tues for lunch and dinner. Gourmet international cuisine, with a menu that changes daily, including homemade pasta, paninis, wild seafood, naturally raised meats and poultry, locally grown organic produce, fresh cheeses, and an awesome chocolate crème brûlée. $$–$$$

Where to Stay

St. Charles Hotel. 16-18 Park Place; (518) 822-9900; www.stcharleshotel.com. Full-service hotel with several large rooms for families. Complimentary continental breakfast. $–$$

Union Street Guest House. 349 Union St.; (518) 828-0958 or (888) 477-7906; www.union streetguesthouse.com. A variety of unique suites with one, two, three, or four bedrooms are available, with wireless Internet, DVD library, cable TV, refrigerators, and a massage therapist a block away. $$–$$$$

Kinderhook

Head north on NY 9.

First settled by the Dutch in the 1660s, Kinderhook, or "children's corner," is perhaps best known today as the hometown of Martin Van Buren, our country's eighth president, and, incidentally, the first one to be born a citizen of the United States. Van Buren had several nicknames, among them "the Little Magician" (for his size and political skill) and "the Red Fox" (for his red sideburns), but it was his nickname of "Old Kinderhook" that may have given us the expression "OK."

Martin Van Buren National Historic Site (ages 6 and up)
1013 Old Post Rd., off NY 9H; (518) 758-9689; www.nps.gov/mava. Visitor center open mid-May through Oct daily 9 a.m. to 4 p.m. $. Grounds open year-round 7 a.m. to dusk and are free.

When Martin Van Buren purchased the thirty-six-room Lindenwald mansion in 1839, he planned to live here after he retired from politics. His failure to win a second term as president in 1841 (despite his Amistad actions) brought about retirement somewhat earlier than expected. A guided tour of the house may be of interest to older children, and special events include a coach and carriage show, a picnic and band concert in period costume, campfire talks, and naturalist-guided nature walks.

Luykas Van Alen House (ages 6 and up)
Route 9H, Lindenwald; (518) 758-9265; www.cchsny.org/prog_links_sites_1.html. Open Memorial Day through Columbus Day, Sat 10 a.m. to 4 p.m. and Sun noon to 4 p.m. $, children under 12 free.

Hudson River National Estuarine
Research Reserve

Created to protect and manage the biologically diverse Hudson River coastal wetlands, this network of four different ecosystems stretches along 100 miles of the river's estuary and encompasses 4,838 acres. Each of the sites offers frequent public field programs. For more information, call (845) 758-7010 or (845) 889-4745, or visit www.nerrs.noaa.gov/hudsonriver or www.dec.ny.gov.

Iona Island. US 9W, Bear Mountain.

Piermont Marsh. US 9W, Piermont.

Tivoli Bays. US 9, Annandale-on-Hudson.

Stockport Flats. US 9, Hudson.

Martin Scorsese's film *The Age of Innocence* was filmed in this restored 1737 Dutch Colonial farmhouse. Also on the thirty-acre site is the Ichabod Crane Schoolhouse, named for a local schoolteacher who was the inspiration for the character in Washington Irving's tale *The Legend of Sleepy Hollow.*

Where to Eat

Carolina House. 59 Broad St. (US 9); (518) 758-1669; www.carolinahouserestaurant.com. Southern cuisine served in a log cabin. $$

Kinderhook Diner. 333 NY 9H, Valatie; (518) 758-1399. Diner delights, especially the homemade blueberry pie. $–$$

Where to Stay

Blue Spruce Inn & Suites. US 9, Valatie; (518) 758-9711; www.bluespruceinnsuites.com. Family-run business for almost forty years, located on ten landscaped acres with a seasonal outdoor pool and a coffee shop (open May through Nov) serving local specialties like pear hotcakes. Rooms and fully furnished suites available. $–$$

Kinderhook Bed & Breakfast. 67 Broad St. (US 9); (518) 758-1850; www.kinderhookbandb.com. Near the village green; four rooms with feather beds (the Green & White room is the largest and best suited for families), and a friendly French poodle named Therman; Well-behaved children are welcome. $$

The Chathams and New Lebanon

Take NY 203 south into Chatham, or NY 203 north into North Chatham; NY 295 leads to East Chatham, and US 20 heads east to New Lebanon.

German and Dutch farmers settled here in 1758, and by the late nineteenth century the area was a railroad hub. The Chathams—which include the village of Chatham, Chatham Center, East Chatham, North Chatham, and Old Chatham—are spread out over miles of pastoral scenery. If you're in the neighborhood Labor Day weekend, you won't want to miss the Columbia County Fair, the oldest festival of its kind in the country. Nearby New Lebanon was the site of the most successful utopian communal society in America for 160 years, the Shakers.

Shaker Museum and Library at
Mount Lebanon Shaker Village (ages 7 and up)

Darrow Road, New Lebanon; (518) 794-9100; www.shakermuseumandlibrary.org. The Shaker Museum and Library of Old Chatham is currently being relocated to the Mount Lebanon Shaker Village, so the complex is temporarily closed. Please check the Web site for updates.

This was the site of the first permanent Shaker community in New York, originally covering more than 6,000 acres, with 120 buildings and 600 believers. Shaker founder Mother Ann Lee was thrown in jail in England for preaching her beliefs in communal living, celibacy, equality, and pacifism, so she and her followers sailed for America in 1774, seeking religious freedom. Children lived apart from the adults, with girls attending school in summer and boys in winter. Older children will appreciate the Shakers' imaginative solutions to everyday problems—the clothespin, circular saw, cut nails, and water-repellent fabric. The new 50,000-square-foot museum will house more than 15,000 artifacts and 20,000 archival items—the largest collection of Shaker craftsmanship in the country. Restoration of the Great Stone Barn as well as ten other historic buildings, new classrooms, a museum store, a seasonal cafe, and a variety of family programs and activities are planned.

Where to Eat

O's Eatery. 309 Rigor Hill Rd., Chatham; (518) 392-1001; www.oseatery.com. Creative American diner cuisine including specialty sandwiches, wraps, a variety of burgers, terrific meat loaf, homemade soups, fresh-baked pies and a children's menu. $

Ralph's pretty good Café. 20 Main St., Chatham; (518)392-3291; www.ralphspretty goodcafe.com. Casual eclectic cuisine, including burritos, mac and cheese, veggie chili, ciabata sandwiches, homemade soups, and daily specials. $

Where to Stay

The Inn at Shaker Mill Farm. 40 Cherry Lane, off NY 22, Canaan; (518) 794-9345; www.shakermillfarminn.com. Bed-and-breakfast with a stream and pond to explore; breakfast and afternoon tea included. $–$$

Shaker Meadows Bed & Breakfast. 14209 NY 22, New Lebanon; (518) 794-9385; www.shakermeadows.com. Nestled among fifty acres of woods and meadows, this B&B has room for large families. The Creamery has three suites and sleeps up to fourteen guests, while The eighteenth-century Farmhouse has six bedrooms and can sleep six to twelve guests. All have fully furnished kitchens, free wireless Internet, private decks or lawn areas, and free passes to the town's private sandy beach on Queechy Lake, with towels and folding chairs provided. $$–$$$

Hillsdale and Copake Falls

Take the Taconic State Parkway south to NY 23. Take NY 23 east to Hillsdale, then NY 22 south to Copake Falls.

These peaceful villages lie along the edge of Taconic State Park and offer a variety of seasonal and scenic outdoor activities.

Catamount (ages 2 and up)

3200 NY 23, Hillsdale; (518) 325-3200 or (800) 342-1840 (snow report); www.catamountski .com. Ski resort open weekdays in season 9 a.m. to 4 p.m., weekends 8:30 a.m. to 4 p.m. Check for seasonal night skiing sessions online. Adults, seniors, and children 7 through 13 $$$$, children 6 and under $$$. Special ski packages available. Adventure Park open mid-May, 9 a.m. to 5:30 p.m., on Fri, Sat, and Sun until mid-June, then open daily in summer. Fall hours not announced yet. $$$$.

This family-oriented year-round recreation park has something for everyone. In winter the ski resort has thirty-two trails, six lifts, snowboarding slopes, and instruction available for snow bunnies age four and up. Babysitting is available for children ages two to six. In warmer months, Adventure Park, an aerial forest rope course complete with zip lines, becomes the focus for kids eight and older, and mountain bikers will appreciate the new Gravity Skills Park and the variety of challenging trails.

Taconic State Park—Copake Falls Area (all ages)

NY 344, Copake Falls, off NY 22; (518) 329-3993, camping reservations (800) 456-2267; www .nysparks.com/parks. Campground is open May through Oct, and park is open year-round sunrise to sunset. Summer parking fee $$; camping $.

Nestled in the Taconic Mountains, this is the northern section of a lush 5,000-acre preserve. The Copake Falls area offers swimming, hiking, boat rentals, picnic areas, playgrounds, trout fishing, and a variety of tent sites and cabins. A highlight is spectacular Bash-Bish Falls, and the new Iron Works Museum offers a look at the lives of the local ironworkers of the mid-nineteenth century. Nature programs and special children's activities are offered year-round. In winter, trails are groomed for cross-country skiing and snowshoeing.

Where to Eat

Hillsdale House. Village Square, NY 23, Hillsdale; (518) 325-7111. Regional American specialties, burgers, chicken fingers, and wood-fired pizza. They'll do half orders for children if you ask. $$$

Random Harvest. 1785 NY 23, Craryville; (518) 325-5103. Farm market and gourmet deli shop. $

Where to Stay

Oleana Family Campground. 2236 CR 7, Copake; (518) 329-2811. www.oleanacamp ground.com. Open May through Oct, with playground, lake for swimming and fishing, video arcade, basketball, softball, and hayrides. $

Swiss Hutte. NY 23, Hillsdale; (518) 325-3333; www.swisshutte.com. Originally a nineteenth-century farmhouse and expanded in the 1970s to contain twelve rooms, this lovely inn has an outdoor pool, a brook-fed pond, big trees, beautiful gardens, and a fabulous gourmet restaurant that features locally grown produce and naturally raised meats and poultry, cheese fondue in front of a fireplace, and seasonal outdoor patio dining. All the rooms have an outdoor porch or balcony. $$–$$$

Millerton and Stanfordville

Head south on NY 22 to Millerton, then NY 199 west to NY 82 and south to Stanfordville.

Taconic State Park—Rudd Pond Area (all ages)

59 Rudd Pond Rd., Millerton, off NY 22; (518) 789-3059; www.nysparks.com/parks. Open daily year-round sunrise to sunset; campgrounds open the first Fri in May through Labor Day. Summer parking fee $$; camping $. Call ahead to confirm changes to hours, activities available, and possible closures due to pending state budget cuts.

The 210-acre Rudd Pond area, the southern part of Taconic State Park, offers swimming, sand beach and bathhouse, a playground, canoe and rowboat rentals, fishing, hiking and biking trails, campsites, and a nice picnic area, with ice-skating, cross-country skiing, and snowmobiling possible in winter.

Thompson Pond Preserve (all ages)

Lake Road, Pine Plains; turn at the Pine Plains firehouse; (914) 244-3271; www.nature.org. Preserved by the Nature Conservancy. Stissing Mountain Fire Tower (518) 398-5673. Open daily year-round. Free.

This 507-acre gem, a registered National Natural Landmark, formed 15,000 years ago when melting glaciers created a kettle at the base of Stissing Mountain. More than 387 plant species, 162 bird species, and 27 mammal species have been identified at the preserve, displaying the amazing diversity of a wetlands. An easy two-hour-loop trail starting from Lake Road will lead you through fields, forests, and swamp, with opportunities for some of the best bird-watching in the Hudson Valley. Scale the fire tower at Stissing Mountain's summit and, on a clear day, you can see all the way to Albany.

Wilcox Memorial Park (all ages)

NY 199, Stanfordville; (845) 758-6100; www.dutchessny.gov/countygov/departments/dpw-parks/ppwilcox.htm. Park hours are Jan through Mar, 9 a.m. to 4 p.m.; Apr through May, 9 a.m. to 6 p.m.; Memorial Day through Labor Day, weekends 9 a.m. to 8 p.m. and weekdays 9 a.m. to 7 p.m.; Labor Day through Memorial Day, weekends only, 9 a.m. to 7 p.m. $.

This lovely 615-acre park has two small lakes, one with a sandy beach, paddleboats, miniature golf, a children's playground, bike paths, hiking trails, campsites, and a snack bar

Where to Eat

Taro's NY Style Pizzeria. 18 Main St., Millerton; (518) 789-6630. Friendly-family place serving great pizza, pasta, and salads. $–$$

Where to Stay

Roseland Ranch. North of town on Hunn's Lake Road, Stanfordville; (845) 868-1350 or (800) 431-8292; www.duderanch.com. Open all year. This wonderful western-themed family resort, located on 1,000 acres of land hugging a lake, offers horseback riding and

lessons, skiing, tennis, volleyball and basketball courts, indoor and outdoor swimming pools, sauna, petting zoo, paddleboats, playground, a video arcade with pool tables, children's activities, **free** babysitting, a tepee you and your child can sleep in, a twenty-four-hour cafe, outdoor barbecue lunches, and family-style dinners. $$$$

Millbrook

Head south on NY 82 to NY 44A.

Settled by Dutch Quakers in the late eighteenth century, the town's name was derived from the old gristmill located on the nearby Wappinger's Creek.

Wing's Castle (ages 6 and up)

717 Bangall Rd., 0.5 mile north of CR 57, northeast of Millbrook; (845) 677-9085; www.wing castle.us. Tours offered after Memorial Day through Labor Day, noon to 4:30 p.m., weekends only in the fall. $$.

Created from recycled and recovered treasures, this whimsical stone castle has been the work and home of Peter and Toni Ann Wing and family for more than four decades. A work in progress, the castle sits atop a hill overlooking the Hudson Valley. Inside are more than 2,000 antiques, oddities, and artifacts. Have a picnic on the grounds, where the Wings built Stonehenge East from 12-foot hand-hewn slabs of rock. A new B&B is scheduled to open soon, featuring rooms as unique as the castle, continental breakfast, and an evening bottle of Millbrook wine.

Innisfree Garden (all ages)

Innisfree, Tyrell Road, 1 mile off US 44 west of Millbrook; (845) 677-8000; www.innisfree garden.org. Open May through Oct, Wed through Fri 10 a.m. to 4 p.m., weekends and holidays 11 a.m. to 5 p.m. $, children under 4 free.

Painter Walter Beck and his wife, Marion, created this serene sanctuary using the landscape as their canvas. Although they never visited the Orient, the Becks studied Japanese scroll paintings and sculpted a series of "cup gardens" based on Eastern principles of design. The peaceful 150 acres surrounding a small glacial lake is laced with streams, stones, waterfalls, and terraces connected by carefully laid paths that are wonderful for strolling.

Cary Institute of Ecosystem Studies (ages 6 and up)

2801 Sharon Turnpike (US 44); (845) 677-5343; www.ecostudies.org. Gifford House Visitor and Education Center, 181 Sharon Turnpike. Open Apr through Dec, Mon through Sat 9 a.m. to 6 p.m., Sun 1 to 6 p.m.; closed Nov 1 to Mar 31 for deer hunting. Free.

For the budding botanists in your family, this is a combination gardening education center and wetland ecology laboratory. Pick up a permit and map at the Gifford House Visitor and Education Center, then tour the grounds. A tropical greenhouse, unusual plant

Sybil Ludington **Statue**

This statue is dedicated to the sixteen-year-old heroine of the American Revolution who rode her horse Star all night for more than 40 dangerous miles (twice the distance Paul Revere covered) to warn her father's militia of the advancing British troops. For more than thirty years, a 50-kilometer footrace has been held in Carmel, retracing the approximate path of Sybil's historic ride. For more information contact the Putnam County Tourist Bureau, www .visitputnam.org.

collections, and a variety of nature trails in and around the 1,924 acres are interesting to explore, and fun family workshops are offered.

Trevor Zoo (all ages)

Millbrook School, 131 Millbrook School Rd.; (845) 677-3704; www.trevorzoo.org. Open daily year-round 8:30 a.m. to 5 p.m. $.

This small six-acre zoo, founded in 1936 and located on the grounds of a picturesque prep school, is home to more than 180 exotic and indigenous species of animals, from red-tailed hawks to coatimundis. Care of the creatures is part of the school curriculum in the hopes that familiarity will breed appreciation. A 1.25-mile self-guiding nature trail and a boardwalk overlooking a marsh are both stroller accessible.

Where to Eat

Charlotte's Restaurant. 4258 US 44; (845) 677-5888; www.charlottesny.com. Local seasonal menu changes daily and may feature free-range venison, kobe burgers, truffle-tossed fries, and grilled salmon. The restaurant also has a children's menu. $$$–$$$$

Millbrook Diner. 3266 Franklin Ave. (US 44); (845) 677-5319. Hometown diner classics. $–$$

Where to Stay

The Cottonwood Motel. 2639 US 44, 4 miles east of Taconic State Parkway; (845) 677-3283; www.cottonwoodmotel.com. Located on three and a half acres of meadows with the Berkshires in the distance, this peaceful place has standard and deluxe rooms, a suite, and a large cottage that sleeps six. $$–$$$$

The Harrison House. 1 Flint Rd., Verbank; (845) 677-3057; www.harrisonhouseinn.com. Elegant new country inn with eight bedrooms, two with fireplaces. $$$$

Brewster

Head west on NY 44A, then south on the Taconic State Parkway, connecting with I-84 east.

Green Chimneys (all ages)

400 Doansburg Rd.; (845) 279-2995; www.greenchimneys.org. Open weekends year-round 10 a.m. to 3 p.m. Donation.

Founded in 1947 as a school where challenged children could interact with farm animals, today the grounds have expanded to over 500 acres, with a day and residential school for 200 students who care for more than 300 animals and birds. Many special events for families are scheduled throughout the year, along with regular tours of the Farm & Wildlife Rehabilitation Center, including a hayride.

Also in **the Area**

Chuang Yen Monastery. NY 301, Kent; (845) 225-1819.

Southeast Museum (ages 6 and up)

67 Main St.; (845) 279-7500; www.southeastmuseum.org. Open Apr through Dec, Tues
through Sat 10 a.m. to 4 p.m. Donation.

A small, offbeat museum, located in the lower level of the old Southeast Town Hall, it
offers permanent exhibits on Borden's condensed-milk factory, the Harlem Railroad, local
rocks and minerals, and other interesting oddities. Family programs and craft workshops
are offered throughout the season.

Putnam Children's Discovery Center (all ages)

854 US 6, Mahopac; (845) 276-2076; www.discoveryctr.org. Open Thurs 10 a.m. to 2 p.m.
Class and program dates and times vary. $.

This interactive museum has lots of hands-on science exhibits for toddlers to teens, from fantasy play areas and puppet shows to workshops in magic, art, chess, computers, and drama.

Where to Eat

Bob's Diner. 27 Main St.; (845) 278-2478.
Dishing up diner delights since 1955. $

Red Rooster Drive-In. 1566 NY 22; (845)
279-8046. Fun fast food from fries to franks,
with the added bonus of a miniature golf
course. $

Where to Stay

Heidi's Inn. 1270 NY 22; (845) 279-8011;
www.heidisinn.com. Rooms and efficiencies,
an outdoor swimming pool, **free** wireless
Internet, and free continental breakfast. $–$$

North Salem and Somers

Take NY 121 south, then NY 116.
   Once Somers was the center of a booming cattle industry, but in 1810 it became
famous as the birthplace of American circus entrepreneurship.

New Hammond Museum and Japanese Stroll Garden (all ages)

28 Deveau Rd., off June Road, just north of NY 116, North Salem; (914) 669-5033; www
.hammondmuseum.org. Open May through Oct, Wed through Sat noon to 4 p.m. The Silk
Tree Cafe serves lunch from noon to 3 p.m. $, children under 12 **free.**

These graceful Edo-period gardens were designed by Natalie Hays Hammond, daughter
of the man who discovered the long-lost King Solomon Mines in Africa. Thirteen small

landscapes have been created here, and each component has a special symbolic meaning. Programs for families with East/West themes are offered in season.

Museum of the Early American Circus (all ages)
At intersection of NY 100 and US 202, Somers; (914) 277-4977; www.somersmuseum.org. Open Thurs 2 to 4 p.m., the second and fourth Sun of every month from 1 to 4 p.m., or by appointment. Donation.

Hachaliah Bailey had a sea captain brother who brought him an elephant from London in 1796. As this was the first elephant seen in America, it caused quite a stir, so Bailey toured "Old Bet" up and down the East Coast. Unfortunately, Old Bet's career as a circus star was cut short one day in Maine, when the pachyderm's passion for potatoes prompted a farmer to shoot her. Still, the folks back in Somers were impressed and soon began rounding up all sorts of exotic creatures for similar road shows, But Bailey felt bad about Old Bet, so he erected the Elephant Hotel in her honor in 1824. Now a National Historic Landmark, the third floor houses a small museum that chronicles the cradle of the American circus.

Katonah

Take I-684 south.

This charming village has dozens of historic homes, many of which were moved from the original town of Katonah 0.5 mile away when the area was flooded at the end of the nineteenth century to create the Cross River Reservoir.

Muscoot Farm (all ages)
51 NY 100, 1 mile south of NY 35; (914) 864-7282 ; www.muscootfarm.org. Open daily 10 a.m. to 4 p.m. Closed on Thanksgiving Day, Christmas, and New Year's Day. Families free, but donations accepted; groups must make reservations and pay a fee.

The 777-acre working farm at Muscoot was a model of agrarian efficiency when it was built in 1885, and today it's a delightful place for families to experience home on the range. Many activities are scheduled on weekends, from blacksmithing to beekeeping demonstrations, and more than 7 miles of nature trails wind through surrounding wetlands and meadows.

Caramoor Center for Music and the Arts (ages 7 and up)
149 Girdle Ridge Rd., near intersection of NY 22 and 35; (914) 232-1252 or (914) 232-5035; www.caramoor.org. House open May through Oct, Wed through Fri and Sun 1 to 4 p.m., Sat 1 to 5 p.m. Adults $$, children 16 and under free.

This lavishly romantic mansion was built in the 1930s by financier Walter Rosen to house his fabulous art collection. Each room has a different theme, from alpine cottage to Italian Renaissance. Entire sections were transplanted from European villas, and walking through the fifty-five rooms is like taking an international architectural tour. Every summer the

Free **Natural Attractions**

Hiking trails, petroglyphs, wildlife displays, and family events are all enjoyed **free** of charge at these nature preserves:

Ward Pound Ridge Reservation and Trailside Nature Museum. NY 35 and NY 121S, Cross River; (914) 864-7317; www.westchestergov.com/parks. **Free** admission but $$ parking fee.

Westmoreland Sanctuary. 260 Chestnut Ridge Rd. (off Route 172), Mount Kisco; (914) 666-8448; www.westmorelandsanctuary.org.

Arthur W. Butler Memorial Sanctuary. Chestnut Ridge Road, Bedford; (914) 244-3271; www.nature.org.

Mianus River Gorge & Botanical Preserve. Mianus River Road, Bedford; (914) 244-3271; www.nature.org.

Caramoor Music Festival offers classical, jazz, and opera concerts in the courtyards, and everyone will enjoy a picnic or a stroll through the statue-studded gardens of this 117-acre estate.

Where to Eat

Blue Dolphin Ristorante. 175 Katonah Ave.; (914) 232-4791; www.thebluedolphinny .com. Housed in a diner, this excellent Italian bistro serves homemade pasta, fresh seafood, and delicious desserts. $–$$

Where to Stay

Crabtree's Kittle House. 11 Kittle Rd., off NY 117, Chappaqua; (914) 666-8044; www .kittlehouse.com. More than two centuries old with twelve rooms and a terrific progressive American restaurant. Children welcome, complimentary continental breakfast. $$$

Yorktown Heights

Head north on I-684, then take NY 35 west.

Yorktown Museum (all ages)

1974 Commerce St.; (914) 962-2970; www.yorktownmuseum.org. **Open year-round Tues and Thurs 11 a.m. to 4 p.m., Sun noon to 3 p.m.; closed during lunchtime. Donation.**

This small but charming museum has several theme rooms, including the Bob McKeand Railroad Room, filled with train memorabilia and a working HO-scale model set; the Marjorie Johnson Room, packed with exquisitely furnished dollhouses and miniature displays;

the Arthur C. Lee Room, chock-full of farm tools for every season; the Sylia Thorne Room, a two-room eighteenth-century Yorktown home, and the Woodlands Room, with a Mohegan longhouse in which you can learn about the area's original inhabitants.

Franklin D. Roosevelt State Park (all ages)

2957 Crompond Rd. (entrances off US 202 and Taconic State Parkway); (914) 245-4434; www.nysparks.state.ny.us/parks. Open weekdays June through Labor Day, 9 a.m. to sunset; all other times open year-round 8 a.m. to dusk. Free. Call ahead to confirm changes to hours, activities available, and possible closures due to pending state budget cuts.

Rent a boat and fish for perch, bullhead, pickerel, and the elusive largemouth bass in Lake Mohansic, or take a leisurely stroll along a nature trail. Play disc golf, volleyball, softball, basketball, or soccer; cool off in the swimming pool; then have lunch at the picnic pavilions. Warm up in winter with cross-country skiing and sledding.

Yorktown Golf and Baseball Center (all ages)

2710 Lexington Ave., Mohegan Lake; (914) 526-8337; www.yorktowngolfandbaseball .com. Open year-round 9 a.m. to 9 p.m. $. Miniature golf, driving range, eight softball and baseball batting cages, lessons for all ages, and a snack bar with picnic tables.

Where to Eat

Gaudio's. 2026 Saw Mill River Rd.; (914) 245-0920; www.gaudiosrestaurant.com. Friendly Italian family place with great thin-crust pizza, pasta, chicken, steaks, seafood, and a kid's menu. $$–$$$

Where to Stay

Holiday Inn Mt. Kisco. 1 Holiday Inn, Mt. Kisco; (800) HOLIDAY. Outdoor pool, Internet, cable TV and in-room movies, restaurant, gym, and laundry service; cribs are available. $$

Also in **the Area**

Osceola Beach. 411 E. Main St., Jefferson Valley; (914) 245-3246; www .osceolabeach.com.

Yorktown Stage. 1974 Commerce St., Yorktown Heights; (914) 962-0606; www.yorktownstage.org.

Kitchawan Preserve. Taconic Parkway, NY 134E, Yorktown; (914) 864-7000; www.westchestergov.com/parks.

Croton-on-Hudson and Ossining

Take US 202 west, then US 9 south.

Settled by the Italian stonemasons and Irish laborers who constructed the Croton Reservoir in the nineteenth century, Croton-on-Hudson later became a country retreat of bohemian artists and intellectuals from Greenwich Village during and after World War I.

Van Cortlandt Manor (ages 7 and up)
5 South Riverside Ave., off US 9, Croton-on-Hudson; (914) 631-8200; www.hudsonvalley .org. Open late May through Labor Day, Thurs through Sun and Monday holidays 11 a.m. to 6 p.m., last tour at 5 p.m.; weekends only Nov and Dec, 10 a.m. to 4 p.m., last tour at 3 p.m. Adults $$, children 5 to 17 $, under 5 free.

A gracious Dutch manor house, Van Cortlandt is filled with a mixture of antiques from several different periods. Demonstrations of colonial crafts, herbal medicine preparation, and cooking take place often, and the eighteenth-century flower and herb gardens are lovely. Legend has it that there are six different ghosts haunting this mansion, from a Redcoat and a Hessian soldier to a laughing girl who arrives by a horse-drawn carriage.

Croton Point Park (all ages)
1 Croton Point Ave. (off US 9), Croton-on-Hudson; (914) 862-5290; www.westchestergov .com/parks. Open daily year-round 8 a.m. to dusk; nature center open Tues through Sat 9 a.m. to 4 p.m. Parking fee $$.

Occupying a 504-acre peninsula jutting out into the Hudson, this park has a playground, campground, cabins, a pool, recreation hall, ball fields, miles of hiking and biking trails, and the Croton Point Nature Center, which offers interpretive programs year-round.

Teatown Lake Reservation (all ages)
1600 Spring Valley Rd., Ossining, off US 9; (914) 762-2912; www.teatown.org. Trails open dawn to dusk daily. Interpretive center open Tues through Sun 9 a.m. to 5 p.m. Free.

Long before the Boston Tea Party, there was a similar uprising in this area. Before the Revolution, when King George III tightly controlled and taxed the colonists' favorite beverage, the

Peekskill **Arts**

Downtown Artists' District. Division Street between Main and South Streets, Peekskill; (914) 734-1292 or (914) 737-1646. The company that created Crayola crayons started here, so it seemed like kismet when painters, potters, sculptors, and photographers revitalized the area. During Open Studio events, more than twenty-eight studios and nine galleries give visitors a wonderful opportunity to see artists at work in a variety of media, and perhaps inspire the next generation of the Hudson River School.

Bird's Eye View **by Balloon**

Hudson Valley Enchanted Balloon Tours. 577 Ridgebury Rd., Slate Hill; (845) 386-1402 or (845) 649-9654; www.balloon-rides-ny.com.

Blue Sky Balloons. 34 Lauer Rd., Poughkeepsie; (888) 999-2461; www.bluesky balloons.com.

Fantasy Balloon Flights. 2 Evergreen Lane, Port Jervis; (845) 856-7103; www .fantasyfliers.com.

Above the Clouds. Randall Airport, Airport Road, Middletown; (845) 692-2556; www.abovethecloudsinc.com.

The Balloon Bed & Breakfast. 73 CR 25B, Hudson; (518) 828-3735; www .balloonbedandbreakfast.com.

local women of the settlement heard of a Bronx merchant in the area hoarding a rare stash of tea and stormed his farm demanding a fair share. The women of the merchant's family held the town women at bay until he finally agreed to supply tea for everyone through the black market. Today this 834-acre preserve is laced with 15 miles of trails around a tranquil woodland lake. Tour Wildflower Island, a two-acre sanctuary in the middle of Teatown Lake that's home to more than 230 species of wildflowers, or visit the small nature museum and learn about the preserve's wildlife rehabilitation program. The museum offers family workshops on weekends, ranging from maple sugaring and wildlife tracking to flower identification.

Where to Eat

Goldfish Oyster Bar & Restaurant. 6 Rockledge Ave., Ossining; (914) 762-0051; www.goldfishdining.com. Fresh seafood (no goldfish on the menu), pasta, steak, a great chocolate mousse, and live music on Thurs and Fri evenings. $$–$$$

ümami café. 325 S. Riverside Ave., Croton-on-Hudson; (914) 271-5555; www.umamicafe .com. Using renewable energy and the locally grown bounty of the county, this eclectic cafe offers creative cuisine such as a fabulous Truffled Mac & Cheese, the Evil Jungle Prince Curry Coconut Chicken Stew, and a Warm Sticky Date Cake to die for. Best of all,

the kids' menu is displayed in 3-D images on View-Masters, and they have Fluffernutters! $$–$$$

Where to Stay

Alexander Hamilton House. 49 Van Wyck St., Croton-on-Hudson; (914) 271-6737; www .alexanderhamiltonhouse.com. Overlooking the Hudson River, this lovely Victorian inn has eight beautiful rooms and suites, all with private bath and most with fireplaces, full breakfast, Wi-Fi, outdoor pool, and fresh-baked cookies daily. Portable cribs, computers with printers, picnic baskets, in-room massages, and chocolate-covered strawberries can be arranged. $$–$$$

Yonkers

Continue south on US 9.

Originally named Nappeckamack, this area was a thriving Lenape Indian village before the Europeans arrived. Every town has its ups and downs, but none more so than when inventor Elisha G. Otis introduced his first "perpendicular stairway" here in 1853.

Hudson River Museum (ages 6 and up)

511 Warburton Ave.; (914) 963-4550 or (914) 963-2139 (planetarium); www.hrm.org. Museum open Wed to Sun noon to 5 p.m., Fri to 8 p.m. $. Planetarium has shows Sat and Sun at 12:30, 1:30, 2:30, and 3:30 p.m. $. Fri night planetarium show at 7 p.m. is free.

Combining science, art, culture, and local history is quite a juggling act, but this museum complex does just that. The longest topographic model of the Hudson ever made is on display at Riverama, an interactive exhibit that utilizes computers, videos, and live fish to explore environmental solutions as well as the diversity of "America's First River." At the Victorian mansion Glenview, six period rooms have been restored, including the newest addition, a twenty-six-room dollhouse modeled after several Hudson River estates. The Lifflander Galleries display nineteenth- and twentieth-century American art, and family-friendly tours are offered throughout the year. Weekend workshops range from candy making and tile painting to model boat building, and next door is the **Andrus Space Transit Planetarium,** home to a state-of-the-art star machine.

Greenburgh Nature Center (all ages)

99 Dromore Rd., Scarsdale; (914) 723-3470; www.greenburghnaturecenter.org. Grounds open daily dawn to dusk. Indoor exhibits open Mon through Thurs 9:30 a.m. to 4:30 p.m., Sat and Sun 10 a.m. to 4:30 p.m. Adults $$, children $.

Explore a variety of environments along self-guided trails at this thirty-three-acre nature center. The nature museum houses over 120 animals, and there's a hands-on discovery room, a greenhouse, changing nature art exhibits, along with a variety of family fun activities like owl prowls, campouts, and salamander storytelling sessions.

Where to Eat

La Lanterna. 23 Gray Oaks Ave.; (914) 476-3060; www.lalaterna.com. Great Italian cuisine with a Swiss accent, indoor and outdoor dining, and friendly service. $$$

Also in **the Area**

New Roc City. New Street, Le Count Place, New Rochelle; (914) 637-7575; www.newroccity.com. Entertainment and retail stores.

Other Things to See and Do in the
Hudson River Valley Region

Franny Reese State Park. Haviland Road, Highland; (845) 473-4440; www
.scenichudson.org.

Highland Lakes State Park. NY 211 East, Middletown; (845) 786-2701; www
.nysparks.com/parks.

Norrie Point Environmental Site. 256 Norrie Point Way, Staatsburg; (845)
889-4745; www.dec.ny.gov.

6½ Station Road Sanctuary. 6½ Station Rd., Goshen; (845) 561-2187; www.ny
.audubon.org/sanctuary.

Orange County Fair Speedway. 239 Wisner Ave., Middletown; (845) 342-2573
or (315) 834-6606; www.superdirtcarseries.com

Wilderstein Preservation. 330 Morton Rd., Rhinebeck; (845) 876-4818; www
.wilderstein.org.

Foundry School Museum. 63 Chestnut St., Cold Spring; (845) 265-4010; www
.pchs-fsm.org.

Clove Furnace Historic Site. 21 Clove Furnace Dr. at NY 17, Arden; (845)
351-4696.

Dr. Davies Farm. 306 NY 304, Congers; (845) 268-7020; www.drdaviesfarm
.com.

Orchards of Conklin. 2 South Mountain Rd., Pomona; (845) 354-0369; www
.theorchardsofconklin.com.

Mills-Norrie State Park. Old Post Road (US 9), Staatsburg; (845) 889-4646;
www.nysparks.com.

Edward Hopper House. 82 N. Broadway, Nyack; (845) 358-0774; www.hopper
house.org.

Webatuck Craft Village. NY 22 at Route 55, Wingdale; (845) 832-6522; www
.huntcountryfurniture.com.

Thomas Paine Museum and Cottage. 20 Sicard Ave., New Rochelle; (914)
633-1776; www.thomaspaine.org.

Where to Stay

Royal Regency Hotel. 165 Tuckahoe Rd.; (800) 215-3858; www.royalregencyhotelny .com. Ninety-one rooms, large suites with Jacuzzis, cable TV with movies, Wi-Fi, fitness center, room service, cafe, cribs and refrigerators on request, and complimentary continental breakfast. $$$–$$$$

Rye

Take the Bronx River Parkway to Scarsdale, then I-287 west to Rye.

Settled in the mid-seventeenth century by Connecticut colonials seeking to improve their lives, this suburban seaside town now has lovely tree-lined streets and interesting shops. The town is the birthplace of humorist Ogden Nash, and some say it's where he got his wry sense of humor.

Playland (all ages)

Playland Parkway (exit 19 off I-95); recorded info (914) 813-7000; general info (914) 813-7010; Ice Casino (914) 813-7059; www.ryeplayland.org. Open May through Labor Day, Tues through Sun. Call for hours. All-day wristbands are required for everyone to enter the amusement park $$$$; non-riders $; children under 36 inches are free.

This Art Deco amusement park, built in 1928, was the first family fun park of its kind and is now a National Historic Landmark. Seven of the more than fifty rides are original, like the wooden Dragon Coaster and painted carousel, but many are newer, and younger children will love the toddler-size Kiddy Land. Cool off at the nearby crescent beach with a swim in the Sound or take a dip in the Olympic-size pool. Take a cruise or pedal a boat on the lake, play a round of miniature golf, then stroll the boardwalk to the beat of a 1940s big band. Next door is the 170-acre **Edith G. Read Natural Park and Wildlife Sanctuary** (914-967-8720) if you want to escape the crowds—and Playland can get very crowded on weekends. Wildlife sanctuary $.

Marshlands Conservancy (all ages)

220 Boston Post Rd.; (914) 835-4466; www.westchestergov.com/parks. Nature Center open 9 a.m. to 5 p.m. Wed through Sun and most holidays. Trails open daily dawn to dusk. $.

Three miles of trails wind through this 173-acre wildlife sanctuary protecting a variety of habitats, from fields and woods to a salt marsh along the shore of Long Island Sound. More than 230 species of birds have been sited along this stretch of the Atlantic migratory flyway.

Where to Eat

La Panetiere. 530 Milton Rd.; (914) 967-8140; www.lapanetiere.com. Fancy French cuisine with a gourmet children's menu and beautiful gardens. $$$$

Seaside Johnnies. 94 Dearborn Ave.; (914) 921-6104; www.seasidejohnnies.com. Sushi, shrimp, lobster, salmon, and every other kind of seafood, along with steaks, ribs, chicken, burgers, salads, and beach baskets of fried clams, calamari, or crab. $$–$$$

Where to Stay

Courtyard by Marriott. 631 Midland Ave.; (914) 921-1110 or (800) 321-2211; www.marriott.com. Indoor pool, Internet, restaurant. $$$$

For More Information

Westchester County Office of Tourism. 222 Mamaroneck Ave., Suite 100, White Plains; (914) 995-8500 or (800) 833-9282; www.tourism.westchestergov.com.

Rockland County Tourism. 18 New Hempstead Rd., New City; (845) 708-7300; www.rockland.org.

Orange County Tourism. 124 Main St., Goshen;. (845) 291-2136 or (800) 762-8687; www.orange tourism.org.

Putnam County Visitor's Bureau.110 Old US 6, Building 3, Carmel; (845) 225-0381 or (800) 470-4854; www.visitputnam.org.

Dutchess County Tourism. 3 Neptune Rd., Poughkeepsie; (845) 463-4000 or (800) 445-3131; www.dutchesstourism.com.

Columbia County Tourism. 401 State St., Hudson; (518) 828-3375 or (800) 724-1846; www.columbiacountyny.com.

Long Island

Stretching eastward from New York City for almost 120 miles, Long Island resembles a great whale basking between the Long Island Sound and the Atlantic Ocean. This is the largest island adjoining the continental United States, and it was once home to thirteen Algonquin tribes before the arrival of the Europeans in the seventeenth century. The fertile farmlands and abundant fishing encouraged the Dutch and English settlers to stay, and 300 years later Long Island became synonymous with suburbia. But Long Island's heritage has left us with more than sprawling malls and car-choked highways. There is an ageless beauty and rich history to this place the Native Americans called Paumanok. Divided into five distinct regions, each area offers opportunities to experience a surprising variety of natural and historical treasures. Whether you choose to explore the opulent estates of the North Shore, meander for miles along the barrier beaches of the South Shore, watch for wildlife in the pine barrens of Central Suffolk, feast on the fruitful harvest of the North Fork, or bask in the sun and sand of the South Fork, your family will find a wealth of activities and adventures. Once you've paused in Paumanok, it's likely you'll be lured back again by its charms.

DRIVING TIPS

Bisecting the center of Long Island is the Long Island Expressway (I-495), known as the LIE to the multitude of motorists who ply its pavement daily. Don't even think about trying to travel the LIE on Friday afternoons in summer or during rush hour, unless you enjoy seemingly endless miles of bumper-to-bumper traffic. Along the North Shore, travel along NY 25 and NY 25A, or the Northern State Parkway, and along the South Shore follow Montauk Highway (NY 27A and CR 80), Sunrise Highway (NY 27), or the Southern State Parkway. For north and south travel, there are dozens of roads cutting across the 20-mile-wide girth of Long Island, including the Seaford–Oyster Bay Expressway and the Sunken Meadow, Wantaugh, and Meadowbrook State Parkways.

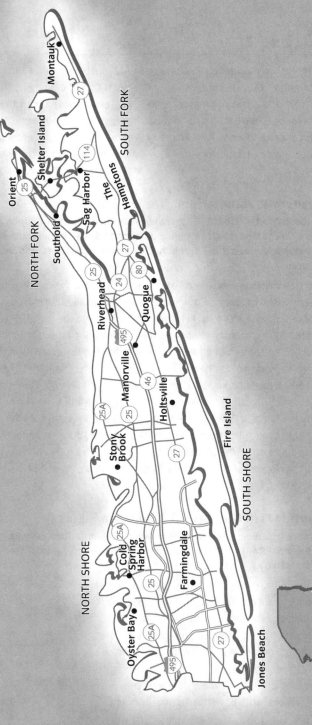

LONG ISLAND

NORTH SHORE

Oyster Bay

Cold Spring Harbor

Farmingdale

Stony Brook

Manorville

Holtsville

Riverhead

NORTH FORK

Orient

Southold

Shelter Island

Sag Harbor

Quogue

The Hamptons

SOUTH FORK

Montauk

Fire Island

SOUTH SHORE

Jones Beach

North Shore

Turn-of-the-twentieth-century captains of commerce and industry created a fabled land of fabulous mansions and exquisite gardens along the "Gold Coast" of Long Island's North Shore. Many of those extravagant estates no longer exist, but the ones that do are awesome. There are other treasures to be found here, as well. Thousands of years of Native American culture and a rich Revolutionary War heritage offer an interesting counterpoint, and farsighted philanthropy has provided numerous nature preserves to explore.

Vanderbilt Museum & Planetarium (ages 6 and up)

180 Little Neck Rd, Centerport; (631) 854-5555; www.vanderbiltmuseum.org. Open Tues through Fri noon to 5 p.m., Sat 11 a.m. to 5 p.m., Sun noon to 5 p.m. Planetarium shows Fri, Sat afternoon and evening, and Sun afternoon. Closed Mon, Christmas, and New Year's Day. Adults $$, children $.

Called Eagle's Nest, this forty-three-acre estate was once the home of William Kissam Vanderbilt II, great-grandson of Comm. Cornelius Vanderbilt. He filled his mansion with an amazing array of art and artifacts from his family travels around the world, devoting a wing to wildlife dioramas and natural-history exhibits. The Marine Museum, next door, houses more than 2,000 specimens of aquatic interest. Added to the complex in 1971, the Vanderbilt Planetarium, one of the best equipped in the country, features a 60-foot Sky Theatre and a 16-inch telescope open to the public on clear evenings. During the day, sunspot and solar flare activity can be viewed on monitors in the lobby, and laser light shows backed up by the Beatles, Pink Floyd, or Led Zeppelin sound tracks are very popular. Special children's programs are offered throughout the year, but in summer they are invited to join Wizard University, where classes are offered in astronomy, history, almost magical creatures, crafty crafts, and potions. Cauldrons will be provided, but students may not bring their owls, toads, or brooms.

Cold Spring Harbor Fish Hatchery & Aquarium (all ages)

1660 NY 25A, Cold Spring Harbor; (516) 692-6768; www.cshfha.org. Open daily year-round 10 a.m. to 5 p.m., Memorial Day to Labor Day Sat and Sun 10 a.m. to 6 p.m. Closed Easter, Thanksgiving, and Christmas. $, 2 and under free.

Opened in 1883, this is New York's oldest fish hatchery and a National Historic Landmark. Feed the fish at several outdoor trout ponds, then ogle the aquariums that hold the largest collection of native freshwater fish, reptiles, and amphibians in the state. For families who like to fish, every Fri through Tues they can keep brook and rainbow trout caught in the tidal raceway, and enroll in a variety of workshops, programs and events from turtle pageants to egg stripping demonstrations.

St. John's Pond Preserve (all ages)

NY 25A, Cold Spring Harbor; (631) 367-3225; www.nature.org. Open daily 10 a.m. to 5 p.m. Donation.

While you're at the hatchery, ask for a key to the gate of this 14-acre Nature Conservancy gem next door. A trail winds through woodlands filled with mountain laurel and moss and past ponds and marsh. Rabbits, red fox, muskrats, river otters, and turtles make their home here, and the wildflowers in spring are lovely.

Cold Spring Harbor Whaling Museum (ages 4 and up)

279 Main St. (NY 25A), Cold Spring Harbor; (631) 367-3418; www.cshwhalingmuseum.org. Open year-round Tues through Sun 11 a.m. to 5 p.m. Open Memorial Day and Labor Day and on Mon in summer. Closed Christmas and New Year's Day. $.

Most children would probably prefer to see their whales alive, but this interesting museum traces the rich maritime history of Long Island with kid-friendly hands-on exhibits, exquisite scrimshaw, and a fully equipped nineteenth-century whaleboat. Programs for families include Ocean Science Sundays, Monday Minnows for small fry, and sea-chantey workshops.

Uplands Farm Sanctuary (all ages)

250 Lawrence Hill Rd., Cold Spring Harbor; (631) 367-3384; www.nature.org. Trails open year-round, dawn to dusk; donation.

Home to the Long Island chapter of the Nature Conservancy, this 97-acre former dairy farm features several miles of level trails looping through meadows and woodlands of red cedar, black cherry, and oak, with thickets of mountain laurel abloom in summer. Wood frogs, spotted salamanders, bluebirds, and bobolinks live here, along with more than forty butterfly species.

Dolan DNA Learning Center (ages 8 and up)

334 Main St., Cold Spring Harbor; (516) 367-5170; www.dnalc.org. Open year-round Mon through Fri 10 a.m. to 4 p.m. Closed holidays. Free.

This is the world's first biotechnology museum, a branch of the Cold Spring Harbor Laboratory, with kid-friendly interactive exhibits that explore the brave new world of DNA. The main exhibition, "The Genes We Share," offers hands-on activities and a tour of the human genome, while two multimedia presentations, "Long Island Discovery" and "DNA: The Secret of Life," are screened during the week several times a day and on request.

Garvies Point Museum and Preserve (all ages)

50 Barry Dr., Glen Cove; (516) 571-8010 or (516) 571-8011; www.garviespointmuseum.com. Preserve open daily 8:30 a.m. to dusk; museum open Tues through Sat 10 a.m. to 4 p.m. Closed winter holidays, open summer holidays. $, under 5 free.

Five miles of nature trails meander through this sixty-two-acre preserve, once the campsite of Matinecock Indians, now the habitat of 140 species of birds, as well as raccoons, opossums, and woodchucks. Exhibits and dioramas at the museum include animatronic figures demonstrating various aspects of Native American culture, and archaeological and geological displays. Outside there's a tulip tree dugout canoe and a wigwam to explore, as well as the first and only dinosaur footprints found on Long Island.

Sea Cliff Village Museum (ages 6 and up)

95 Tenth Ave., Sea Cliff; (516) 671-0090; www.seacliff-ny.gov. Open Sat and Sun 2 to 5 p.m., closed mid-July to mid-Oct. $.

Artifacts and albums of photographs highlight the history of this Victorian resort overlooking Hempstead Harbor, including a collection of costumes from the turn of the century and a fully outfitted Victorian kitchen.

Cinema Arts Centre (ages 6 and up)

423 Park Ave., Huntington; (631) 423-7611 or (631) 423-3456; www.cinemaartscentre.org. Call for schedule. Adults $$, children $.

International and independent films are screened at this theater, along with frequent showings of silent movie classics accompanied by live music. Special events include book signings and discussions by notable film actors and writers.

Walt Whitman Birthplace (all ages)

246 Old Walt Whitman Rd., West Hills; (631) 427-5240; www.waltwhitman.org. Open year-round; mid-June to Labor Day, Mon through Fri 11 a.m. to 4 p.m., Sat and Sun 11 a.m. to 5 p.m.; after Labor Day to mid-June, Wed through Fri 1 to 4 p.m., Sat and Sun 11 a.m. to 4 p.m. Closed major holidays. $.

In 1819, Walt Whitman, one of America's most beloved poets, was born in this finely

Other Parks and **Nature Preserves** of the North Shore

David Weld Sanctuary. Boney Lane, Nissequogue; (631) 329-7689; www .nature.org.

Welwyn Preserve and Holocaust Memorial and Educational Center of Nassau County. Crescent Beach Road, Welwyn Preserve County Park, Glen Cove; (516) 571-7900; www.nassaucountyny.gov. Holocaust Museum: (516) 571-8040; www.holocaust-nassau.org.

Shu Swamp Preserve. c/o North Shore Wildlife Sanctuary, Frost Mill Road, Mill Neck; (516) 671-0283; www.nswildlife.org.

Caumsett State Historic Park. 25 Lloyd Harbor Rd., Lloyd Neck; (631) 423-1770; www.nysparks.state.ny.us.

crafted farmhouse built by his father. Although his family moved to Brooklyn when he was 5, Whitman returned to Long Island to become a schoolteacher at 16 and founder and editor of a newspaper at 19, a period in which he also wrote his classic collection of poems *Leaves of Grass*. Ask about a driving-tour map of some of Whitman's favorite places to amuse the muses, including the highest point on the Island, Jayne's Hill. Special events are scheduled throughout the year, including marathon readings of Whitman's poetry, Victorian tea parties, spooky Halloween tale-telling, and a Yuletide Family Day, complete with craft and cookie making.

Governor Alfred E. Smith/ Sunken Meadow State Park (all ages)

NY 25A and Sunken Meadow Parkway, Kings Park; (631) 269-4333; http:// nysparks.state.ny.us/parks. Open year-round daily sunrise to sunset. $$.

Enjoy a mile of beach along Long Island Sound at this popular 1,266-acre park. Swim in Smithtown Bay, hike or bike along 6 miles of nature trails through a salt marsh, have a picnic, visit the small nature museum for interesting eco-exhibits, and play a round of golf at the three-hole golf courses on the grounds.

Sweetbriar Nature Center (all ages)

62 Eckernkamp Dr., Smithtown; (631) 979-6344; www.sweetbriarnc.org. Open daily 8:30 a.m. to 4:30 p.m. year-round. $.

Home to a variety of wild animals unable to be released back into their habitats, this center provides for their care and rehabilitation. There's also a Butterfly & Moth Vivarium, the first one on Long Island, and wonderful programs for families are offered year-round, including seasonal storytelling, photography expeditions, nature detectives, fantastical creature explorations, and owl prowls.

American Merchant Marine Museum (all ages)

At bottom of Steamboat Road, Kings Point; (516) 773-5391 or (866) 546-4778; www.usmma .edu. Grounds open daily 8 a.m. to 4:30 p.m. Museum open Tue through Fri 10 a.m. to 3 p.m., Sat and Sun 1 to 4:30 p.m.; closed federal holidays and during summer and winter leave periods. Free.

Located on the campus of the United States Merchant Marine Academy, this museum has a wonderful collection of model ships, marine artifacts, and maritime art, as well as interesting interactive exhibits.

Joseph Lloyd Manor (all ages)

Lloyd Lane, Lloyd Harbor; (631) 692-4664; www.splia.org. Open Memorial Day through Labor Day, Sun 1 to 5 p.m. $.

Built in 1766, this was the estate of Griselda and James Lloyd, as well as the home and workplace of Jupiter Hammon, a slave and the first published black poet in America. Tour

New York **Trivia**

The Little Prince, by Antoine de Saint-Exupéry, was written on Long Island.

the restored mansion, then step outside and stroll through the fragrant formal gardens overlooking the sound.

Northport Historical Society Museum　(ages 4 and up)　

215 Main St., Northport; (631) 757-9859; www.northporthistorical.org. Open year-round Tues through Sun 1 to 4:30 p.m. Closed holidays. Donation. Self-guided tours $.

The shipbuilding heritage of this charming village, once known as Cow Harbor, is high-lighted here with exhibits, artifacts, and memorabilia. Self-guided walking tours of Main Street are available, including use of an MP3 player with audio information, and a book of historic photographs of the town. Throughout the year, special events are scheduled, including holiday parties, parades, auctions, and antique shows.

Earle-Wightman House Museum　(ages 7 and up)　

20 Summit St., Oyster Bay; (516) 922-5032. Open year-round Tues through Fri 10 a.m. to 2 p.m., Sat 9 a.m. to 1 p.m., Sun 1 to 4 p.m. $.

Home of the Oyster Bay Historical Society, this 1720 landmark house is filled with authentic eighteenth-century furnishings, and outside is a lovely restored eighteenth-century garden of flowers and medicinal herbs. A recent addition is the Discovery Cen-ter, where kids can dress up in Revolutionary War uniforms and play colonial games. Special events are scheduled year-round, and the Old Fashioned Country Fair is a family favorite.

Planting Fields Arboretum State Historic Park　(all ages)　

1395 Planting Fields Rd., Oyster Bay; (516) 922-8600 or (516) 922-9210; www.plantingfields .org. Grounds open daily year-round 9 a.m. to 5 p.m., except Christmas; visitor center open Apr through Oct, 11 a.m. to 4:30 p.m.; Coe Hall (1039 Van Buren St., Oyster Bay) open Apr through Sept daily, 11:30 p.m. to 3:30 p.m., except Christmas. $.

Formerly the Gold Coast estate of William Robertson Coe, this 409-acre verdant plantation has spacious lawns, woodlands, cultivated gardens, and an arboretum designed by Fred-erick Law Olmsted Jr. The sixty-five-room Tudor Revival Coe mansion is an architectural delight, and its restored rooms are filled with beautiful antiques. Special events through-out the year include dog shows, flower exhibitions, and concerts.

Raynham Hall　(ages 7 and up)

20 W. Main St., Oyster Bay; (516) 922-6808; www.raynhamhallmuseum.org. Open early Sept through June, Tues through Sun 1 to 5 p.m., July through Labor Day noon to 5 p.m.; closed major holidays. $.

Built in 1738, this was the home of Samuel Townsend, whose son Robert was Gen. George Washington's top spy during the Revolutionary War. The house was occupied by the British Queen's Rangers during the war, and reportedly several ghosts from that era remain.

Sagamore Hill National Historic Site (ages 5 and up)
20 Sagamore Hill Rd., Oyster Bay; (516) 922-4788; www.nps.gov/sahi. Grounds open year-round dawn to dusk; visitor center open year-round, Wed through Sun 9 a.m. to 5 p.m., closed Mon and Tues. Closed major holidays. $.

Operated by the National Park Service, this Victorian mansion was the permanent home and summer White House for President Theodore Roosevelt and his wife and six children. The Old Orchard House contains exhibits and a short documentary highlighting Roosevelt's life and times. Kids can become Junior Rangers by going on a history hunt and completing an activity booklet. Afterwards, take a walk along the Sagamore Hill Nature Trail, now a wildlife sanctuary, for a swim in Cold Springs Harbor.

Theodore Roosevelt Sanctuary (all ages)
134 Cove Rd., Oyster Bay; (516) 922-3200; http://ny.audubon.org/trsac.htm. Open year-round 9 a.m. to 5 p.m. Donation.

Despite Roosevelt's passion for hunting, he was a strong supporter of environmental conservation. This twelve-acre sanctuary is the first owned by the National Audubon Society and offers eco-education programs for all ages, such as raptor rehabilitation and flight demonstrations, endangered-species survival, animal tracking, and aquatic ecology. The Trailside Museum and Nature Center has lifelike dioramas and displays, and the Injured Wildlife Care Center attends to hundreds of wounded birds, mammals, reptiles, and fish every year. The former president's grave is located in the cemetery next door.

North Shore Play Places

Nathan's Fun House. 6137 Jericho Turnpike, Commack; (631) 462-6019; www.longislandtourism.com.

Laser Kingdom. 544 Middle Country Rd., Coram; (631) 698-0414; www.laserkingdoms.com.

Castle Golf Amusements. 1878 Middle Country Rd., Centereach; (631) 471-1267; www.longislandtourism.com.

Fun 4 All. 200 Wilson St., Port Jefferson; (631) 331-9000; www.fun4all-ny.com.

The Rinx. 660 Terry Rd., Hauppauge; (631) 232-3222; www.therinx.com.

Muttontown Preserve (all ages)

Muttontown Lane, (south side of NY 25A) East Norwich; (516) 571-8500; www.nassaucounty ny.gov. Open year-round. $.

Three country estates cobbled together comprise a pastoral patchwork of meadows and woodlands, threaded with seven easy trails offering opportunities to spot the elusive Cooper's Hawk or a Great Horned Owl. Wildflower walks and autumn leaf talks are some of the many activities offered outside, at the county's largest nature preserve.

Mount Sinai Marine Sanctuary Nature Center (all ages)

Harbor Beach Road, Mount Sinai; (631) 473-8346. Open daily June through Sept 10 a.m. to 2 p.m. Hours may vary. Free.

Outdoor touch tanks and indoor aquariums house a variety of local marine life, from fish, turtles, clams, and moon snails to a rare blue lobster.

Christopher Morley Park (all ages)

500 Searington Rd., Roslyn Heights; (516) 571-8113; www.nassaucountyny.gov. Open daily dawn to dusk year-round. Park free, some facilities $$.

This ninety-eight-acre county park, site of writer Christopher Morley's cabin, "Knothole," offers ball fields and courts, a nine-hole golf course, an outdoor ice rink, a model-boat pond, an outdoor Olympic-size swimming pool, and a recently renovated playground and fitness trail.

North Shore **Boats & Ferries**

American Phoenix Lines and the Schooner *Phoenix.* 76 Shore Rd., Glen Cove; (631) 765-3502 and (516) 744-2353; www.discoverourtown.com.

Martha Jefferson Bay Cruises. Port Jefferson Harbor; (631) 331-3333; www .marthajefferson.com.

Port Jefferson Ferry. 102 W. Broadway, Port Jefferson; (631) 473-0286; www .bpjferry.com.

Thomas Jefferson Paddle Steamer. 128 Shore Rd., Glen Cove; (516) 671-5563; www.byy.com.

Liberty Cruises. 377 Jerusalem Ave., Hempstead; (516) 486-3057; www.lady libertycruises.com.

Discovery Wetlands Cruise. 111 Main St., P.O. Box 572, Stony Brook 11790; (631) 751-2244; www.longisland.about.com.

Other Parks of the **North Shore**

Cedarmere. Bryant Avenue, Roslyn Harbor; (516) 571-8130; www.nassau countyny.gov.

Blydenburgh County Park. Smithtown; (631) 854-3713; www.co.suffolk.ny.us.

West Hills County Park. Old Country Road, Huntington; (631) 854-4423; www.co.suffolk.ny.us.

Hempstead Harbor Beach Park. West Shore Road, Port Washington; (516) 571-7930; www.discoverlongisland.com.

The Science Museum of Long Island (all ages)
1526 N. Plandome Rd., Plandome; (516) 627-9400; www.smli.org. Open daily year-round. Call for more information. $.

Interactive exhibits and hands-on activities designed to encourage children's curiosity about the physical sciences are offered here, but you must preregister for most workshops, which can range from holiday celebrations to animal encounters.

Sands Point Preserve (all ages)
95 Middleneck Rd., Port Washington; (516) 571-7900 or (516) 571-7901; www.sandspoint preserve.org. Open year-round daily 9 a.m. to 7:30 p.m. $.

Two opulent mansions occupy this 216-acre Gold Coast estate, Hempstead House and Falaise, but unfortunately children ten and under are not allowed inside them. The grounds will probably be more interesting to kids, anyway, as will the Kilkenny Castle knockoff, Castlegould, now a visitor center. Several natural history displays are inside the castle, and maps of the six marked nature trails are available at the desk. Many interesting programs are offered throughout the year, but a favorite family event is the Sands Pointe Medieval Faire that arrives every Sept.

Old Westbury Gardens (all ages)
71 Old Westbury Rd., Old Westbury; (516) 333-0048; www.oldwestburygardens.org. Open late Apr through Oct, daily 10 a.m. to 5 p.m., Sun in Nov, and holiday celebrations in Dec; closed Tues. Adults $$, children $, 6 and under free.

Steel magnate John S. Phipps built this 200-acre palatial country estate as a wedding present for his heiress wife, Margarita Grace, in 1906. The Charles II manor house and surrounding gardens were patterned after her childhood home in England, and the results are breathtaking. The mansion is filled with beautiful furniture, art, and family mementos, and the formal English gardens surrounding the house are considered to be the best in the country. Children will enjoy exploring playhouses, from a miniature thatched cottage complete with a tiny tea party for dolls inside to three rustic kid-size log cabins. Programs and events for families include Fairy Tale Friday evenings, tea parties with your favorite doll, and scarecrow creations for the garden.

The Long Island Museum (all ages)

1200 NY 25A, Stony Brook; (631) 751-0066; www.longislandmuseum.org. St. James General Store and Post Office, 516 Moriches Rd.; (631) 862-8333. Deepwells, NY 25A; (631) 862-6080. Open year-round Fri and Sat 10 a.m. to 5 p.m., Sun noon to 5 p.m. Closed Mon through Thurs, Thanksgiving, Christmas, and New Year's Day. Adults $$, children $, under 6 free.

Now an affiliate of the Smithsonian Institution, this nine-acre complex of several museums, a blacksmith shop, a one-room schoolhouse, an 1870 barn, and beautiful gardens offers a window into the history and art of Long Island. The Melville Carriage Museum has more than one hundred vehicles, including ornate European coaches, shiny fire engines, cheery omnibuses, and rare gypsy wagons. The Art Museum's collection of American paintings, sculpture, and decorative arts depicts rural Islander life and includes works by Winslow Homer, Norman Rockwell, and Louis Comfort Tiffany. The Margaret Melville Blackwell History Museum features a great duck decoy collection, but children will be drawn to the fifteen miniature furnished sixteenth- to twentieth-century period rooms. Field trips and special events are scheduled year-round, from food festivals to holiday celebrations.

Stony Brook Grist Mill (all ages)

Harbor Road and Main Street, Head of the Harbor; (631) 751-2244; www.wmho.org. Open May through Oct, Sat and Sun noon to 4:30 p.m. $.

Built in 1751, this is Long Island's most completely equipped working mill. Milling demonstrations are offered during the tour; afterwards, walk down to the millpond to feed the ducks cracked corn from the mill.

Saddle Rock Grist Mill (all ages)

Grist Mill Lane, Great Neck; (516) 571-7900; www.saddlerock.org. Open on Sun, May through Oct, 1 p.m. to 5 p.m. Free.

This is the oldest continually operating tidal gristmill in the country, built in 1702, and it has undergone several restorations over the past 300 years. Demonstrations are offered on Sunday afternoons in season.

The Nassau Veterans Memorial Coliseum

1255 Hempstead Turnpike, Uniondale; (516) 794-9300; www.nassaucoliseum.com.

Situated on a former air force base, the Coliseum is home to the New York Islanders Hockey team, as well as a venue for a variety of concerts, ice shows, exhibitions, and circuses.

Flax Pond Marine Laboratory (all ages)

Shore Drive, off Crane Neck Road, off NY 25A, Stony Brook; (631) 632-8709; http://alpha1
.msrc.sunysb.edu. Lab is open weekdays 8 a.m. to 3 p.m.; marsh is open daily. **Free.**

Budding biologists will enjoy touring this research and instructional laboratory, operated
by the State University of New York, where the ecology of crustaceans, fish, mollusks, and
algae is studied. Surrounding the lab is a 146-acre salt marsh preserve with an interesting
nature trail winding through the tidal wetlands.

Where to Eat

Louie's Oyster Bar and Grille. 395 Main
St., Port Washington; (516) 883-4242; www
.louiesoysterbarandgrille.com. Raw bar, crab
cakes, fish-and-chips, lobster, and other seafood specialties, with views of Long Island
Sound. $$$

Steve's Pier I. 33 Bayville Ave., Bayville;
(516) 628-2153. Seafood, steak, and lobster,
plus home baking, children's meals, and out-
door deck dining in season. $$$

Three Village Inn. 150 Main St., Stony
Brook; (631) 751-0555; www.threevillageinn
.com. Colonial homestead serving steak, seafood, regional specialties, along with home
baking and a children's menu. $$$$

Where to Stay

Chalet Inn & Suites. 23 Centershore Rd.
and NY 25A, Centerport; (631) 757-4600.
Rooms and suites with kitchens, overlooking
a pond; **free** Wi-Fi and newspaper; children
under twelve stay **free.** $–$$

East Norwich Inn. 6321 Northern Blvd.,
East Norwich; (516) 922-1500 or (800) 334-
4798; www.eastnorwichinn.com. Seventy-two
rooms and suites, some with kitchenettes, a
cottage, heated outdoor pool, gym, sauna,
laundry service, cable TV, Internet, and complimentary continental breakfast. $$–$$$

South Shore

Pristine sugar sand beaches line the southern coastline of Long Island, beckoning beach-
combers, sun worshipers, and sports enthusiasts. There are enough malls in the area to
shop till you drop, but that doesn't usually appeal to the preteen-and-under crowd. What
will impress them are the seemingly endless barrier beaches, the eclectic assortment of
museums, mills, and mansions, and the wide variety of indoor and outdoor playgrounds.

The Hicksville Gregory Museum (all ages)

1 Heitz Place, Hicksville; (516) 822-7505; www.gregorymuseum.org. Open Tues through Fri
9:30 a.m. to 4:30 p.m., Sat and Sun 1 to 5 p.m.; closed Mon and major holidays. $.

The largest collection of rocks and minerals on Long Island is displayed inside this historic
former courthouse, along with interesting plant and animal fossils, a bevy of butterfly
specimens, and a 1915 jail cell.

New York **Trivia**

The widest point in the state east to west (not including Long Island) is 330 miles.

Heckscher State Park (all ages)

Heckscher Parkway, Field 1, East Islip; (631) 581-2100; www.nysparks.state.ny.us. Open year-round 7 a.m. to sunset; campgrounds open May through Sept. Parking fee $. Call ahead to confirm changes to hours, activities available, and possible closures due to pending state budget cuts.

Covering 1,657 acres, this is a great family park, with three sandy beaches, a swimming pool, hiking trails, ball fields, a playground and picnic area, fishing in Great South Bay and Nicoll Bay, recreation programs, and campsites. This is also a trailhead where hikers can enter the Long Island Greenbelt Trail, a path winding past woodlands and wetlands, stretching 34 miles to Sunken Meadow State Park.

Long Island Children's Museum (ages 2 to 12)

11 Davis Ave., Garden City; (516) 224-5800; www.licm.org. Open daily July and Aug, 10 a.m. to 5 p.m.; Sept through June open Tues through Sun 10 a.m. to 5 p.m. Closed Memorial Day, Labor Day, Thanksgiving, Christmas, and New Year's Day. $$, under 1 free.

Multimedia, interactive, and hands-on exhibits in twelve galleries are offered at this learning laboratory housed in a 40,000-square-foot former airplane hangar. You can blow big bubbles, explore the senses, dance to music from all over the world, or be a TV star at the Communication Station. Throughout the day, special programs are offered, from story and art classes to theater presentations.

Cradle of Aviation (all ages)

1 Davis Ave., Garden City; (516) 572-4066; IMAX schedule (516) 572-4012; www.cradleof aviation.org. Open Tues through Sun 9:30 a.m. to 5 p.m. $$, under 2 free.

Housed in hangars near where Charles Lindbergh in the *Spirit of Saint Louis* took off on his daring transatlantic solo flight is an incredible collection of seventy historical aircraft, from balloons to biplanes to lunar land rovers. The IMAX Dome Theater screens three different films daily, and if you'd like to have lunch on Mars, stop by the Red Planet Café for authentic Martian cuisine.

Long Island Museum of Science and Technology (ages 8 and up)

1 Davis Ave., Reckson Visitor's Center, Garden City; (516) 390-5174; www.limsat.org. Open Tues 10 a.m. to 2 p.m., Wed through Sun 10 a.m. to 5 p.m., and holiday Mondays 9:30 a.m. to 5 p.m.; free.

This new museum, part of the Museums at Mitchel complex, has interactive exhibits on robotics, color mixing, electronic music, weather radar, and radiation. As this museum is still a work in progress, new exhibits will be added in the future, designed to inspire the next generation of scientists and engineers.

Firefighters Museum and Education Center (all ages)

1 Davis Ave., Garden City; (516) 572-4177; www.ncfiremuseum.org. Open daily Tues through Sun 10 a.m. to 5 p.m. and daily in summer. $.

Frank Pendl, a fire service academy instructor, and Andy Stienmuller, a Nassau County fire marshal, dreamed of creating a museum to display a growing collection of firefighting memorabilia, and a year-round fire-safety education center. Opened in 2006, today the 10,000-square-foot facility, adjacent to the Long Island Museum of Science and Technology, houses antique and contemporary fire apparatus and gear, and a variety of hands-on exhibits designed to reinforce fire safety. A new addition is the Junior Firefighter Academy, where kids can pretend to ride a fire truck, rescue a gingerbread child, give first aid to the gingerbread family, then put out a faux fire. The museum gift shop carries a nice selection of firefighter toys and souvenirs.

Amityville Historical Society–Lauder Museum (ages 8 and up)

170 Broadway, Amityville; (631) 598-1486; www.amityvillehistoricalsociety.org. Open Sun, Tues, and Fri 2 to 4 p.m. Closed Easter, Christmas, and New Year's Day. Donation.

Artifacts and memorabilia from Amityville's past include paintings, photographs, carriages, and china, as well as a replica of an old schoolroom.

Sagtikos Manor (ages 4 and up)

NY 27A, West Bay Shore; (631) 661-8348; www.sagtikosmanor.org. Open Wed, Thurs, and Sun in July and Aug, 1 to 4 p.m.; Sun in June, 1 to 4 p.m. $.

Other South Shore Indoor Play Spaces, Laser Parks, and Arcades

Fun Zone. 229 NY 110, Farmingdale; (631) 847-0100; www.longislandtourism.com.

Fun Station USA. 40 Rocklyn Ave., Lynbrook; (516) 599-7757; www.funstationfun.com.

Laser Kingdom. 133 Milbar Blvd., Farmingdale; (631) 694-6148; www.laserkingdoms.com.

Q-Zar. 151 Voice Rd., Carle Place; (516) 877-7200; www.longislandtourism.com.

Dave and Buster's. 261 Airport Plaza Blvd.; (631) 249-0708; www.daveandbusters.com.

Built in 1697, this forty-two-room mansion served as headquarters for the British during the Revolutionary War, and in 1790 George Washington really did sleep here.

Clark Botanic Garden (all ages)

193 I.U. Willets Rd., Albertson; (516) 484-2208; www.clarkbotanic.org. Open daily year-round 10 a.m. to 4 p.m. Closed winter weekends, Christmas, and New Year's Day. Donation

Wander through twelve acres of wooded sandy moraine dotted with three ponds and adorned with fragrant wildflower, herb, perennial, annual, rose, and rock gardens. Special events include walking tours, a nighttime Halloween Spooky Walk, and a daytime Halloween Not-So-Spooky Walk and Scary Tales for younger folks.

Bellport-Brookhaven Historical Society Museum (ages 4 and up)

31 Bellport Lane, Bellport; (631) 776-7649 ; www.bbhsmuseum.org.

Exchange shop open Memorial Day through mid-Dec, Thurs through Sat 11 a.m. to 5 p.m.; museum complex open Fri and Sat 1 to 4 p.m. $, children 12 and under **free.** Exhibits of Long Island life are on display at this museum complex of six buildings, from farm tools and antiques to decoys, vintage toys, and Native American artifacts.

East Rockaway Grist Mill Museum (all ages)

Wood and Atlantic Avenues, Memorial Park, East Rockaway; (516) 887-6300; www.villageof eastrockaway.org. Open Sat and Sun, June until Labor Day, 1 to 5 p.m. Free.

Housed in a 300-year-old mill, on the Mill River, this small but charming museum has displays about the early days of Long Island. Exhibits explore the history of the original inhabitants of the area, the shipping industry, and early firefighting. There's also a collection of century-old artifacts and memorabilia, as well as an 1898 schoolroom.

Center for Science Teaching and Learning (all ages)

1 Tanglewood Rd., Rockville Center; (516) 764-0045; www.cstl.org. Open year-round; programs offered morning and afternoon. $.

Art on **Long Island**

Parrish Art Museum. 25 Job's Lane, Southampton; (631) 283-2118; www.parrish art.org.

Pollock-Krasner House and Study Center. 830 Springs-Fireplace Rd., East Hampton; (631) 324-4929; www.naples.cc.sunysb.edu.

Heckscher Museum of Art. 2 Prime Ave., Huntington; (631) 351-3250; www .heckscher.org.

Nassau County Museum of Art. One Museum Dr., Roslyn Harbor; (516) 484-9337; www.nassaumuseum.com.

Nestled on seventeen acres of this pastoral preserve, in nineteenth-century buildings, is a place where people can design their own science experience. Utilizing an inquiry-based teaching philosophy, challenges and experiments are offered to children, sometimes solo, sometimes with an adult, involving crafts, nature hikes, turtle talks, pumpkin picking, photography, rocketry, owl prowls, weather watches, and family field trips. Amazing Animals, a 3,000-square foot environment, is home to reptiles, amphibians, birds, and small mammals, and there's an activity area with puppets, puzzles, footprint stamping, and a fossil dig.

Adventureland Amusement Park (all ages)
2245 NY 110, Farmingdale; (631) 694-6868; www.adventureland.us. Open daily Mar through Oct, 11 a.m. to 6 p.m. Adults $$$$, children $$$.

Thirty rides will rock and roll you, there's a haunted house to spook you, and a mini-golf course for terra-firma types. The arcade features more than 300 games and attractions, and aspiring singers and actors can make a recording and video on-site.

Woodcleft Canal (all ages)
Woodcleft Avenue, Freeport. Open year-round.

Once the territory of the Merokes, an Algonquin tribe, the town was later named Freeport because ship captains were not charged customs duties to land their cargo. Today, the "Nautical Mile" parallels the canal, with interesting shops, open-air seafood markets, outdoor cafes, miniature golf, and charter fishing boats at the docks. A small extension of the South Street Seaport is here as well, with maritime memorabilia and models of a variety of sailing vessels.

Bayard Cutting Arboretum State Park (all ages)
440 Montauk Hwy., Great River; (631) 581-1002; www.bayardcuttingarboretum.com and www.nysparks.state.ny.us. Open year-round Tues through Sun, Nov to Apr, 10 a.m. to 4 p.m., and Apr through Oct, 10 a.m. to 5 p.m. $.

Located along the Connetquot River, this 690-acre estate was designed by Frederick Law Olmsted in 1887, and features five marked trails that wind through gardens, meadows, and marshes and past artistic arrangements of century-old oaks, elms, maples, and the largest conifer collection on Long Island. A Tudor mansion houses a small nature museum of mounted birds and other local flora and fauna, and the lovely cafe overlooks the grounds through Tiffany windows

African American Museum (ages 4 and up)
110 North Franklin St., Hempstead; (516) 572-0730; www.aamoflongisland.org. Open year-round Tues through Sat 10 a.m. to 5 p.m. Donation.

Dedicated to preserving the art, history, and culture of African Americans on Long Island, this small but interesting museum has permanent displays as well as special exhibits from the Smithsonian Institution and the Brooklyn Museum.

Old Depot (all ages)

South Broadway and South Third Street, Irmisch Park, Lindenhurst; (631) 226-1254; www
.villageoflindenhurst.com. Open June through Sept, Mon, Wed, and Fri 2 to 4 p.m., and Oct
through May, Wed, Fri, and Sat and the first Sun of each month, 2 to 4 p.m. Free

Artifacts and memorabilia of the railway era are displayed at this restored 1901 depot and
freight house, including a working telegraph system, with the history of the town written
in Morse Code.

Connetquot River State Park Preserve (all ages)

Sunrise Highway, 0.5 mile from Connetquot Avenue, Oakdale; (631) 581-1005; www.nysparks
.state.ny.us. Preserve open year-round, Apr through Sept, Tues through Sun 6 a.m. to 4:30
p.m., and Oct through Mar, Wed through Sun 8 a.m. to 4:30 p.m. $. Call ahead to confirm
changes to hours, activities available, and possible closures due to pending state budget cuts.

Once a private game reserve for the Vanderbilts, Whitneys, and other Gold Coast elite,
this 3,473-acre preserve, Long Island's largest state park, is now a nature preserve open
to everyone, with more than 50 miles of hiking and cross-country trails winding through
woods filled with wildlife. Deer, rabbits, foxes, wild turkeys and nesting osprey make
their home here, as do many rare plants. The former clubhouse has a small nature exhibit
depicting Long Island habitats, a touch tank, and a collection of bird eggs. Environmental
interpretive programs are offered, from Bat Safaris to scavenger hunts, as are catch-and-
release fly-fishing for an additional fee. With the oldest fish hatchery in Long Island about
a mile upstream, the odds are in your favor if you care to cast out a line.

Quogue Schoolhouse Museum (all ages)

90 Quogue St. East, Quogue; (631) 653-4224; www.suffolk.lib.ny.us. Open July and Aug,
Wed and Fri 3 to 5 p.m., Sat 10 a.m. to noon. Free.

In 1822 this was the biggest and best school in Suffolk County and cost about $350 to
build. Today it houses photographs, maps, and memorabilia of the town's early years, as
well as a collection of toys, household items, and farm tools.

Quogue Wildlife Refuge (all ages)

3 Old Country Rd., Quogue; (631) 653-4771; www.quoguewildliferefuge.com. Refuge and
Distressed Wildlife Complex open daily year-round sunrise to sunset; nature center open
Tues and Thurs 11 a.m. to 4 p.m., and Sat and Sun 11 a.m. to 4 p.m. Free.

Surrounded by farms and fields, this refuge has 7 miles of trails
snaking through 305 acres of swamps, bogs, and pine barrens.
Visit the Charles Banks Belt Nature Center, which overlooks the Old
Ice Pond, for a variety of nature exhibits and a touch table, and also
the Distressed Wildlife Center, home to injured animals that would
not be able to survive in the wild. Special events throughout the
year include an Earth Day Celebration, an Easter Egg Hunt, Halloween Trails, and summer ecology programs.

Islip Grange (all ages)

10 Broadway Ave., Sayville; (631) 472-7016; www.sayville.com. Open daily year-round 9 a.m. to 5 p.m. Free.

Spread over twelve acres, this complex of historic nineteenth-century structures saved from demolition includes a water-powered mill, barns, cottages, and a Dutch Reformed church.

State Parks in the Area

For more information visit www.nysparks.state.ny.us or call the individual park offices.

Belmont Lake State Park. Southern State Parkway, exit 38, North Babylon; (631) 667-5055.

Bethpage State Park. 99 Quaker Meeting House Rd., Farmingdale; (516) 249-0701.

Hempstead Lake State Park. West Hempstead; (516) 766-1029.

Valley Stream State Park. Valley Stream; (516) 825-4128.

Natural Nassau County. For more information visit www.nassaucountyny.gov or call the individual park offices.

Eisenhower Park. 1899 Hempstead Turnpike, East Meadow; (516) 572-0348.

Bay Park. First Avenue, East Rockaway; (516) 571-7245.

Cantiague Park. West John Street, Hicksville; (516) 571-7056.

Cedar Creek Park. 3340 Merrick Rd., Seaford; (516) 571-7470.

Cow Meadow Park & Preserve. South Main Street, near Ann Drive South, Freeport; (516) 571-8685.

Grant Park. Broadway and Sheridan Avenue, Hewlett; (516) 571-7821.

Nickerson Beach Park. 880 Lido Blvd., Lido; (516) 571-7700.

North Woodmere Park. Hungry Harbor Road, North Woodmere; (516) 571-7801.

Wantagh Park. 1 King Rd., Wantagh; (516) 571-7460.

Rev. Arthur Mackey Sr. Park. Lakeside Drive and Washington Road, Roosevelt; (516) 571-8692.

Massapequa Preserve. Merrick Road and Ocean Avenue, Massapequa; (516) 541-2461.

Tackapausha Museum and Preserve (all ages)

Washington Avenue, between Merrick Road and Sunrise Highway, Seaford; (516) 571-7443; www.nassaucountyny.gov. Open year-round Tues through Sat 10 a.m. to 4 p.m., Sun 1 to 4 p.m. Closed Mon and holidays. $, under 5 free.

Five miles of trails wind through this 84-acre nature preserve, home to the ruby-throated hummingbird and 170 other bird species, as well as raccoons, muskrats, gray squirrels, and opossums. The museum has exhibits explaining the ecology of Long Island, with wetlands displays of amphibians and reptiles, and interactive activities for children.

Jones Beach State Park (all ages)

1 Ocean State Parkway, Wantaugh; (516) 785-1600; www.nysparks.state.ny.us and www .jonesbeach.com; Open daily year-round. Vehicle fee $. Call ahead to confirm changes to hours, activities available, and possible closures due to pending state budget cuts.

In 1692 privateer Thomas Jones purchased 6,000 acres of marshland and beachfront in this area and opened a whaling station. In 1929 the legendary Robert Moses developed 2,413 acres of this into what is now the most popular beach on the East Coast, welcoming more than 8 million visitors every year. Stretching for over 6 miles along the Atlantic Ocean, plus a half mile of bay beach, this is a great place to soak up the sun and surf. A 2-mile boardwalk, deck games, beach volleyball, miniature golf and pitch-and-putt courses, two swimming pools, picnic areas, and playgrounds offer plenty of outdoor options, and top-line concerts take the stage on summer nights. Nearby, on a barrier island within the park, is the Theodore Roosevelt Nature Center, with an environmental boardwalk winding through the sand dunes and opportunities to spot the local wildlife. Inside the center are marine touch tanks, kid-size microscopes, whale-bone digs at the Discovery Bone Cove, and a variety of interpretive programs for families.

Lakewood Stables (ages 1 and up)

633 Eagle Ave., West Hempstead; (516) 486-9673; www.lakewoodstables.com. Open daily year-round, Mon through Sat 10 a.m. to 7 p.m., Sun 10 a.m. to 5 p.m. Fee depends on ride.

Recently renovated, Lakewood Stables offers equestrian enthusiasts trail rides through nearby Hempstead Lake State Park, with English- and western-style lessons available, as well as pony rides for the younger set.

Long Island Maritime Museum (ages 4 and up)

86 W. Avenue, West Sayville; (631) 854-4974; www.limaritime.org. Open year-round Mon through Sat 10 a.m. to 4 p.m., Sun noon to 4 p.m.; closed New Years Day, Easter, Thanksgiving, and Christmas. $.

Located on the waterfront, five historic buildings spread out over fourteen acres highlight Long Island's maritime heritage. The main museum houses a collection of ship models, and exhibits about shipwrecks and the U.S. Lifesaving Service. Nearby is the nineteenth-century Rudolph Oyster House, typical of the culling cottages where Dutch immigrants worked in the booming oyster industry until the hurricane of 1938 wiped out all the South Shore oyster beds. The Beebe Cottage, home to a family of nine, had all the modern

Other Outdoor **Spaces**

Long Beach Island Resort. 350 National Blvd., Long Beach; (516) 432-6000; www.iloveny.com.

Nassau-Suffolk Greenbelt Trail. (631) 360-0753; www.hike-ligreenbelt.com.

Captree State Park. Ocean Parkway, Babylon; (631) 669-0449; www.nysparks .state.ny.us.

Gilgo State Park. Ocean Parkway, Babylon; (631) 669-0449; www.nysparks .state.ny.us.

conveniences of the day, including a coal stove, a dry sink, and a three-holer outhouse out back. Over thirty unique boats are displayed inside the Everitt-Lawrence Small Craft Exhibition Hall, and boat building and restoration programs are ongoing at the Frank Penny Boat Shop. Moored outside in the Boat Basin is a floating collection of historic watercraft, including the oyster sloop *Priscilla,* the tugboat *Charlotte,* and *Vixen,* a 1930s clam boat. A boardwalk overlooks 200 acres of wetlands of the Great South Bay, and special events include concerts, regattas, seafood festivals, ecology programs, pirate encampments, and the annual Halloween Boat Burning.

Fire Island National Seashore (all ages)

Park Headquarters, 120 Laurel St., Patchogue; (631) 687-4750; www.nps.gov/fiis. Robert Moses State Park (631) 669-0470; www.nysparks.state.ny.us. Fire Island Lighthouse (631) 321-7028. Sailors Haven Visitor Center (631) 597-6183; open mid-May through Oct. Watch Hill Visitor Center (631) 597-6455; open mid-May though mid-Oct. Wilderness Visitor Center (631) 281-3010; open year-round Wed through Sun. Smith Point County Park (631) 852-1313. William Floyd Estate, 245 Mastic Beach; (631) 399-2030; open mid-May through mid-Nov, Fri, Sat, Sun, and holidays, 9 a.m. to 5 p.m. Fire Island Ferries (631) 665-3600; www.fireislandferries.com. Sayville Ferry Service (631) 589-0810; www.sayvilleferry.com. Davis Park Ferry (631) 475-1665. Sunken Forest Ferry Service (631) 589-0810; www.long island.com. Park is open year-round sunrise to sunset, and lifeguards are on duty at main beaches from Memorial Day to Labor Day. Cars not allowed on most of Fire Island. Free, but parking fees and/or transportation fees $–$$$.

Running for 32 miles along the Atlantic shore of Long Island, this scenic strip of sand was established as a National Seashore in 1964 and is the only developed barrier beach in the country without roads. More than 237 diverse plant species tenaciously tangle their roots in this uniquely beautiful place, and more than thirty mammals, from finback whales to the tiny masked shrew, live within the park's boundaries, along with snakes, turtles, terrapins, and, unfortunately, ticks and poison ivy, so stay on the boardwalks! Numerous ferries ply the waters of Great South Bay between Robert Moses State Park and Smith Point County Park, providing access to seventeen resort communities catering to a variety of lifestyles, linked together by boardwalks. The visitor centers at Sailors Haven, Watch Hill, and Otis Pike Fire Island High Dune Wilderness offer excellent maps and information, and nature trails wind through several diverse habitats. The 875-acre Robert Moses State Park, the oldest state park on Long Island, can be reached by car via the Robert Moses Causeway and offers 5 miles of pristine beaches, a pitch-and-putt golf course, and a historic light-house to explore. Local legends tell of pirates who lit bonfires on the beach to lure ships to their doom, thereby giving the island its name. But since 1826, sailors have looked to the Fire Island Lighthouse for guidance, with its counterclockwise flash every seven and a half seconds. Visible from 20 miles at sea, it was often the first sight of America that waves of new immigrants saw as they sailed toward New York, the "City of Golden Dreams." A small museum is housed in the keeper's cottage, and tower tours are offered in summer.

Almost 7 miles down the beach is the Sunken Forest at Sailors Haven, a below-sea-level stunted woodland of endangered century-old holly, sassafras, and shadblow. Farther down the beach is Watch Hill, a seven-acre area of windswept dunes next to the only federally designated wilderness area in the state, the Otis Pike Fire Island High Dune Wilderness. There's a walk-in campground with twenty-six sites at Watch Hill. Wilderness camping is available with a permit for the Otis Pike area, and at the eastern end of the park is Smith Point County Park, with 270 campsites, showers, snack bars, playgrounds, and picnic places. Activities along this barrier island are endless, and include swimming, boating, hiking, sightseeing, fishing, and wildlife watching. Special events occur year-round, with ranger-conducted programs, tours, seining demonstrations, and seaside stories and crafts. Kids can become Junior Rangers by completing the activities in a park booklet, and then receive a patch or badge from the visitor center. A new program for kids online is the National Park Service's WebRangers (www.webrangers.us), which allows cyber folk to learn about all the federal parks through Internet games and quizzes. Also on the island is the ancestral home and estate of William Floyd, a Revolutionary War general and one of the signers of the Declaration of Independence. Guided tours are offered of the 25-room Old Mastic House, twelve outbuildings, and the family cemetery, surrounded by 613 acres of trail-laced forests, fields, and marsh.

Old Bethpage Village Restoration (all ages)

1303 Round Swamp Rd., Old Bethpage; (516) 572-8401; www.nassaucountyny.gov. Open Apr through Dec, Wed through Sun 10 a.m. to 4 p.m., summer 10 a.m. to 5 p.m. Closed Mon and Tues. $$, under 5 free.

Step back in time as you stroll through this 209-acre farm village, a collection of fifty-one historic buildings and seven reconstructions that recreate mid-nineteenth-century Long Island life. While this village never really existed as such, the structures, moved here from various locations, are authentic. Costumed interpreters offer tours, and although many of the buildings are not yet ready for prime time, it's an interesting place. A new addition is the Restoration Farm, a seven-acre area dedicated to sustainable, organic agricultural principles, with the bounty of Bethpage available for purchase at the stand in the parking area. Special events for families include nineteenth-century baseball games, Civil War reenactments, concerts, candlelight evenings, and the Long Island Fair in Oct.

Where to Eat

56th Fighter Group. NY 110, Republic Airport Gate 1, East Farmingdale; (631) 694-8280; www.56thfgrestaurant.com. WWII aviation ambience, complete with Big Band music. Serving soups, salads, sandwiches, Kobe burgers, seafood, pasta, steaks, home-made pot roast, and a Junior Pilot's menu. $$–$$$$

The Hideaway. Houser's Hotel, Bay Walk, Ocean Beach; (631) 583-8900. Casual contemporary cuisine, including seafood, steaks, and duck, with indoor and outdoor deck dining and terrific water views. $$–$$$$

Molly Malone's. 124 Maple Ave., on the Fire Island Ferry Pier, Bayshore; (631) 969-2232; www.mollymalonesbayshore.com. Irish classic cuisine, including shepherd's pie and corned beef and cabbage, plus fresh seafood, pasta, soups, salads, sandwiches, and a children's menu. Daily live music on the waterfront deck. $$–$$$$

Where to Stay

Clegg's Hotel. 478 Bayberry Walk, Ocean Beach, Fire Island; (631) 583-9292 and (631) 583-5399; www.cleggshotel.com. Facing Great South Bay, within a five-minute walk to the ocean, European-style design, with rooms with shared bathrooms, suites, and studio apartments; **free** use of bicycles, board games, beach chairs, and umbrellas; weekly rates available, and children under eight **free,** except for one-time bed charge. $$$–$$$$

Fire Island Hotel and Resort. 25 Cayuga Walk, Ocean Bay Park, Fire Island; (631) 583-8000; www.fireislandhotel.com. Formerly Coast Guard buildings, and recently renovated, with rooms, suites, apartments, and cabins, a heated pool, restaurant, playground, bike shop, gift shop, and nearby tennis courts. Three-night minimum on weekends. $$$$

Central Suffolk

The heart of Long Island is a tapestry of pitch pine and scrub oak forests threaded by the Carmans and Peconic Rivers and hemmed in by sandy Atlantic beaches and the rocky shores of the Long Island Sound. Within Central Suffolk's borders lies the Pine Barrens Preserve, a 100,000-acre wilderness area crowning a giant aquifer and providing an Eden for wildlife. Other opportunities for animal observation are available at the numerous zoos, farms, and marine labs in the area, and there's even a ten-ton duck to check out.

Wildwood State Park (all ages)

North Wading River Road, Wading River; (631) 929-4314; www.nysparks.state.ny.us. Open daily sunrise to sunset; campgrounds open Apr through Oct. Summer parking fee $.

On beach-trimmed bluffs overlooking Long Island Sound, and with twelve miles of trails traveling through undeveloped hardwood forests, this scenic Long Island Sound spot is special. There are 2 miles of beach for swimming or fishing, plus picnic places, a playground, basketball courts, ball fields, bike paths, a nature trail, and line or square dancing on starry summer nights.

Peconic River Herb Farm (all ages)

2749 River Rd., Calverton; (631) 369-0058; www.prherbfarm.com. Open late Apr through June, 9 a.m. to 5 p.m.; July through mid-Oct, 9 a.m. to 4 p.m.; closed mid-Oct through Mar. $.

More than 700 varieties of unusual and unique plants grow at this fourteen-acre working riverfront farm, landscaped to inspire a new generation of growing gardeners.

The Big Duck (all ages)

1012 Flanders Rd. (NY 24), Flanders; (631) 852-8292 or 283-6055; www.co.suffolk.ny.us. Open May through Labor Day, Tues through Sat 10 a.m. to 5 p.m., Sun 2 to 5 p.m. Free.

Where does a ten-ton duck sit? Anywhere she wants, and this one sits patiently along NY 24, a tribute to the area's duck farm heritage. Inside Long Island's most famous landmark, which is listed on the National Register of Historic Places, is a small gift shop offering duck-a-bilia and tourism information. In Dec, local schoolchildren celebrate the annual Holiday Lighting of the Big Duck, with "Duck" carols, hot chocolate, and cookies.

Long Island Game Farm Wildlife Park (all ages)

Chapman Boulevard, about 1 mile north of CR 111, Manorville; (631) 878-6644; www.long islandgamefarm.com. Open daily early May through early Oct, Mon through Fri 10 a.m. to 4:30 p.m., Sat and Sun 10 a.m. to 5:30 p.m. $$$, under 2 free.

For four decades this zoo and wildlife park has entertained and educated children with a menagerie of animals, from alligators to zebras. Follow the nature trails to Bambiland, the Nursery, and Old McDonalds's Farmyard, where kids can pet and sometimes feed the baby pigs, rabbits, chickens, ducks, and ponies. A new addition in the animal show lineup is Tiger Time, featuring rare tigers from around the world. An assortment of amusement rides, slides, spinning teacups, a tiny train, and an antique carousel are available, plus pony rides for pint-size equestrians.

The Animal Farm Petting Zoo (all ages)

296 Wading River Rd., Manorville; (631) 878-1785; www.afpz.org. Open Apr through Oct, Mon through Fri 10 a.m. to 5 p.m., Sat and Sun 10 a.m. to 6 p.m. $$$, under 2 free.

Many of the animals here are former exotic pets, abandoned by their owners, and not able to be cared for at regular shelters. From macaws to Japanese snow macaques, hamsters to horses, and bobcats to bunnies, this is an oasis of safety for these beautiful creatures. Board the Safari Train for a tour of the terrain, and enjoy encounters with a variety of these animals at scheduled shows. Don't miss the "Super Cow" musical puppet show, the Turtle Train ride, and a chance to bottle feed the baby pigs, cows, goats, and lambs. Be advised, many of these animals need a good home, and some are available for adoption.

Harold Malkmes Wildlife Education and Ecology Center at Holtsville Park (all ages)

249 Buckley Rd., Holtsville; (631) 758-9664. Open daily 9 a.m. to dusk; zoo closes at 4 p.m.; closed Christmas, Thanksgiving, New Years Day, and Easter. Donation.

Built atop a garbage dump, this scenic park offers a triple pool complex, a fitness trail, picnic and playground areas, a zoo housing injured wildlife, including mountain lions, and a barnyard of friendly farm animals to pet. A Halloween Happening happens in late Oct, a Menorah Lighting in Dec, and Holtsville Hal makes his annual appearance on Groundhog Day to determine if spring will come soon, or not.

Hallockville Museum Farm (all ages)

6038 Sound Ave., Riverhead; (631) 298-5292; www.hallockville.com. Open Fri through Sun 11 a.m. to 4 p.m. Docent-led tours, adults $, children $.

Built in 1765, this was home to the Hallock family for five generations. Follow a forty-point self-guided tour, marked by numbered and informative signs, or a docent-led time-travel trip through 200 years of Long Island farm life. The eighteen buildings in the twenty-eight-acre complex include the Homestead, a big barn, a smokehouse, cobbler's shop, and a workshop, making this one of the oldest intact farms on the island. Special events throughout the year include Tractor Pulls, Bird Walks, a fall festival, and a Victorian Christmas, complete with Santa's arrival in a cheery red antique truck.

Atlantis Marine World (ages 4 and up)

431 East Main St., Riverhead; (631) 208-9200; www.atlantismarineworld.com. Open year-round daily 10 a.m. to 5 p.m. Closed Christmas. Adults $$$$, children $$$, under 3 free. Separate fees for behind-the-scenes tour, shark dive, trainer program, snorkel adventure, aqua adventures, and tour boat trips. Riverhead Foundation for Marine Research and Preservation; www.riverheadfoundation.org. Stranding Hotline: (631) 369-9829.

Considered to be one of the top aquariums for kids in the country, Atlantis lives up to its reputation. Indoor exhibits re-create the Legendary Lost City, an Amazon rain forest, and the largest all-living, closed-system Coral Reef in the Western Hemisphere, holding 20,000 gallons of water and more than 800 types of fish. The 120,000-gallon Shark Exhibit is home to a variety of formidable fish, plus a 300-pound loggerhead turtle, but if you'd like a closer look, those over twelve may climb into the tank's underwater cage, with equipment provided, and create their own *Jaws* memories. Stop at the Ray Bay and Touch Tanks to feel the fish, sea stars, clams, and stingrays, and don't miss the new interactive 3,000-gallon saltwater Tidal Marsh exhibit, where kids can pop up through tunnels and be surrounded by hundreds of fiddler crabs! Outside, walk past the Ancient Reptile Ruins, home to lizards and snakes, towards the Koi Pond, goldfish relatives that can live 200 years. The Lost Temple looms ahead, home to three bachelor Japanese snow monkeys who recently moved here from New York City's Central Park Zoo. Penguins, otters, seals and sea lions swim in humane habitats, animal demonstrations are offered throughout the day, and guided tours of the salt marsh outside are always interesting.

Other Aquatic Adventures include a Pirate Snorkel Adventure, a Trainer Program, Sea Lion Kisses, and a Sleep With The Fishes overnight slumber party. The adventure continues with a one-and-a-half-hour voyage down the Peconic River and into Flanders Bay aboard the *Atlantis Explorer,* guided by knowledgeable ecologists. For arcade activities, stop by Nemo's Family Fun Center for skeeball and shootouts, or pause at Poseidon's Peak & Playground along the Peconic. Unearthing Atlantis is also a new addition, with gemstone mining, wall rubbings, and archeological fossil digs. But Atlantis Marine World is more than a great place to explore the seas—it's also home to the state's only authorized stranding and research facility, the Riverhead Foundation for Marine Research and Preservation. They rescue, rehabilitate, and release, when possible, injured seals, sea lions, sea turtles, whales, dolphins, and porpoises, and offer seal cruises, ecology walks, and beach cleanups in season.

Dinosaur Walk Museum (all ages)

221 East Main St., Riverhead; (631) 369-6556; www.dinowalk.com. Open year-round daily 10 a.m. to 5 p.m. $$.

This small two-story space has sculptured life-size dinosaur replicas, a faux fossil pit to excavate, and a dino-themed library, movies, and an activity area.

The Fauna Society Serpentarium (all ages)

213 East Main St., Riverhead; (631) 722-5488. Open year-round daily 11 a.m. to 6 p.m. $$.

More than two hundred snakes, lizards, frogs, turtles, and alligators live here, incased in seventy exhibits, with live reptile presentations offered throughout the day.

Suffolk Historical Museum (ages 5 and up)

300 West Main St., Riverhead; (631) 727-2881; www.suffolkcountyhistoricalsociety.org. Open year-round Tues through Sat 12:30 to 4:30 p.m. Closed holidays. Donation.

The county's colorful history is highlighted here, drawn from a collection of more than 20,000 artifacts, with exhibits on Native Americans, whaling, transportation, farm life, the Civil War, and arts and crafts of the area.

Railroad Museum of Long Island (all ages)

416 Griffing Ave., Riverhead; (631) 727-7920; www.rmli.us. Open spring through fall, Sat and Sun 10 a.m. to 4 p.m. $.

Ride the rails aboard the tiny train that travelled the New York World's Fair in 1964–65, or climb aboard a caboose, a vintage steam engine, a sleek commuter car, or a massive

New York **Trivia**

The hottest day on record in the state is 108 degrees Fahrenheit, which was recorded on July 22, 1926, in Troy.

Activities and **Amusements**

When the kids need to work off some energy, try one of these entertainment centers:

Country Fair Park. Long Island Expressway, exit 64, Medford; (631) 732-0579; www.countryfairpark.com.

Karts Indoor Raceway. 701 Union Parkway, Ronkonkoma; (631) 737-5278; www.karts1.com.

Laser Kingdom. 544 Middle Country Rd., Coram; (631) 698-0414; www.laser kingdoms.com.

locomotive at this charming museum. Rolling stock is parked outside, and restoration projects are ongoing. The museum has another smaller branch in Greenport Station, with train memorabilia, photographs, and artifacts of the Long Island railways.

Silly Lily Fishing Station (ages 4 and up)
99 Adelaide Ave., East Moriches; (631) 878-0247; www.sillylily.com. Open Mar to Nov, 6 a.m. to 4 p.m. $$$$.

Fish for fluke, flounder, striped bass, and bluefish in Moriches Bay, aboard 16-foot row-boats, with an 8-horsepower engine optional. Poles, tackle, live bait, and nets are available for rent, as are kayaks and sailboats for less piscatorial people.

Suffolk County Farm and Education Center (all ages)
4600 Yaphank Ave., Yaphank; (631) 852-4600; www.ccesuffolk.org. Open daily 9 a.m. to 3 p.m., with weekend programs; closed Thanksgiving, Christmas, and Easter. **Free.**

Workshops and demonstrations at this 300-acre, century-old working farm offer families the opportunity to learn about home on the grange. There are sheep, goats, pigs, chickens, and cattle to feed and care for, daily hayrides in summer, and the annual Pumpkin-Fest, complete with a Parent Calling Contest and Cow Chip Bingo, followed a few weeks later by the October catapult celebration known as the Pumpkin Fling.

Splish Splash Water Park (all ages)
2549 Splish Splash Dr., Calverton; (631) 727-3600; www.splishsplashlongisland.com. Open May through Sept; hours vary. $$$$.

Ninety-six acres of aqua action at this water world for all ages, with slippery serpentine tubes and tunnels twisting through a terrain of typhoons, lagoons, and past pirates marooned. Check out cabana rentals, complete with chairs, shaded areas, locker, refrigerator, and food delivery service to your door throughout the day.

Boomers (all ages)

655 Long Island Ave., Medford; (631) 475-1771; www.boomersparks.com. Open year-round, Fri 4 p.m. to 10 p.m., Sat 11 a.m. to 9 p.m., Sun 11 a.m. to 7 p.m.; tickets $, all day passes $$$$.

Bumper boats, batting cages, go-karts, mini-golf, a climbing wall, a carousel, a tiny train ride, a roller coaster, and an arcade offer action adventures for everyone.

Where to Eat

Cooperage Inn. 2218 Sound Ave., Baiting Hollow; (631) 727-8994; www.cooperageinn .com. Fresh seafood, steaks, salads, chicken potpie, meat loaf, roast duckling, pasta, barbecue ribs, and homemade desserts. $$–$$$$

Jerry & the Mermaid. 469 East Main St., Riverhead; (631) 727-8489; www.jerryandthe mermaid.com. Casual outdoor dining with a water view; serving fresh seafood, chicken, and steak, with karaoke on weekends. $–$$

Lobster Roll. 3225 Sound Ave., Riverhead; (631) 369-3039; www lobsterroll.com. The new Northside branch of the legendary South Shore seafood spot, serving chowder, chili, crab cakes, cheeseburgers, lobster rolls, and homemade desserts, with outdoor deck dining in season. $–$$

Where to Stay

Best Western East End. 1830 NY 25, River-head; (631) 369-2200; www.bestwesterneast end.com. One hundred rooms, with **free** Wi-Fi, cable TV, outdoor heated pool, fitness center, restaurant, room service, complimentary continental breakfast, and children under 18 **free** with adult. $$$$

Holiday Inn Express Hotel & Suites. 1707 Old Country Rd., Riverhead; (631) 548-1000; www.ichotelsgroup.com. Eighty-nine rooms and forty-one kitchenettes, some with microwave and mini fridge, cable TV, WIFI, movies and games available, fitness center, and outdoor pool. $$$$

Wading River Motel. 5890 NY 25, Wading River; (631) 727-8000; www.wadingrivermotel .net. Rooms and kitchenettes, barbecue pits, lawn games, and heated outdoor pool surrounded by five landscaped acres. $–$$

South Fork

Home to the Shinnecock Native Americans, celebrities, and sybarites, the South Fork is an interesting mosaic of farmland, rolling dunes, deep harbors, and sparkling wave-washed beaches. The hamlets of the Hamptons are here, as are one of the oldest lighthouses in the country and possibly the best fishing in the state.

East Hampton Town Maritime Museum (all ages)

301 Bluff Rd., off NY 27, Amagansett; (631) 324-6850; www.easthamptonhistory.org. Open Memorial Day weekend through Columbus Day weekend, Sat and Sun 10 a.m. to 5 p.m. $.

Housed in a former U.S. Coast Guard barracks, this museum contains an interesting collection of maritime memorabilia highlighting the seaworthy history of Amagansett. Artifacts from the Revolutionary War–era HMS *Culloden* shipwreck of 1781, exhibits on

The Long Island National **Wildlife Refuge**

Composed of nine nuggets of nature, strung along 6,500 acres of the Atlantic Flyway and the Long Island Pine Barrens, this refuge provides important nesting, wintering, and migratory rest stops for hundreds of bird species. Over 500 species of plants thrive in this green path, along with 35 species of mammals, 30 species of reptiles and amphibians, and over a 100 kinds of fish. For trail maps and more information, visit the **U.S. Fish & Wildlife Service** Web site at www.fws.gov/northeast/longislandrefuges.

Wertheim National Wildlife Refuge

Target Rock National Wildlife Refuge

Lido Beach National Wildlife Refuge

Oyster Bay National Wildlife Refuge

Seatuck National Wildlife Refuge

Amagansett National Wildlife Refuge

Conscience Point National Wildlife Refuge

Sayville National Wildlife Refuge

Elizabeth A. Morton National Wildlife Refuge

aquaculture and commercial fishing methods, and offshore whaling expeditions fill three floors with oceanic objects, plus there's a hands-on Discovery Room for smaller sailors. Outside is a jungle gym trawler to board, and a wooden vessel collection that includes a catboat and a whaleboat, and the Indian Field Gunning Shanty.

Pine Neck Nature Sanctuary (all ages)

Head of Lots Road, East Quogue; (631) 367-3384; www.nature.org. Open year-round dawn to dusk; donation.

Trimming Shinnecock Bay with a Spartina grass skirt and a coastal forest coat of pine and oak, this seventy-seven-acre pristine preserve is a major migratory stopover and wintering grounds for ducks, egrets, ibis, herons, gulls, songbirds, raptors, and great horned owls, as well as deer and mink.

Amagansett National Wildlife Refuge (all ages)

Atlantic Avenue, off NY 27, Amagansett; (631) 286-0485; www.fws.gov. Open year-round, depending on nesting season, dawn to dusk; free.

This unique thirty-two-acre double-dune ecosystem of swales and fens is filled with rare plants, orchids, stunted oak scrub, and cranberry bogs, the habitat and haven for a multitude of birds, from songbirds and shorebirds to hawks, owls, and the eastern hognose snake.

Home Sweet Home Museum (ages 6 and up)

14 James Lane, East Hampton; (631) 324-0713; www.easthampton.com/homesweethome. Open May through Sept, Mon through Sat 10 a.m. to 4 p.m., Sun 2 to 4 p.m.; Apr, Oct, and Nov, Fri and Sat 10 a.m. to 4 p.m. and Sun 2 to 4 p.m.; closed holidays. $.

This was the boyhood home of John Howard Payne, actor, playwright, and poet, best remembered for writing the lyrics to "Home Sweet Home." Explore Payne's extensive china collection, then step outside to see the picturesque 1804 Pantigo windmill.

Old Hook Mill (all ages)

North Main Street, East Hampton; (631) 324-0713. Open June through Sept 10 a.m. to 4 p.m., grounds accessible year-round. Short guided tours are given in summer. $.

There are more windmills in this town than anywhere else in the country, and this one, built in 1806, was restored to working condition in 1939.

Mulford Farm House (all ages)

10 James Lane, East Hampton; (631) 324-6850; www.easthamptonhistory.org. Open Memorial Day Weekend through Columbus Day weekend, Sat 10 a.m. to 5 p.m., Sun noon to 5 p.m. $.

Built in 1680, this restored colonial farm is unique in that it was home to one family for eight generations. All the structures are intact and in their original locations. Farm tools and furnishings tell the tale of seventeenth- and eighteenth-century agrarian activities,

Suggested **Reading**

Treasure Island, by Robert Louis Stevenson

By the Sword, by Selene Castrovilla and Bill Farnsworth

Forgotten Tales of Long Island, by Richard Panchyk

The Battle of Long Island, by Scott Ingram

Neil Armstrong Is My Uncle and Other Lies Muscle Man McGinty Told Me, by Nan Marino

The Wainscott Weasel, by Tor Seidler

Eleven Kids, One Summer, by Ann M. Martin

Samuel's Choice, by Richard J. Berleth

Walt Whitman: Words For America, by Barbara Kerley

My Secret War: The World War II Diary of Madeline Beck, Long Island, New York 1941, by Mary Pope Osborne

Horsing around the **South Fork**

Deep Hollow Ranch. Off Montauk Highway, Montauk; (631) 668-2744; www .deephollowranch.com.

Rita's Stables & Petting Farm. 3 W. Lake Dr., Montauk; (631) 668-5453.

Sears Bellows Stables. Flanders Road, NY 24, Hampton Bays; (631) 668-5453.

and special events throughout the season include historical reenactments, lantern tours, holiday workshops, poetry marathons, and performances by the resident Mulford Barn Repertory Theater.

Montauk Point Lighthouse (all ages)

2000 Montauk Hwy., Montauk State Park, Montauk; (631) 668-2544 or (888) MTK–POINT; www.montauklighthouse.com. Open Mar through early May, Sat and Sun; early May through Sept, daily sunrise to sunset; call for schedule Nov through Dec. Montauk Point State Park. 50 S. Fairview Ave.; (631) 668-3781; www.nysparks.state.ny.us. Park open year-round. Adults $$, children $.

Commissioned by George Washington, this is the oldest operating lighthouse in the state, flashing every five seconds. Built on the easternmost tip of the Island where the British Navy set signal bonfires for its ships during the Revolutionary War, this area was heavily fortified during World War II against a possible German U-boat invasion. Tour the small museum next to the lighthouse-keeper's cottage, and check out the electrified exhibit of miniature eastern seaboard lighthouses. Folks over 41 inches can take the 137-step trek to the top for a breathtaking view of the forested 724-acre Montauk Point State Park, and of the race of converging tides from Long Island Sound and the ocean.

Viking Fishing Fleet Ferry Service (all ages)

462 West Lake Dr., Viking Dock, Montauk Harbor, Montauk; (631) 668-5700; www.viking fleet.com. Operating daily Memorial Day through Columbus Day, 8 a.m. to 6 p.m. Fee depends on trip.

Choose from naturalist-led whale-watching expeditions, fishing charters, and ferry service to Block Island.

Sag Harbor Whaling and Historical Museum (all ages)

200 Main St., Sag Harbor; (631) 725-0770; www.sagharborwhalingmuseum.org. Open daily mid-May through Oct, Mon through Sat 10 a.m. to 5 p.m., Sun 1 to 5 p.m. $, children under 3 **free.**

Housed in the Greek Revival mansion of a nineteenth-century whaling captain, this museum has an eclectic collection of artifacts and memorabilia from Sag Harbor's colorful maritime past.

County Parks of the **South Fork**

Cupsqoue Beach County Park. Westhampton; (631) 852-8111.

Dwarf Pines Plains Preserve. West Hampton; (631) 852-8111.

Cedar Point County Park. East Hampton; (631) 852-7620.

Sears Bellows County Park. Hampton Bays; (631) 852-8290.

Shinnecock East County Park. Southampton; (631) 852-8899.

Meschutt Beach County Park. Hampton Bays; (631) 852-8205.

Theodore Roosevelt County Park. Montauk; (631) 852-7878.

Custom House (ages 4 and up)　　　　　

912 Main St., Sag Harbor; (631) 725-0250; www.splia.org/hist_custom.htm. **Open Memorial Day weekend through Columbus Day, Sat and Sun 1 to 5 p.m. $.**

More than 200 years ago, when Sag Harbor was one of two official U.S. ports of entry, this was the home office of customs inspector Henry Packer Dering, his wife, and their nine children. It also served as Long Island's first post office.

Elizabeth A. Morton National Wildlife Refuge (all ages)　　

784 Noyack Rd., Sag Harbor; (631) 286-0485; www.fws.gov/refuges. **Open daily sunrise to sunset. $ per car or pedestrian/cyclist.**

Two-thirds of this 187-acre sanctuary stretches out between Little Peconic and Noyack Bays like a long sandy finger beckoning birds. More than 220 avian species have been sighted here, from osprey to the endangered piping plover and least tern, and there are also resident red fox, rabbits, raccoons, weasels, and white-tailed deer as well.

Halsey Homestead Museum (ages 4 and up)　　　

249 S. Main St., Southampton; (631) 283-2494. **Open July through mid-Oct, Fri, Sat, and Sun 11 a.m. to 4 p.m. $, under 17** free.

Built in 1648 by Southampton's founder, Thomas Halsey, this is the oldest English frame house in New York. Inside are seventeenth- and eighteenth-century furnishings, with a vintage apple orchard and herb garden outside.

Rogers Mansion (ages 4 and up)　　　　　

17 Meeting House Lane, Southampton; (631) 283-2494; www.southhamptonhistorical museum.org. **Open year-round Tues through Sat 11 a.m. to 4 p.m. $.**

Built by a sea captain in 1843, this Greek Revival home and surrounding grounds feature exhibits in twelve buildings, ranging from displays on Shinnecock and Montauk Native

Americans to artifacts from the Revolutionary War and antique toys. Outside are a one-room schoolhouse, a barn, a carriage house, blacksmith, cobbler, and carpentry shops, a country store, a saloon, and an apothecary shop.

Water Mill Museum (all ages)

41 Old Mill Rd, Water Mill; (631) 726-4625; www.watermillmuseum.org. Open mid-May to mid-Sept, Thurs through Mon 11 a.m. to 5 p.m., Sun 1 to 5 p.m. $, children **free.**

For more than 300 years, this wooden water mill has served the community, grinding grain, weaving cloth, spinning yarn, and even manufacturing paper. The small museum has displays of colonial crafts and grinding tools.

Hither Hills State Park (all ages)

50 South Fairview Ave., Old Montauk Highway, Montauk; (631) 668-2554; www.nysparks .state.ny.us. Open year-round daily, with lifeguards on duty in summer. Be aware that hunting is allowed in fall and winter. Summer parking fee $$.

This 1,755-acre state park is adjacent to two large nature preserves, making the area a wonderfully wild place to explore. Hike through pine and oak forests, past a cranberry bog, and around advancing sand dunes dotted with beach plum and rugosa roses. Follow the path to the crest of the dune for panoramic views of Napeague Harbor, Block Island Sound, and the legendary site of Captain Kidd's treasure, Gardiner's Island. For families planning to spend more time in the area, the 168-site campground on the beach has nearby hiking and biking trails, 2 miles of ocean beach, ball fields and courts, a general store, bathhouse, playground, picnic areas, movies, magic shows, children's summer the-ater, folk and line dancing, and environmental interpretation programs.

Camp Hero State Park (all ages)

50 S. Fairview Ave., Montauk; (631) 668-3781; www.nysparks.state.ny.us. Open year-round, dawn to dusk. $.

An urban legend suggests that this once top-secret military base was the site of the Mon-tauk Project, a research facility that conducted experiments exploring the time-space continuum and possibilities of invisibility and time travel, issues that intrigued Nikola Tesla and Albert Einstein. Designated a state park in 2002, this newly accessible 415-acre area has a long stretch of pebbly beach famous for surf fishing, overshadowed by bluffs, and miles of hiking and biking trails through majestic maritime forests and freshwater

South Fork **Open Spaces**

Montauk Mountain Preserve. Montauk; (631) 329-7689; www.nature.org.

Wolf Swamp Preserve. North Sea; (631) 329-7689; www.nature.org.

Kirk Park Beach. Montauk; (631) 324-2417; www.easthampton.com.

wetlands. The giant forty-ton radar dish that dominates the scene is the SAGE, the last of its kind, able to spot incoming fighters at 200 miles away, but soon made obsolete by spy satellites. A small museum is being planned for the future, with exhibits on WWII and the Cold War era, at this National Historic Site.

Accabonac Harbor (all ages)

Springs Fireplace Road, East Hampton; (631) 329-7689; www.nature.org. Open daily sunrise to sunset. Free.

A self-guided nature trail winds through 200 acres of woodlands and meadows and leads down to the cordgrass-lined Accabonac Harbor. This diverse tidal marsh is home to deer, raccoon, red fox and the piping plover. Depending on the tides, the path can get a bit swampy, so bring your rubber boots.

Where to Eat

Gosman's Dock. 500 W. Lake Dr., Montauk; (631) 668-5330; www.gosmans.com. Originally and currently a fish market, this family place has expanded into a great restaurant, serving homemade chowder, seafood sandwiches, sushi, lobsters, steaks, and burgers, with an outdoor raw bar and cafe, and wonderful water views. $$–$$$$

Inlet Seafood Restaurant. 541 E. Lake Dr., Montauk; (631) 668-4272; www.inletseafood .com. Six skippers helm this new waterfront fresh seafood spot, serving literally their catch of the day, prepared with an Asian fusion twist, and chocolate lava brownies for dessert. $$–$$$$

The Lobster Roll Restaurant. 1980 Montauk Hwy., at Napeague Beach, Amagansett; (631) 267-3740; www.lobsterroll.com. Wonderful beach place, specializing in char-grilled

fish, chowder, homemade desserts, and, of course, lobster rolls. $–$$$

New Moon Cafe. 524 Montauk Hwy., East Quogue; (631) 653-4042; www.nmcafe.com. Great Tex-Mex and barbecue, plus homemade desserts, a children's menu, and delivery service. $$

Where to Stay

Colonial Shores Cottages. 83 W. Tiana Rd., Hampton Bays; (631) 728-0011; www .colonialshoresny.com. Rooms, suites, and cottages with full kitchen, cable TV, private beach, pool, marina, and rowboats and paddleboats; children under 12 stay free. $$$–$$$$

Driftwood on the Ocean. 2178 Montauk Hwy., Montauk; (631) 668-5744; www.dune resorts.com. Rooms, suites, efficiencies, and cottages, on the beach, with a heated pool, cable TV, **free** Internet, refrigerator, tennis courts, and playground on ten secluded acres. $$$$

The Southampton Inn. 91 Hill St., Southampton; (631) 283-6500; www.south amptoninn.com. Ninety rooms and suites, refrigerators, cable TV, Wi-Fi, game room, outdoor heated pool, tennis court, lawn games, library with fireplace, children's play area, and a restaurant. $$$$

North Fork

More rural than the South Fork, this region also has a rich maritime and farming heritage. Colonial saltboxes and a dozen award-winning vineyards grace the historic hamlets settled more than 300 years ago. Shelter Island, nestled between the Forks' prongs, is the jewel of the Peconic, harboring a rare white-pine swamp and a large population of nesting osprey.

Cutchogue Village Green (ages 5 and up)
Route 25 at Case's Lane, Cutchogue; (631) 734-7122; www.cutchoguenewsuffolkhistory.org. Guided tours offered late June through Labor Day, Sat, Sun, and Mon 1 to 4 p.m. Donation.

The village green that's the heart of this picturesque hamlet is surrounded by historic wooden buildings dating back to the seventeenth century. The oldest house in New York is here, built in 1649 and named, appropriately, Old House. Next door is the 1704 Wickham Farmhouse, with agrarian articles and the earliest school in the area, the 1840 Old Schoolhouse Museum, housing a collection of antique toys, books, maps, and artifacts of the Corchaug Indians.

East End Seaport Museum (ages 4 and up)
End of Third Street, on the North Ferry dock, Greenport; (631) 477-2100; www.eastend seaport.org. Open mid-May through June, and Sept, Sat and Sun 11 a.m. to 5 p.m.; July and Aug, Mon, Wed, Thurs, and Fri 11 a.m. to 5 p.m., and Sat and Sun 9:30 a.m. to 5 p.m. Donation.

Housed in a former train station, this nautical niche has exhibits highlighting the maritime heritage of the North Fork, from Fresnel lighthouse lenses to the rise and fall of the menhaden and oyster industries. Nearby is the Village Blacksmith, with fiery forge demonstrations on summer weekends, and the annual Maritime Festival, with whaleboat races, chowder contests, and children's activities at Captain Kidd's Alley in autumn.

Orient Beach State Park (all ages)
North Country Road/NY 25, Orient; (631) 323-2440; www.nysparks.state.ny.us. Orient Point Ferry (860) 443-5281 or (631) 323-2525; www.longislandferry.com. Open daily sunrise to sunset. Lifeguards on duty in summer. Parking $. Call ahead to confirm changes to hours, activities available, and possible closures due to pending state budget cuts.

Reaching westward into Gardiner's Bay, this 357-acre sliver of sand has miles of polished pebble beach to stroll, a small maritime forest to explore, and a great sandy swimming spot. Osprey circle overhead, a herd of deer roam the bayberry and beach plum thickets, and endangered piping plovers nest in shallow dimples in the sand. From the tip of the spit you can see the restored Long Beach Bar Lighthouse, better known as "Bug Light." Playgrounds, picnic places, showers, and environmental tours are available in season. At Orient Point ferries can be boarded for travel to New London, Connecticut, past Plum Island, the site of a top secret U.S. biomedical research center.

Natural **North Fork**

For more information contact the **North Fork Promotional Council** at (631) 298-5757 and www.northfork.org.

Mill Road Preserve. 1900 Mill Rd., Mattituck

Downs Farm Preserve. 23800 NY 25, Cutchogue

Cedar Beach County Park. 3690 Cedar Beach Rd., Southold

Arshamomaque Pond Preserve, Southold

Inlet Pond Park. 65275 CR 48, Greenport

Dam Pond Maritime Reserve. 11855 CR 48, East Marion

Orient Point County Park. 41425 NY 25, Orient

Oysterponds Historical Society (ages 4 and up)

1555 Village Lane, Orient; (631) 323-2480; www.oysterpondshistoricalsociety.org. Open Thurs, Sat, and Sun 2 to 5 p.m. Call for exhibition dates. $, under 12 free.

An interesting collection of six buildings traces the history of everyday eighteenth- and nineteenth-century East End life. Visit Village House, a furnished Victorian boardinghouse; the Hallock Building, once a cookhouse and dormitory for the farm workers; the vintage carriage collection inside the Red Barn; the eighteenth-century Webb House; and two one-room schoolhouses.

Mashomack Preserve (all ages)

79 S. Ferry Rd., Shelter Island; (631) 749-1001; www.nature.org. Open 9 a.m. to 5 p.m., Mar through Sept, and 9 a.m. to 4 p.m., Oct through Feb. Preserve is closed Tues, except in July and Aug, when it is open daily; open weekends in Jan. Donation.

On the southeastern third of Shelter Island, 20 miles of trails lace through 2,039 acres of oak and beech forests, with 10 miles of coastline cut by tidal creeks and a rare 4,000-year-old white-pine swamp. This "Jewel of the Peconic" is home to one of the densest populations of nesting osprey on the east coast, as well as habitat for more than 200 species of birds, including the endangered piping plover and least tern. Stop at the Nature Conservancy Visitor Center for maps of the six trails, including a marine trek, and information about forest scavenger hunts, bird searches, night hikes, Halloween hikes, family hikes, and live animal presentations.

Southold Historical Society Museum Park (ages 3 and up)

54325 Main Rd., Southold; (631) 765-5500 or (631) 765-5551; www.southoldhistoricalsociety .org. Open July through Oct, Sat, Sun, and Wed 1 to 4 p.m. Donation.

Stewards of Southold's heritage, this historical society has amassed and restored a dozen authentic buildings spanning three centuries. Most are clustered at the Maple Lane complex, filled with an ever-expanding collection of antiques, from farm tools to Victorian dollhouses and their denizens. A gift shop and consignment store are open in season, and special events include art auctions, ice-cream socials, concerts, dance performances, candlelight tours, and Step Back In History programs.

Southold Indian Museum (all ages)
1080 Main Bay View Rd., Southold; (631) 765-5577; www.southoldindianmuseum.org. Open June and Sept, Sun 1:30 to 4:30 p.m.; and July and Aug, Sat and Sun 1:30 to 4:30 p.m. Donation.

More than 300,000 Algonquin artifacts are housed at this archaeological museum. Permanent exhibits include arrowheads and spears, agricultural displays, and the largest collection of Algonquin pottery in the country. A children's area has been added, with puppets, puzzles, and props that offer hands-on experiences, and Artifact Identification Day is a chance to find out what that odd object is you found on the ground.

Custer Institute (ages 6 and up)
1115 Main Bay View Rd., Southold; (631) 765-2626; www.custerobservatory.org. Public observing every Sat after dusk until midnight. $.

Stargaze on a Sat night at this observatory that's usually available for members only. Opened in 1927, this is Long Island's oldest public observatory, and the equipment is stellar. A recent addition is the 11-foot-tall, 25-inch-diameter Obsession, a Newtonian Dobsonian reflecting scope, making it the largest one on Long Island. The museum has an assortment of rare astronomical devices, a Civil War bullet collection, and a display of fossils, rocks and meteorites, including one from Mars. Check the Web site for viewing conditions, space station sightings, satellite spotting, star parties, and other outer-worldly events.

Horton Point Lighthouse (all ages)
Lighthouse Road, Southold; (631) 765-5500; www.southoldhistoricalsociety.org. Open Memorial Day to Columbus Day, Sat and Sun 11:30 a.m. to 4:30 p.m. $.

Overlooking Long Island Sound, this nineteenth-century lighthouse has a restored keeper's cottage, a nautical museum filled with maritime artifacts, and a whale display focusing on East Coast leviathans, accompanied by the acoustical stylings of humming

North Fork **Action**

Greenport Skatepark. (631) 477-1133; www.greenportvillage.com.

Drossos' Mini Golf Arcade. Main Road, Greenport; www.drossosmotel.com.

Island Bike. Shelter Island; (631) 477-1133.

humpback whales. The grounds surrounding the restored green, ten-second light have picturesque panoramic picnic areas, just a short stroll to the beach.

Where to Eat

Claudio's. 111 Main St., Greenport; (631) 477-0627; www.claudios.com. The oldest same-family-run restaurant in the country, serving victuals since 1870, including fresh lobster, broiled flounder, baked shrimp, shellfish samplers, baskets of broiled or fried seafood combos, a Friday Night Bake, and a Little Mate's menu. $$–$$$$

The Dory. 185 North Ferry Rd., Shelter Island; (631) 749-4300; www.doryrestaurant .com. Scenic deck dining on the waterfront. Serving chowder, coconut shrimp, mussels marinara, fish and chips, steaks, stuffed chicken, seafood specials, and Devil's Food Cheesecake for dessert.

Where to Stay

Heron Harbor Suites. 61600 Main Rd., Southold; (631) 765-5121. Seventeen one- and two-bedroom suites, with full kitchen facilities, **free** Internet, flat-screen cable TV, swimming pool, playground, beach passes, and massage therapy available. $$$$

Pridwin. Shore Road, Shelter Island; (631) 749-0476 or (800) 273-2497. Forty rooms, water-view cottages, fireplace cottages, and contemporary-style cottages, plus a private pool, beach, kayaks, paddleboats, bicycles, a game room, a tennis camp, a Kids Movie Night, and an on-site massage therapist. $$$–$$$$

Sunset Motel. 62005 CR 48, Greenport; (631) 477-1776; www.sunsetgreenport .com. Rooms, suites, and a cottage, with refrigerators, sun deck, private beach, and a chaise-checked lawn overlooking the Sound. $$–$$$$

For More Information

Long Island Convention & Visitors Bureau and Sports Commission. (877) FUN-ON-LI; www.discoverlongisland.com.

Long Island Farm Bureau. (631) 727-3777; www.lifb.com.

Long Island Guide. www.long.island .lodgingguide.com.

Nassau County. www.nassaucountyny.gov.

Suffolk County. www.co.suffolk.ny.us.

Fire Island. www.fireisland.com.

Shelter Island. www.shelterislandtown.us.

East Hampton www.easthampton.com.

Southampton Chamber of Commerce. (631) 283-0402; www.southamptonchamber .com.

Southampton Town. www.town.south ampton.ny.us.

Sag Harbor Chamber of Commerce. (631) 725-0011; www.sagharbor.com.

Hampton Bays Chamber of Commerce. (631) 728-2211; www.hamptonbayschamber .com.

Greater Westhampton Chamber of Commerce. (631) 288-3337; www.whbcc .org.

East Quogue Chamber of Commerce. (631) 653-5143; www.eqny.com.

Hamptons. www.hamptonstravelguide.com.

Montauk. www.montaukyguide.com.

Index